WANDERING

ISBN: 0-9903820-0-1
ISBN-13: 978-0-9903820-0-3
Library of Congress Control Number: 2014941679
Wanderers Press
Koloa, HI

To Shanti and Andy, my travel muses.
Thank you for your love and directions.

As I approached my 40th birthday, it was becoming more and more apparent that a lifetime of good luck wasn't enough. I was born with a lot of positive attributes: I'm tall, adventurous, smart, and pretty – great qualities that many people are not fortunate enough to have. But I slowly started to freak out, so I set out to prove to myself that everything was great and nothing would change. A birthday is just another number, I told myself; it's nothing to be afraid of.

At 39, I paddled a standup board 17 miles down the Na Pali coast on Kauai, where I live. I ran my first marathon. I paddled in a six-man canoe across the Kaiwi channel, from Molokai to Oahu, then paddled a one-man canoe across the same channel a few months later.

40 finally came and I was even more dissatisfied with my life. All of my big, adrenaline-pumping events were over, leaving

in their place an emptiness I didn't know how to fill. My personal life was full of friends – all couples, all starting to have babies. My drinking buddies now drank water and had an 8 o'clock bedtime. I was seeing a guy, but he was recently divorced and unwilling to become any more involved in my life than dinner and an occasional movie; any dreams of a family of my own were starting to fade away. I was tired of my job; I had been a bookkeeper at the same company for six years and had no desire left to sit behind a desk. Everything in my life was boring me. I needed a change.

Just as my midlife crisis was picking up momentum, my friend Shanti suggested it was time I left the island to see how other people around the world live. She has been across the globe and considers herself a traveler. She told me stories of hostels, all-night parties, and wonderful people from different cultures. I've been places, but certainly not as a true traveler, more as a tourist: two weeks in Italy, a short stay in Paris, a little bit of Canada and the Caribbean; my trips were planned by the people I went with – planning is not in my skill set.

To just take off on a trip to a different country with nothing but a few changes of clothes, a water purifier, a laptop and a camera for a year sounded great. Adventure. New friends. I could learn some new skills, like how a bus schedule works or how to get lost in a foreign country and find my way again. I could do this. And maybe along the way I'd figure out what I wanted to do with my life; maybe a change in career, and, fingers crossed, maybe meet the man of my dreams.

I wasn't excited about going solo, though. Kauai has one road and I still manage to get lost. Sometimes I'm too anxious to talk to people I don't know; what if I'm too old to start a trip, and no one wants to hang out with me? A year without friends would be pretty sad. But the idea was planted, and so began my story of a 40-year-old directionally confused, socially anxious woman on her first adventure around the world.

The first thing I did was give my notice at work and buy a one-way ticket to Mexico. I chose Central America as a good place to jump off into the world on my first solo trip. I enrolled in a Spanish school at my first stop; I love learning languages. I considered my arrangements done for the time being. Packing my apartment into a storage unit, selling my truck, and saying my goodbyes occupied me for the next few weeks.

I started making a giant pile of stuff in my apartment of things I might take when it occurred to me that I didn't even have a backpack. That's how bad I am at planning – I forgot the first essential piece of gear. Some moments of panic and a phone call to Shanti and a pretty blue pack with a matching daypack came from REI five days later.

Packing up the apartment went fairly well. I'd only lived in that apartment for a year, but the amount of crap I'd accumulated was amazing. If I didn't move so much, I'd probably be one of those crazy hoarders with years of junk piled up, waiting to bury me in an avalanche of tchotchkes, books and the other collected detritus of years in one place.

The next phase of my plan was to move my couch and some boxes into my storage unit, sell my books at Kauai's only bookstore and drop off clothes at Habitat for Humanity. Instead, I helped break in the new engines on a Zodiac at the boat company where I used to work. We puttered around and jumped in the water when we were surrounded by dolphins, then spent the rest of the day drinking. Since it was Friday night, it was time to go out. I could try again Monday. There were only a couple weekends left before I departed and I couldn't waste them by getting work done.

Then came the momentous day of starting the journey, becoming officially homeless. After a great breakfast saying goodbye to some friends, I did the final cleanout of my apartment. Moving out had been in the works for a month, but seeing my cramped, gloomy apartment empty actually made me sad and anxious. I was sad because it wouldn't be long until I had to say goodbye to everyone, and anxious because I still couldn't believe the trip was really happening. Pretty scared, actually. I've never put all my stuff in a backpack and just wandered around, and I really have no idea what to expect. Everyone told me I'd have a great time and meet lots of new friends and love it, but until I got started I was kind of freaked out. This is where planning might have helped. I kept wondering why I still hadn't just Googled my destinations. I'm a great Googler; I'll look up anything at any time for anyone. But I still hadn't found a single picture of San Miguel de Allende, my first destination.

Until I left on Saturday I was roommates with Sol, an 11-month-old, and all I had left to do was make the final decision on what was going in the backpack and what was staying in storage, and clean out my truck to sell. That was tough; I've had my Jeep for 13 years, but she went to a good home. I would need the extra dollars for margaritas.

It was my last day in the United States, for who knew how long. I used it to test the blog app on my phone. God only knew if I'd have Wi-Fi anywhere I went, but I could always use it to send an SOS.

MEXICO
JUNE 4ᵀᴴ, 2012

SAN MIGUEL
DE ALLENDE

Viva Mexico! I wasn't sure I'd make it, but I got there. One easy airport and two hard ones, and I could begin my wandering around the world. I was a bit worried when I couldn't find my flight out of Lihue, possibly the easiest airport in the world with a whopping 10 gates. But Honolulu and Houston later, and

I was an expert. I should mention that I have a healthy fear of public transportation. I used to ride the bus to work downtown when I lived in Seattle, and I was so afraid I'd miss my stop I'd end up standing behind the driver annoying him for the last five minutes of every ride. Every day he'd say, "Here's your stop," and every day he would be slightly less friendly. An utter lack of a sense of direction made every trip look different, and I tried to explain that to him, but I think he thought I was just a well-dressed crazy person.

I flew into Leon, Mexico, and my first sight was armed men lounging on the runway, making me feel safe. Customs was a breeze, except that they aren't fond of purple ink pens and made me go to the back of the line to fill out all my forms again in the black ink of bureaucracy. I found my bag and a cute little man holding a sign with my name on it. Before I left I asked Pablo to teach me some Spanish phrases, like "Which bus to San Miguel" and "How much does the taxi cost," but in the end, I just went online and paid someone $30 to pick me up. All in all, getting to my first port-of-call was easier than I expected.

San Miguel de Allende is about an hour and a half from the Leon airport, and it was an insane trip. The car was new and clean, my driver was dressed in typical "hired car" attire of slacks, a dress shirt and a tie, and we flew across the countryside on a one-lane highway just like at home but skinnier, with totally optional traffic rules. It was great. The only times we slowed from "holy shit" speed were to avoid hitting cows in the road. I'm not sure there was a speed limit. Because he was conscientious, he used his turn signal when he drove on the wrong side of the road to pass.

Habla Hispana Spanish School is in the heart of San Miguel, set on the main street, thank God. I was told all roads lead back to it, which was exactly what I needed. Even so, after I checked into my dorm and was leaving to find food, my teacher said *bueno suerte*. It was like she knew me already. I took a picture of the front door in case I had to show it to a cab driver to find my way home. I managed to find an ATM, a café for lunch, and a run-down market with sad vegetables. Lunch was great, though. All the Spanish I learned from drinking at my favorite Mexican restaurant on Kauai came in handy. *Enchiladas con pollo, por favor. Uno mas cerveza, por favor.* I already felt like a local. Finding useable currency and feeding myself aren't much to brag about, but I was quite proud of myself. I didn't even need to flash the picture of my school and beg for directions home.

My first day of Spanish class was awesome. There were three of us. Tracy is a personal trainer from Texas with two kids; her father owns a house in San Miguel and her pilot husband flies them down to visit for vacations. I had previously thought all Texans know Spanish, but I was wrong. Tracy had been coming here for several years and showed me her running routes, although I couldn't imagine going out the front door to run – I'd get flattened by a bus on these pencil-thin roads or break my ankle on the cobblestones. Susan is an actress/singer/chant leader/sound healer (I could go on forever). She moved here two months before I showed up to be near her brother and make her retirement fund stretch to infinity. She wore long, flowing cotton clothing and was dripping turquoise jewelry.

Socorro was our grammar teacher and Enrique was our conversation leader, and we learned a good deal in our first four hours. Every time we tried to say more than we knew words for, Enrique would stop us and say "You talk pretty one day" – he loves David Sedaris – meaning, "Use only the words you know, be patient and it'll come". Or, "You have less vocabulary than a

Mexican two-year-old, so you're going to sound stupid regardless of what you say".

After class I took a walk with Susan and her dog, Alma, who came to class with her. We went to an organic café for lunch; I ordered vegetarian tamales without onions, the worst vegetable ever, and they were fantastic. This was where Susan spent time telling me about her many talents as a singer, artist, actress, healer, et cetera, and she fit very nicely into the general category of "eccentric." When I arrived and was wandering the town, I didn't find a single English-speaking person. That day, thanks to Susan, I found myself in an entire room of non-Spanish speakers. They weren't at all like I imagined they would be, like the ex-pats in a Hemingway book; I could drink with those people. These were all dressed up for the country club, but too old to play tennis anymore. I was by far the youngest gringo, and I'm not young by far. But that's what I get for wandering around with a new-age tour guide.

Susan had blatantly ignored the "No dogs allowed" sign, written in English, and Alma was stretching her leash to the limit to beg under everyone's tables. Susan was completely oblivious to the fact that dogs aren't welcome everywhere and that this wasn't Southern California.

This was quite noticeable when we walked up through the artists' alley and into the open markets. Susan was walking on one side of the alley and her dog on the other, basically clotheslining anyone who tried to walk by, and being the only white people around, it was pretty embarrassing. I don't think she noticed.

She did notice, however, the old Mexican woman waving the pointy end of a knife at her dog. Susan got upset, but it was actually very funny. This poor old woman, dressed in raggedy clothes and sitting on an overturned five-gallon bucket in a stiflingly hot room, was making food to sell, and some crazy white woman's dog wanted to stick its nose in? I thought the knife-waving was a great warning. No translation needed.

When I finally got back to my dorm to start homework, I made some sad discoveries. Hulu doesn't work in Mexico, and I may never get to see who passed their board exams on Grey's Anatomy. Google quickly learned where I was and all of my searches came back in Spanish, directing me to Spanish-only websites. Great. Since my homework didn't put me to sleep, I was desperately trying to find online TV, and eventually I found a website with every episode of the Simpsons. In Spanish. I thought subliminal learning might be the way to go, but the only thing I could say when I woke up was *aye carumba*.

Here's an interesting fact about San Miguel: there are no permanent signs for stores or cafés. A shop opens, they put out a small sign, they close, and the sign goes away. Different stores are open at different times of the day; some take siestas, some are open on weekends. The few streets I've worked up the courage to explore never looked the same two days in a row. With my severe geographical handicap, this was devastating.

I went for a walk on Sunday after I arrived and there wasn't much going on. I managed to find a run-down grocery store about a tenth the size of a 7-11. The next day I was walking with my eccentric new friend and we found a fantastic grocery store with everything I could think of. I went back later and couldn't find it, but it hadn't occurred to me that it would be closed, all traces of its existence swept away. I walked and walked and got lost, finally discovering that the "all roads lead back" advice I received was complete bullshit. Roads led to more roads which led to the other side of town which led to a taxi and having to use the picture of my Spanish school to get home.

I learned that I needed to find more concrete landmarks, and I set out after class on Wednesday with Tracy, who was much more my style for a walking companion. She took me to an even more fantastic grocery store than the first. We parted ways after shopping and I had to retrace my steps back to my dorm as Tracy was living at her father's house across town, and that was when I discovered my second geographical handicap in Mexico. I spend so much time watching my feet so I don't trip down a curb or stumble on the uneven cobblestones or fall in a hole or trample a beggar that I completely forget to look at the street signs. I was completely lost again. Thank God for the picture.

I guess it was good that I could walk the same streets every day and it would always seem like a new adventure, but I was beginning to doubt my ability to make it out of this town, much less to other countries. The school offered a walking tour of the city and I should take advantage of it. And find someone to teach me how to ride the buses that don't seem to have any stops. Baby steps.

I also discovered that I don't mind being lost as much if I have an ice cream cone.

My first week in Mexico was finished, and so far it seemed pretty dull. I went to school for a few hours, walked a few blocks to get lunch, stopped by the grocery store for supplies, did some homework, walked a few more blocks for dinner, wandered around and went back to my dorm. I would probably shoot myself if that was my everyday life in the States. But it was so exciting! Everything was in Spanish! Stepping off the curb was an adventure. Even a can of tuna fish was so much more awesome when I couldn't read the label.

I finally managed to permanently etch the location of the Bonanza grocery store into my brain, "Walk out the front door, cross to Relox, walk three blocks, left on Messones and it's on the left." I had to repeat this to myself about 40 times, but I could start eating regularly.

I got better at reading price tags, converting pesos to dollars, and understanding the amount the cashier told me. I was seriously shocked when I learned that the exchange rate was about 14 pesos to a dollar. I thought it was about eight or 10, so I wasn't impressed at all by how cheap I was told things were in Mexico – but 14 changed everything. The beer that I thought was $4 was actually only $2.60! Knowing that, I could start drinking more. The amazing gordita I had for lunch was less than a dollar. And I was told that I should never pay a taxi driver more than 30 pesos to go anywhere. $2! I swore I wouldn't walk ever again.

At the *jardin*, I met some new friends, Benito and Luis. Although their English was better than my Spanish it still wasn't great, so we were practicing on each other. I spoke in Spanish, they spoke in English, and we tried very hard to understand what we were talking about. Benito asked if I had seen the San Miguel skyline yet; I hadn't, so he ran down the block and came back on a motorcycle. I hopped on and off we went. My mother would have had a heart attack. He seemed harmless enough, cute, kind of chubby and missing a tooth, but overall he looked like a teddy bear.

I thought we were only going a few streets up; San Miguel is surrounded by hills so steep I didn't even want to walk up them, but Benito just kept driving. I was holding him in a death grip so I wouldn't fall off the back. Fifteen minutes later, we were on the highway and I was wondering if our destination got lost in translation; maybe he was going to sell me to a brothel. He spoke so fast I probably wouldn't have caught that.

But in the end, he took me to an overlook where I could see the entire city, thousands of twinkling lights. Just as promised, he dropped me off at my doorstep, where he then tried to get his tongue in my mouth. I definitely missed the part about payment when we were planning.

I had only been in Mexico for a week, but it felt like this adventure had lasted months already. Time moves really slowly when you don't have much to do, which is great for vacation. I was learning how to relax and do nothing, which seemed to be the national pastime. Just sit and watch and be, a skill that's harder than I would have thought.

I had started feeling guilty that I hadn't worked out in more than a week. I dragged my running shoes a few thousand miles to sit in a closet. There was Yoga and TRX and a gym and all I really wanted to do was eat gorditas. And that brought up a potential problem: Mexican clothes for when I inevitably get fat. I had been visiting the shops and trying on cute local shirts, but the Mexican garment industry is just not prepared for a girl my size. They're all like clothes for dolls. I kept asking, *"Mas grande?"* and they always said no. The woman in the bra shop just laughed.

My main activity after school was hanging out in the *jardin*, where I'd met all of my non-school friends. It's a giant square with the *parroquia* (church) on one side and stores and cafés on the other sides, with benches and trees and pathways in the middle, about the size of a small city block. Everyone goes there at about 9 p.m. to sit and watch. Dozens of people hung out in the *jardin* all day, but it really got going at night. Each corner had a shoeshine man and his regular customers; Mexicans apparently love to wear shiny shoes. There were carts and carts of street food served in used Dorito bags, beggars, gypsies selling dolls and woven hats and lots of beautiful toys that I have no desire to buy, toddlers, old

people, wandering mariachis dressed in matching outfits looking for tourists to play to, anyone you could imagine. There I met
Jose, an old man who was born and raised in San Miguel. He's
been to New York, Mexico City, all over the world, and he can't
imagine living anywhere else than his hometown. He had a thing
for tall women so he was happy to sit and tell me about his city.
And we had a date the next day, and he taught me how to dance
to the mariachi bands.

The main thing I noticed was that San Miguel specialized in
fiestas. The town should; it got a lot of practice with some sort of
party every night with fireworks and the parroquia bells ringing.
The feast of Corpus Christi was Thursday night, and every block
had an altar with flowers and candles and pictures of their saints
and, of course, fireworks. Each group of people with an altar was
trying to outdo the next with louder music and more fireworks;
it was total madness to walk a few blocks, and almost impossible
not to get hit.

Enrique, one of my Spanish teachers, asked "What do you call
fireworks?"

"Poor people staying poor."

Fireworks every night for any reason. Socorro used the word
fiestero, an actual adjective describing this town and how much
its people love their parties.

Even after staying out late and drinking, there was no point
in trying to get to sleep at any respectable hour. Someone will
always think that fireworks several hours after your bedtime is
still a respectable hour, and maybe a full-on band as well. Getting
home at 2 a.m., there is still a danger of being awoken at 4 if, say,
a baby is born.

But for Corpus Christi, the town splurged on a light show for
the *parroquia*. At precisely 9:15, all the lights in the *jardin* went

out and booming opera, classical, and Mexican music blared from giant speakers all around the square. There were choreographed lights on the front of the building that lasted for about 15 minutes. Squiggling serpents, angels, saints and revolutionary war – basically the entire history of Mexico swirling on the front of a building.

I met my new friends there to view the celebration. Afterward, I suggested we should have a couple beers and they took me to Mama Mia's, a sort of Mexican-Italian bar and restaurant with three floors playing '80s music, filled with obnoxious drunk Americans. Benito and Luis taught me all the bad words in Spanish they thought I should know. At the end of the night our check came, and they both just sat there staring at me, not moving for their wallets like I was. Ok, I'm sure I have more money than they do, Benito is a taxi driver and Luis is a part-time property manager, so I paid for our drinks. At $2 each, it didn't come to much. But I did find out later from Socorro about a custom here that whoever invites people out always picks up the tab. These guys have probably never paid for a drink in their lives. Way to work the tourist.

I had been dreading the first sighting of wildlife here. The cockroaches and spiders in Hawaii aren't too bad, but my way of coping with them at home is to chase them down with a spray bottle of Clorox so I don't have to get up close or do any squishing, then scoop them up when the legs stop kicking. Thinking about traveling Mexico and Central America really brought my bug phobias into perspective. There was no way I could avoid the interaction, and I imagined that the cockroaches would be way bigger and more ferocious and maybe have some teeth. I finally saw one while walking home and although it was big and gnarly, it wasn't anything that my flip-flop couldn't handle. Phew. I also saw my first scorpions. They were dead already so no extra courage was required on my part, but they were sort of cool to look at. I imagined I'd change my mind about that when I'm screaming and throwing a phone book someday soon. Tracy was with me, and being from Texas, she's seen plenty of scorpions. She remarked that they were teensy babies; actually, I think she looked at them and said, "Where's your daddy?" That gave me some pause, but it was better to see some then than be wondering when I'd get my first surprise.

Two other things I'd been dreading were the post office and the *lavenderia*. Those seem like fairly simple things, but in my day-to-day, life-skills-challenged world they were mountains to be climbed. I wanted to find a post office and mail something. It's so easy at home; there are stacks of boxes and all I need is an address, a pen and some tape. I had no idea what it would be like here, so I hadn't bought any cute trinkets for my friends yet for fear that I'd end up carrying them in my backpack for the next nine months. Tracy's father told me that there's a 50/50 chance of the mail actually getting to its destination. Reliable mail is something I've always taken for granted. Laundry, too. Who doesn't have a washing machine in their house or nearby? I was afraid of the *lavenderias* here. There were no laundromats so I had to give my clothes to someone, more than likely a short, round, old woman in a hot, dark room with a single washer and dryer. Being six feet tall, I have so much trouble finding clothes that fit me and I didn't know what I'd do if I lost all of my clothes. I wasn't assigning blame to these women in advance, but a real concern was leaving my clothes and never finding the shop again. A dire possibility for the geographically challenged. I took a lot of pictures on my way so I could retrace my steps.

I was also a bit self-conscious of another concern: were these small-town Mexican women prepared for my thong underwear?

I was bored and signed up for a "parade of homes" tour – me and 30 old married white folks. We followed a woman in impossibly high heels walking the cobblestones, and just watching her accomplish that was worth the 130 pesos. I could barely manage it in flip-flops. You can't really see any houses from the streets, all of the blocks are enclosed by walls, and you only know if you're in a good neighborhood if the walls are freshly painted and aren't crumbling. But enter the gates and there are hidden parks with fountains and a 12-bedroom house and rumors swirling that a guy from Microsoft owns this place, or a drug lord keeps it for his girlfriend. Places I couldn't afford if I saved every peso my entire life, and I have to admit I was envious. But to keep things in perspective, I was typing my blog on a computer that costs more than the average Mexican makes in a year.

My first cooking lesson was from an American guy who teaches yoga in Peru. Tracy took me to his house and we made stuffed jalapeños. Mix the cream cheese with garlic and cumin to stuff the peppers, after taking out the seeds for those who can't do too hot, mash in a couple small shrimp, wrap them in bacon, dip in egg whites, roll in breadcrumbs, then fry till crispy. Trying to keep weight off my thighs wasn't even on my mind.

The day after the stuffed jalapeños I went for my first run with Tracy. I'm pretty sure it was the margaritas that decided it was a good idea, but I committed and had to show up. Six a.m. was bad enough; add in a spicy dinner the night before and sneaking some cigarettes at the bars, top it off with 6,500 feet of elevation, and my first day back to exercise couldn't have been much worse. We only went about three miles, but I swear I almost vomited out my lungs.

Tracy met me and took me on her "easy" route with mostly flat cobblestones, and that was more than enough. Tracy is a personal trainer; envision a slim Texas girl running backwards when I fell behind, yelling "Come on Melissa, move it!" It was only about 15 minutes until I was pretty sure I would die, but she wouldn't let me turn around until I made it to the top of a hill, and then she tried to be sneaky and trick me into going down the backside. No, thanks.

While we were on our way back, I was breathing loud enough to wake up all the people who barely got to bed after the last round of fireworks, and Tracy stopped. Oh, thank God. But no, we're doing single leg lunges off the curb. I still had a bit of ego left and couldn't let her do them on her own. I was almost happy when we started running again, giddy when we slowed down, and...seriously? Pushups? Finally we ran back, where Tracy left me at my doorstep after she guilted me into a small round of jump squats. This was not the Mexican experience I had envisioned, so I made a note to myself: drink more tequila and ignore Tracy.

After explaining my fear of the *lavenderia* and losing my clothes, the school headmistress Marta offered to escort me to *El Cisne* (the swan), where she knows the women. Just as I had imagined, it was run by a large, round Mexican woman. We made jokes about my having to walk around town naked if I forgot where I left my clothes, and I felt good about leaving everything I owned there. She was still probably going to laugh at my underwear, but not to my face. Washed, dried, ironed and folded into obsessively neat squares for a little over $2. My first mission was accomplished.

I had an interesting language lesson the next day. In general, Socorro was a patient, helpful teacher for grammar, and Enrique liked to keep things fun and teach us Mexican-isms during his hours of conversation. When I was worried about losing my laundry I was trying to say that I was afraid, *tengo miedo*. But I got it twisted up a bit and was saying *tengo mierda*, or "I have shit," which would be a logical reason to need a laundromat. I found out I'd been walking around town telling people I have shit. When I told Socorro, she was the first person who wasn't polite enough to correct my error, and she was laughing so hard I thought she would *tiene mierda*. As the tears were streaming down her face, I tried to say that I was now embarrassed, and it turned out that *embarazada* means "pregnant." Awesome. I have shit and I'm pregnant. I had really tried not to be the class clown.

Another time, I was trying to ask if it was Thursday, and Benito looked at Luis and said "I don't know about him, but I have two balls." I didn't even know where that went wrong.

Enrique liked to teach us local sayings and slang so we could better understand the people we met on the street. This was always my favorite part of class. When you want to remark on the weather, *esta haciendo calor*, it's hot. But if I say I'm hot, *estoy caliente*, I just told everyone that I'm horny. Hot guys are *mangos* or *un taco de ojo* (eye taco). And we could use *vomitar* when sick, or better yet, *saludar al monster*, saying hello to the monster. I love idioms.

I met an ex-pat named Billy and he explained some slang as well. The teens greet each other *Hola, wey*. *Buey* means ox. They figure that the ox is the dumbest animal alive because it's the biggest animal, yet does all the work for the tiniest animal, the people. It could easily turn around and trample a man and never have to work, but it doesn't, so it must be incredibly stupid. *Buey* was shortened to *wey*, which now is basically "dude."

I had absolutely no doubt that I would continue to unintentionally tell people about my bodily functions or parts when I was innocently discussing the weather, but it was a great way to get people to talk to you. Someday when I go back I'm going to walk into a bar and "accidentally" announce that I'm horny. Maybe then I won't have to buy drinks.

After two weeks a new student started at school, Juniper. She'd been traveling for a few months and had just arrived from South America, so her Spanish was pretty advanced. She was living in the big house with me, and it was nice that I had someone to drink with. We visited Cañada de la Virgen, a pyramid complex about 10 miles from San Miguel with seven structures, a ball field and processional roads, very nicely kept. We found a taxi to take us to the office, but the tour bus had broken down so we had to wait with some of the workers until it could pick us up, which was fine because it was way too hot to walk. I was trying to tell the men that I forgot something and was using the word *dimentico*; I guess it was left over from my Italian-speaking days. *Dimentico* means crazy in Spanish, which these gentlemen were kind enough to point out. Which brings me back to my laundry. Now I know that I was saying that I have shit and am crazy. Sigh.

Juniper and I took a tour to Guanajuato with Jorge, the historian at the Spanish school. Jorge was very funny and quite inappropriate; he'd be talking about his children one moment and remark on my cleavage the next. His favorite saying was "This is Mexico, anything is possible," and that was usually his answer to a question regarding whether something was legal or not. Guanajuato is a bit older than San Miguel and is home to the university, so the population is much younger. We went to the childhood home of the artist Diego Rivera, a pretty amazing place. His parents were landlords by trade, which seems strange for the late 1800s, but they built a house on the side of a mountain when there weren't many houses and every time they needed more space they simply excavated further into the mountain for another room. Very smart people. A lot of his work was on display, along with smaller versions of his murals.

I learned about *micheladas*, which are basically beer, fruit juice, and salsa. And I realized while sitting in the bar that I don't know any famous Mexicans.

Our final stop on the tour was the mummy museum, El Museo de las Momias, which was seriously creepy. When I think about a mummy I think about the ones from Scooby Doo, wrapped in bandages, arms out, comical. But these were naked, dead people with tortured looks on their faces, and the sight of them was really disturbing. Jorge had been there about 500 times, leading tours or classes, and knew it by heart. He started going there when he was a child and the bodies were just propped up against the walls, not in temperature-controlled glass cases, with puddles of water on the floor and horrible smells. He had nightmares from it. I couldn't imagine taking a child there now, much less back then, yet there were children of all ages. I love the cultural differences.

On the way back we stopped at a tortilla stand; restaurants were some of my favorite places to work on my Spanish. About a dozen local people were standing around, and I marched right up to the woman at the counter and said "I am a cheese quesadilla." Whatever, I still got fed.

Further along on our way home from Guanajuato, Jorge pulled the car to the side of the road. He rummaged in the cooler in the trunk and pulled out cups, ice, El Jimador tequila and Squirt. Another Mexican lesson, he made us *palomas*. We stood watching the cars and horses go by and got drunk while Jorge told increasingly inappropriate stories about sex workers and the various bars we shouldn't enter. He called for a toast and we raised our glasses, toasting *"Salud."* A passing driver happened to hear and held his beer out the window, toasting with us. *Me gusta Mexico.*

El dia de los Locos is something that shouldn't be missed if you happen to be in San Miguel in mid-June. Juniper and I left our dorm early to get a good seat on the curb before all the families and kids arrived. Not that I wouldn't be able to see over everyone's heads, but it was nice to have a place to sit for a day-long parade. While we were waiting for the dancers a raggedy, homeless-looking man walked up and stood in front of me, staring. I said, *"Hola,"* and he told me, in Spanish, how much he loved me. I had begun to notice days ago that the men here paid extra attention to me, a 6-foot tall, slim brunette, whom they all called "blondie" in a land of short, plump, dark women. I tried to explain it to Juniper, but until that day she hadn't really noticed. The man was still standing in front of me staring, and eventually all the families around us began to laugh and tell me that he must be my boyfriend. It was an uncomfortable few minutes of unrequited declarations of love before a couple local men finally drove him off.

By the time the parade made its way to our spot, half of Mexico must have smashed its way onto the sidewalks. There were floats on trucks with stacks of speakers blaring music, and hundreds of people in costume dancing in the streets. Some were throwing treats to the crowd, and when I say throwing, I mean they were literally pelting people with gum and horrible-flavored candy. That was not a good time to be the tallest person around; I had a welt on my forehead by the time the day was done. The kids loved it though; they just waited by my feet for everything to hit me and drop to their level.

The dancers were amazing. The simplest costumes were rubber masks, but with this town being such a festive place, most people went elaborate with huge papier-mâché heads and painted bodies. Each neighborhood had a different theme and there were dozens of Simpsons, Avatar characters, clowns, devils, transformers, traditional Mexican dress, cross-dressers, men in diapers with giant baby heads, and every cartoon character imaginable. Each barrio had a truck with a generator and 7-foot stacks of speakers blaring Mexican music, and every few minutes the entire parade would just stop and dance in place. This lasted for hours, and the pitcher of margaritas that Juniper and I brought was gone long before the end.

I was developing a couple addictions from my two weeks here in San Miguel: corn tortillas and Catrinas. The tortillas are pretty obvious – grind up corn and fry it, I couldn't stop eating them. The Catrinas are super fun, skeletons dressed up in formal clothes. Created by Jose Posada, they represent corruption by the wealthy class. Although he only created the basic form they now came in every style and color, pictures or statues, big or small. But it's always a skeleton in some form of fancy dress. I wanted to buy every one I saw, but I didn't want to carry them around the world in my backpack for the next several months, because by then I learned what a horrible place a Mexican post office really is.

I bought some organic Mexican coffee for Shanti and Pablo, friends from home, and a couple gifts for their son's first birthday. I found a nice sized box, so I figured I'd fill it before I sent it – fewer gifts to send later. Tracy and I walked to the post office and the first thing I was told was that I couldn't mail coffee beans, which was exactly the opposite of what the man at the coffee shop told me, which was frustrating but not surprising. Tracy's birthday was coming up; maybe she'd get coffee.

I was still going to mail Sol's presents, so I gave my box to the clerk and she told me it would cost $135 US to mail everything.

It might not have been that bad if the contents of the box were worth more than $20. Ok, whatever, I'll still mail it, I told myself. The Spanish children's book was super cute. This was the beginning of my trip and I still felt rich with all my saved money. But the post office didn't take credit cards and I only had about 200 pesos in my pocket, and the nearest ATM was a 10-minute walk. What post office in a tourist town full of art galleries doesn't accept credit cards?

Tracy's children were now the recipients of Sol's giant wooden crayons. Merry Christmas. They were made out of actual tree branches, too, and perfect for a child's tiny hands. Oh, well.

After repurposing most of the gifts I had bought, I still had the book and I wasn't sure what to do with it. It was a Spanish-language version of Dr. Seuss' "Oh, The Places You'll Go," for a boy who will grow up bilingual. It was way too cute to leave behind and there was definitely no return policy at the book store. I guess I'm going to haul a children's book around the world till I make it back home, I thought. Then when I'm old and frail, I can call Sol to come over and take out my trash and carry my groceries and remind him what I did for his first gift.

I had one more week in San Miguel and I spent a couple nights drinking margaritas and planning my next destination. This was where the real adventure would begin. I had been relatively safe and comfortable at the Spanish school and now that I had a basic grasp of the language, it was time to start riding buses and exploring. I've always been a bad planner and have a bit of a mass transportation phobia, but I had to see if I could do this or go home with my tail between my legs. I booked a room in Mexico City for four days at a place that was rated "safe" on Trip Advisor. I felt I needed to be a little cautious going to the biggest city in the world solo, so it was a little over my budget. Then, while perusing the map, I got stuck on the word "Mazatlan;" it's so fun to say out loud that I decided go there for some much-needed beach time. I missed the beaches at home. Both places were more expensive than I liked, but I had saved enough money to get me through a year of budget travel, so why not book a room on the beach once in a while, live like a queen, and only travel for 10 months? I thought the tradeoff was worth it; I already knew how to scrimp and save and be frugal, but when would I get the chance to spoil myself again? Certainly not when I was back home, working but broke. But if I kept making travel plans while drinking margaritas, I might be out of money and back home in a couple months.

The next class with Enrique was extremely informative; new words and conjugations like any normal day, but also with a great geography and cultural lesson. I was asking him about places in Mexico and what they're like, and which ones shouldn't be missed. The subject veered off to violence in certain areas, the drug cartels, and other current events in Mexico.

The basic lesson was that I shouldn't be afraid to go to any specific area of Mexico, regardless of the scary reports we hear in the news. Sure, there are bad neighborhoods, but you wouldn't stay away from the entire city of New York just because a couple places aren't safe – same idea in Mexico. Every town has its bad streets, but no place is completely unsafe. Even in the areas of mass killings, tourists have never been targets. You'd have a better chance of getting robbed by a random guy on the metro than being a victim of drug crime.

The big drug traffickers are pretty careful about who they kill and behead; they don't just shoot whoever is around – that's just in the States. Mexicans don't have a term similar to "going postal," and they don't have kids who bring guns to school and spray their classmates with bullets. Large-scale violence against strangers doesn't occur there; almost every person found dead was killed purposefully, and everyone knows why.

I couldn't bet my life that this was true, but Enrique told a story about his father who lives in Chihuahua. He was sitting at a table in a bar playing cards with his friends, like he does every afternoon, when a man with a gun walked in and asked for a specific man by name. The man answered, and got shot in the head. No one was surprised, nor did they do anything about it, because this man had a small hardware store in a small town, yet somehow made enough money to have several houses, and all his kids had cars and studied in Europe. It was understood that he must have gotten too greedy in his other business.

Before I left Kauai, several people told me that I was stupid to even think about going to Mexico because it was too dangerous. But with a bit of common sense, there was no reason I shouldn't go wherever I wanted there.

Enrique also expanded my list of places I should visit, although it would have taken me the entire year and I wouldn't even have made it to Central America. There's a train that goes to Copper Canyon, which is deeper than the Grand Canyon but not as wide. And if I was going to Mazatlan, why not go a bit further north and check out the desert right next to the ocean in Baja California? And as long as I was there, it would be a shame to miss Tijuana. But there are so many other places in the world, I had to decide how long to give each country. I don't know if there's a term for "sugar daddy" in Mexico; I needed to ask Enrique.

Three weeks was how long it took me to get seriously out of shape. When I first got there I thought I'd actually lose weight from all the walking I had to do; every time I was hungry I had to walk somewhere, and at 6,500 feet, even going to the corner store made me break a sweat. So I started running with Tracy two or three times a week. We got out while it was still pitch-black outside and ran out of town on the side of the highway. Cars and buses were screaming past, making us jump off the side of the road; I think the painted lines were completely optional. We were breathing unregulated exhaust fumes; add to that the extreme altitude, and it made for some seriously unhappy lungs. The first run was awful; I thought I was going to die on the side of the road, and two weeks later it didn't get any better.

Tracy took me for mostly flat runs, but the tiny hills still felt like Mt. Everest. Little by little, I could run farther, but always breathing like an obese asthmatic woman trying to climb stairs. We ran hills one Friday and that was the worst run yet; we went about four miles total, but the first half was almost straight uphill and Tracy kept stopping to wait for me and yelling at me because all I wanted to do was sit on the curb and cry. I didn't think it would take this long to acclimate to the altitude.

I started feeling really bad about my plummeting fitness level that weekend, especially after several days of nonstop margaritas and an out-of-control corn chip addiction. I tried to do some TRX cardio and that was just sad – four burpees and I was sprawled out on the floor like I had just finished a marathon.

One afternoon I went swimming with Tracy and her kids. The only reason I could walk out in public after seeing myself in a bikini was that a dozen fat ladies were doing water aerobics in the pool; nothing like using someone else's problems to make myself feel better. They inspired me to swim some laps. But mostly I just wanted to lay on the comfy chair and nap in the sun, which Tracy made me feel good about. "Tan fat looks better than white fat," she said.

The next run was finally better. I went farther than before, and was even able to talk a little bit. I was finally getting accustomed to the altitude, just in time to leave. I kept telling myself that I'll get back into shape when I get to the beach: I'll swim every morning, surf, maybe run on the sand. But there were also new bars and restaurants to try. Maybe it was time I just made peace with my inner fat girl and quit torturing myself. Drinking was way more fun.

I had one more language lesson before I left San Miguel. I found out there is only one letter different between saying "I fell" and "I pooped myself." Sometimes Socorro laughed so hard I was afraid she'd have a heart attack.

It was time to leave San Miguel de Allende, and I really enjoyed this town as a the gateway to my adventure, even if there wasn't enough hair conditioner, Chap-Stick or skin lotion to keep me from feeling like I was going to dry up and crack into little dusty pieces in the mountain air. It was a great place to begin a trip for the timid traveler. Tracy and I went to El Gato Negro for a goodbye *michelada* or three, and we spoke Spanish with the owner/bartender and the locals in the bar. But even if we didn't speak Spanish, it would have been easy to find all-American bars if we had wanted. We met a man who has lived there 20 years and doesn't know anything in Spanish except *muchas gracias* and *por favor.* I don't understand how it's possible to live somewhere and not learn the language, but I imagine some people just don't care. It reminds me of the controversy in the U.S. about Mexicans who won't learn English. We do it, too.

I liked San Miguel because everyone was friendly and I could walk anywhere I wanted at any time of the day or night. I don't think there was anywhere I could go where I'd be in trouble. When I saw a group of Mexican guys sitting on a doorstep in their wifebeaters, it didn't send up red flags; they were probably just having a pleasant conversation in front of someone's house wearing something comfortable and cool. I might not always think the same thing in parts of California.

Finally, I liked San Miguel because my Spanish class was great. I came away armed with so much slang, if I could remember it all, that I could get by in most any situation. When Socorro found out I was traveling by myself, she told me that Mexico is filled with "sharks with legs," especially near the beaches. But Enrique taught me multiple ways to say "fuck off," and that's about all I need if I'm in trouble. Not that I haven't learned to speak proper Spanish, but a girl should always have some sharp words at the ready.

It was a memorable week because it was election time; the entire country was voting on Saturday and Sunday. I'd seen election posters on every corner and half the cars, and trucks drove the streets with stacks of speakers blaring music and campaign speeches. The cutoff time for advertising had arrived, so every candidate was in the center of town throwing parties with bands playing and massive fireworks shows. Before I came to Mexico, I never thought I could get tired of fireworks, but every night?

I hadn't spoken to a single person who liked any of the candidates; everyone was trying to figure out who was the least corrupt. But they all put on a good fiesta, which is why I found it so bizarre that the entire country goes dry for the elections. I was in Mexico City during voting and I had to remember to buy tequila on Friday or go all weekend without. I can't imagine the United States curbing liquor sales for an election. We'd have a revolution.

And yes, I do think it's a little pathetic that I was there in a time of possible historic change and all I could think about was where my next margarita was coming from. But whatever, I was on vacation.

MEXICO CITY

My fear of riding the bus made me stupidly nervous while I was waiting at the station. I had no idea what to expect, and I hung out in the loading area just in case the bus tried to leave without me, even though I was there an hour early. But I did manage to get on the correct bus, which seemed like a huge accomplishment for me.

My seat mate was Felipe. I started talking to him before we left, because the driver made an announcement and spoke so fast I only caught about 20 percent of it. Felipe told me we were going to be late because protesters had shut down the highway. For years the locals had been asking for a bridge to cross the highway on foot and no one listened to them, so they formed a barricade of bodies across the road and wouldn't let any cars through; it was quite a spectacle. We finally made our way across town by way of backstreets. It didn't seem like San Miguel had ever seen a protest, so there were just as many people watching the protesters as there were holding signs.

The ride was unexpectedly pleasant; I got to speak Spanglish to Felipe and lay back in a super-comfy chair with a footrest. Mexico really knows how to do buses.

When we finally got to Mexico City, my nerves went out of control. The place was crazy, huge, and crowded – thousands of people everywhere you look. Felipe helped me navigate the taxi system before we parted ways, understanding I may not have even made it out the door of the bus station without his help. Imagine Grand Central Station with 10 times the number of people, all speaking Spanish as fast as they possibly could. My taxi driver was as insane as you need to be to drive in that city; he would start to turn down a street, see the traffic, throw it into reverse into oncoming traffic, try the next street, weave in and out, run lights and barely miss pedestrians, all while laying on the horn. We made it to my hotel without incident; it wasn't as scary as it sounds since he seemed to have everything under control. I did learn, however, that this was not a place to walk out into the street and expect cars to stop.

My hotel was in the Centro Historico, 34 blocks of museums and historic buildings. I wouldn't have been able to guess that from wandering around; I saw dozens of wedding dress stores on one street, another street of camera stores, and an entire street of Jesus stores, with some small cafés in between. The people, the noise, the traffic: Mexico City was slightly terrifying and more than a little intimidating. It was time for some Mexican television in my room. The trip there was enough adventure for one day.

The next day was a great day to be in Mexico City – it was election day and everyone was out voting. There were miles of people standing in lines guarded by police in full riot gear. My hotel overlooked the Zocalo, or Plaza de la Constitucion, which is the absolute center of the city, and is surrounded by government buildings and cathedrals. The square was filled with people lighting candles and holding prayer vigils for their candidates, camera crews filming at the voting stations, and a giant stage under construction. This was definitely the place to be on election night.

I started my grid search of the city, determined to find some cool stuff. The first place I came to was the Mexico City Metropolitan Cathedral, and a lot of people were going in, so I followed. No earthquake or hellfire rained down, despite what my father seemed to think would happen if I walked into a church. As I wandered in I heard the processional start, and that's really the only way to get me into a church – to trap me inside while sightseeing. After years of Catholic school, I think the last time I went to mass I was at the Vatican, about seven years ago. I guess it was time again. The incense brought back mixed memories of Catholic youth: getting paddled by nuns, but also sneaking quick naps in church during school hours. You really have to give the Catholics credit, though – I've been to masses at the Vatican, Mexico City, and Middleburg Heights, Ohio, and there's not a single difference in the ritual. Way to stick to a plan.

The next discovery on my list was Diego Rivera's murals at Palacio Nacional. I walked and walked and couldn't find a single open door in the block-sized building. Whether it was because of the elections or because it was Sunday, I wasn't sure.

Keeping the cathedral's location in mind, I started wandering the streets, not looking for anything in particular – just taking in all of the activity on a day when every Mexican is outdoors. All of the stores were open with the merchandise blocking the roads, and every store had a man with a microphone and speaker calling out what he had for sale. I walked for about three hours before I realized I had no idea which direction I had come from and had a moment of panic. The people in Mexico City weren't easy to approach; they were all in a hurry and spoke way too fast for me to understand, so I had to work up the courage to approach someone and ask for directions. Of course, I picked the only crack whore on the street, and instead of getting directions I was invited to her party, which probably involved taking me to a bar where I would then be parted from all my money. It was an interesting conversation, though. Finally I found a chubby, innocent-looking woman with small children who pointed my way home.

The next day, I went to see the pyramids at Teotihuacan. I signed up for a tour through my hotel and in an eight-hour day, we only got to spend two hours at the site and didn't get to see everything. A van picked me up and we drove around the city picking up two other people: Sasha, a Russian studying in Los Angeles, and Juan Pablo, a flight attendant from Colombia, both also traveling solo. They were both on layovers to their next destination, and along with another American couple on a long layover, they were the only non-Mexicans I'd seen. I thought I was the only tourist in the city right then.

While we thought we were headed straight to the pyramids, we stopped at a market far outside of town where the locals carve statues and make tequila. I should have guessed that we would be forced to stop somewhere to spend money, and with the free tequila shots, that's exactly what happened. I went from feeling like a captive to wondering what cool figurines my friends might like. The one nice thing I can say is that the tequila-hawkers were very generous with the free drinks, although we all spent way more money than it cost to get us drunk – at 10 a.m.

Teotihuacan was an amazing sight, ancient stone streets and structures as far as I could see. Our guide dropped us off, half-drunk, at the entrance and we were told to meet at the other entrance in two hours, which didn't leave time for much. Along the way, we saw mostly Mexican families on vacation, and hundreds of vendors selling strange carvings of jaguar heads that made growling noises when you blew into them. That sound followed us the entire way; by the end I thought if one more person made a jaguar roar, I was going to start smashing them all. We couldn't walk five feet without someone trying to sell us something, which really made the visit disappointing.

The one pyramid we made sure to climb was the Pyramid of the Sun. I was told that there was a piece of silver at the top to touch for good luck. It's also the tallest pyramid with 248 steps to the top, and people were camped out on the crooked stairs almost the entire way, huffing and puffing. This was my first of many examples of things you can do in foreign countries that you could never do in the United States. The steps were crooked and narrow and almost straight up, there were no hand rails, and there was nobody watching you for safety. Later, I tried to Google how many people have died on those steps, but couldn't find any information. I'm guessing a lot.

When we finally made it to the top, walking over dozens of bodies laid out and barely breathing from the climb, and went to find the silver charm, the entire peak was roped off with yellow *cuidado* tape (caution), and workmen were replacing the stones. That must be the opposite of good luck.

I also went to the Museo Nacional de Antropologia, but I went on my own time so I was in no hurry. Just a death-defying cab ride away from my hotel. All-in-all, I was not impressed with Mexico City. I think if I was in a group or had another travel partner, I would have liked it more, but as a single woman with grade-school Spanish, it was very unfriendly. The bars were dark and loud, it was impossible to try to understand anyone speaking, and walking at night had a very sinister feeling to it. I spent a decent amount of time in my room watching Spanish sitcoms trying to absorb more language without actually studying. My hotel was not much nicer. They talked me into an upgrade, for a fee of course, to get away from the construction I should have been away from anyway. Not a lot of money, but all those little extras add up. In the end I think I won since my upgrade got me the all-you-can-eat breakfast buffet.

Four days in Mexico City, completely exhausted from walking, sightseeing and failures at communication, and I was ready for my next destination, Mazatlan. Finally, some beach time.

But first, the Benito Juarez International Airport in Mexico City. That was an adventure in itself for a solo tourist. I tried to check in at an automated kiosk as directed, and it wouldn't give me my ticket. I was sent inside, waited in an almost endless line with my heavy backpack now full of tequila and unnecessary carved trinkets bought in an alcoholic haze, was told I had to go to another room to wait in another line, then told to go back to the first room. It was not hard to fake tears at this point; being a woman does have advantages at times. The man at the counter felt bad and gave me a ticket, but not a guaranteed seat, because the airline overbooked the flight. I begged some more to no avail, went through security and found another man to show some tears, and got on the plane. I bought my ticket two weeks earlier, so I'm not sure why I was only able to get on the plane by threatening a meltdown, but if that's what it took, I was willing to do it. The airport must have a social program to employ people in wheelchairs, and they were the first friendly, smiling faces I'd seen in Mexico City. Nothing like finding happy people, only to get on a plane and never come back.

MAZATLAN

Finally, I made it to Mazatlan. The first thing that happened when I got off the plane – or rather didn't – was I couldn't get a taxi. Usually, tourists get mugged by taxi drivers trying to take them somewhere, all shouting at once, so this was pretty unusual. Every driver was wearing the same uniform and ignoring me – even weirder. I went to the desk and was told that if I didn't have transportation already arranged, I had to sign up for a timeshare to get a ride. All I had to do was spend a morning touring a hotel, El Cyd, and I'd receive gifts and get my taxi money refunded. Total monopoly, total bullshit. I signed up, since it was too far to walk to my hotel with my giant backpack, and paid an outrageous amount of money. The driver took me all the way to the opposite side of town, then turned back, turning my 20-minute ride into an hour. Normally I'd practice my Spanish on drivers, but I was so ticked off I didn't say anything except "you're going the wrong way" while showing him the map to my hotel.

I checked into my room and the hotel seemed pleasant enough. I had a balcony on the third floor, and directly in front of me was a two-lane road, then the *malecón* (boardwalk), then the ocean. There was a lot of activity – skateboarders, rollerbladers, dog walkers, joggers, and people just hanging out. My room was fairly run-down – painted plywood everywhere, and I immediately broke all the doorknobs; I didn't think I wanted my toothbrush anywhere near the bathroom. But there was a sort of Mexican charm to the place, and that made up for a lot.

My first thought was to go swimming to wash off the stress of travel and soak up some saltwater after a month in dry mountain air. On Kauai, I'd swim a couple times a week, go way out in the ocean with a friend and check out the turtles and fish. This water was brown and scary, however; I couldn't even see my fingertips. Fish were jumping next to me, and these giant birds would swoop down and dive at them. Then I swam through a bait ball and wondered what the hell was chasing them? I don't think I've ever swam so fast to get back to the beach. Maybe it was just time to soak up some sun.

I was walking up the beach to get my towel when a man approached with a Tupperware of water and a big blue jellyfish.

I'd noticed a couple on the beach earlier, but I didn't pay them any attention. He told me that the full moon and high tide and a storm in the south meant there would be tons of jellyfish and I shouldn't swim for the next few days. Not that I'd see them in the murky gross water; I'd just get wrapped up in a burning 3-foot tentacle. So much for swimming here. Mazatlan was looking way less attractive, and I'd only been there a couple hours.

So what to do? Sit in a bar and drink margaritas – that's always a good backup plan. I walked the *malecón* and ended up sitting across from some bars listening to music while trying to decide which bar to visit first, and a man strolled up and handed me a Corona. We sat and drank and I worked on my Spanish. Another man sitting a few feet away whistled at me, came running over and pulled me to my feet. *Cucarachas.* I looked behind me, and every time a wave broke, hordes of giant roaches scrambled up the wall. He kicked them back into the ocean. That's how I spent my first night: free cold beer, a whistle, get up, kick the roaches away.

My new friends told me the cops have been cracking down on people drinking by the beach – exactly what we were doing. But I'm a tourist; I figured the most they'd do is pour out my beer. Mexico needs tourists, especially Americans, after all the bad press from drug cartel killings. Moments later, we saw a police pickup truck drive by with two giant men standing in the back wearing black masks and head-to-toe black riot gear, cradling machine guns. They made the cops at home look like Barney Fife. That gave me a little pause, so I waited until they were a block away to pick up my beer again.

I went to my timeshare appointment, mostly because they promised to refund my taxi fare, but also because they were picking me up and taking me to the far end of Mazatlan, where

I hadn't gone yet. I got there and the hotel representative sat me down to breakfast by myself and told me to lie about what hotel I'm staying in so she could get credit. Sketchy right off the bat. Twenty minutes later, a man took me to a presentation room to ask me a few questions before the tour. It was a nice-looking hotel – not any place I'd stay even if I had the money, and certainly not a place I'd consider buying a timeshare, and I told him that. I explained that I was hijacked at the airport, had no interest in whatever he was going to tell me, and all I wanted was my cab fare back. It didn't occur to me that he'd be offended; I figured that with the airport ride setup he'd heard it all before, but he said, "You have a bad attitude and I don't want to waste my time. Please pay for your breakfast and leave." Whatever. I'm a budget traveler and I came to get my money back; go ahead and try to make me leave before that happens. I ended up going to the sales desk and telling the woman there I had finished my tour and I'd like my free gifts now, and she gave me a fully paid boat trip to a bird-watching island and $30 cash.

I caught a taxi out of the hotel marina and walked the rest of the way back to my hotel. I'd now seen all of Mazatlan; I couldn't swim and there was no surf – nothing to do but drink. So I bought a bus ticket to Sayulita, gave my boat trip to the sweet woman at the hotel desk, and packed my gear. I was warned that I wouldn't like Mazatlan, but obviously I was so new at this travel thing that I thought I could be happy anywhere. Lesson learned; on to the next adventure.

SAYULITA

Sayulita was a great place to hang out and just be. Family-style restaurants, hippie smoothie bars, yoga palapas, surf shops, and of course plenty of bars. The town is basically three streets with a central square; there aren't any dangerous places to drunkenly stumble into, and the beach is covered with umbrellas and chairs and cute men who bring you drinks. I didn't have a place to stay when I arrived, so I found a taxi and told him to take me anywhere that wasn't too expensive, then later I could walk around and find a hotel where I'd want to stay for a week or two. I took advantage of the free yoga class at the Hotelito Los Sueños, where I met a vacationing family from Tampico, Mexico. We decided to trade surf lessons for Spanish lessons and we borrowed some soft-top boards and hit the beach. My Spanish class in San Miguel left me completely unprepared to give surf instructions, but thankfully they spoke English well. I was out with two women and their boyfriends, not water people, so when they got tired and went back to the beach, I paddled out to the real surf break and caught a few small waves. I couldn't compete with all the guys on 11-foot boards and didn't want to piss off the "Mexican Surf Mafia," or so all of the stickers on their boards said, so I paddled in and hung out with my new family.

They had a cooler full of cans of tequila, something completely new to me, but quite welcome. And there was a man selling marijuana donuts, so we bought a few of those. Quite a pleasant afternoon, sitting under umbrellas on the beach. I thought I might be high for days. The mother of the family was getting a foot massage when I got back and I mistakenly thought it was from her husband, but it was just some random guy. I wasn't prepared for just anyone to rub my feet, but they told me to sit back and relax and enjoy, and the donut was really kicking in, so I let him work his magic on me, too. Apparently he's a roving foot massager, and I never quite figured out how he got paid, but it's possible he was just a weirdo with a foot fetish who does it for free. At one point, he put my toes in his mouth, and if that was why he was doing it, I guess that's a small price to pay for a foot rub.

I went back to my hotel for some air conditioning and found a boat company online for a snorkel trip, and sent an email to make a reservation. Almost immediately, I received a reply with a request to meet the captain that night for a drink. Again, sort of odd. I have a lot of experience on boats, having worked for a charter boat company on Kauai for six years, and Darrin wasn't much different from the other captains I've met. Fantastic stories of sailing in exotic places. We talked about his boat and walked around town with his little dogs, or "my children," as he called them. When I told him I worked as an accountant for a boat company, he immediately thought that our meeting was fated. I was going to move here and work with him and be his true love and make his company successful. I wasn't quite drunk enough to agree with him just yet.

I was invited to join him on his next charter to Yalapa, a remote fishing village. Waterfalls and caves were promised, and it was a really good pickup line. I was going.

Technically, Sayulita is one hour different from Puerto Vallarta, but since everyone who has ever come here has missed their planes, buses or appointments, the local government decreed that there was no more time change. My iPhone disagreed, so I was never quite sure what time it was. And since most people now rely on their iPhones as watches, people have had a lot of problems with trips they scheduled. Darrin lectured me on this for 20 minutes before he was satisfied that I understood, and we set my pickup time at 8:30 a.m. in front of my cute new cabana at the Bungalos Aurinko.

I've had a good amount of experience on commercial boat trips and private fishing boats, but nothing prepared me for Darrin's boat.

Darrin and his dogs picked me up in his beat-up red Volkswagen Beetle, dogs hanging out the window, cigarette dangling from Darrin's lips. We drove to La Cruz Marina, about 20 minutes away from Puerto Vallarta, and I had coffee with some of his other guests while the crew was getting the boat ready.

The Sayula 1 is a trimaran, about 25 years old, and it was about what you'd expect for a boat company: cushions to lay on, although covered with dog hair; trampolines; a bar in the main cabin, the boat itself maybe not in as good of repair as it used to be, or as clean as it should be. The smell of cigarettes was everywhere, and Darrin was clearly on his way to a nice buzz by 10. I asked when the boat was last dry-docked and he just laughed. This is Mexico, after all; they probably don't have many Coast Guard inspections.

Our group was an interesting mix of gay men and couples from Texas smoking cigars. One of the Texans, Jeff – long scraggly ZZ Top beard and all – told me he paid extra so he could control who else goes on the boat, and he wasn't very happy with the other half of the group in Speedos and Panama hats, oiling each other to maximize their sun time. Darrin was a pretty happy-go-lucky guy, and after a few drinks he didn't even notice that his tourists were shooting dirty looks at each other across the boat. For their part, his tourists didn't notice that their captain had progressed from beer to rum and was lighting a joint as the boat pulled away from the dock.

The crew consisted of three Mexican guys, one of whom thankfully took the helm from Darrin. The others were making drinks and serving us on the trampolines. We started out slowly from the marina and we never picked up speed; I found out later that the propellers had broken and Darrin didn't have the money to replace them, so he had bought a set half the size his boat needed. We went across the bay at about four knots, watching every other boat company reach the destination as we puttered along getting drunk. We stopped to swim a couple times and watch a pod of dolphins, and we finally made it to Yelapa. We had two solid hours of drinking before we started our hike to the waterfall.

At the beach, we boarded a water taxi and went to the palapas on the beach for lunch. Although Yelapa is not an island, there are no cars or major roads, so it's only accessible by boat; there weren't many other tourists. The beach was covered with dozens of beach chairs with umbrellas, and only about four other people. We had more drinks and amazing fresh fish. Darrin's dogs were running around the beach, chasing the local children, and jumping on them and barking if they happened to trip and fall while running away. We continued drinking, and the crew was sitting at a table apart from us rolling fat joints for everyone. This was definitely the first cruise I've been on where the captain and crew were more loaded than the passengers.

The waterfall is at the top of the town and we had to walk up narrow cobblestone streets in the blazing sun. Everyone was pretty messed up and we were by no means certain we'd make it all the way. I kept catching my flip-flops on the stones and skinning my knees and hands. Two of the Texans paid to take horses up, led by a guide. I don't know how Darrin did the hike while chain-smoking. We stopped for a water break, no idea how much longer this hike would be, wondering if we should just go back to the beach and keep drinking. But we finally made it to the top of the road and the waterfall was beautiful, as they all are. The water was cold and we swam until we were almost sober again, then headed back down so the slow boat could make it back to town before dark.

The crew took up a collection so we could buy more booze for the boat, then they unfurled the sails and we made good time back just as a storm rolled in to soak us. No one was even remotely sober enough to care, and happily, the sheer quantity of alcohol and pot eventually bonded our group so we were all having fun together.

As we were getting off the boat, Darrin asked us to pay his crew because he didn't like to deal with money, which was probably why his business was just barely holding on. He told me a couple times he was looking for someone to run his business, and I could definitely see that he needed help. One of the groups made arrangements to meet up with him in a couple days to pay, and the accountant side of me cringed at this. Money collection is a pretty important part of a successful business. But this was Mexico, so nothing really surprised me anymore.

I'd been in Sayulita for a week, and life had fallen into a very pleasant pattern. I got up at about 8 a.m. and walked across town to the Hotelito Los Sueños, the hotel where I spent my first night. I did yoga in Spanish for an hour and a half for only 80 pesos, not quite $6, under a giant palapa on a third-floor terrace. My next stop was the coffee bar across the hotel – all you can drink for 15 pesos with free Wi-Fi. At around 11 I started wandering back towards my hotel and stopped at the smoothie shop for a "Surfer's Brunch," lots of fruit and oatmeal and a chat with the owners, a Mexican woman and her English husband. By then it was incredibly hot out; Mexico in July is maybe why there weren't many tourists around, and it was time for some air conditioning in my room. I liked to hide from the sun from noon to three, using the time to work on my Spanish, play online and make lunch. I bought a Spanish copy of "Harry Potter and the Sorcerer's Stone" that I had been copying and translating, per Enrique's instructions. He might not like my choice of book, but he thought it was very important that I copy Spanish text so I can better understand sentence structure and learn new words. It was pretty slow going; maybe I should have started with an actual children's book. I had to look up half the words, then I ended up forgetting them and looking them up again the next day. I can't say I'd learned much in the three weeks since my class had ended.

Three o'clock was beach time and it was still way hotter than I could possibly describe, but it was becoming bearable. I grabbed a paddleboard from the cute Mexican guys by the water and spent about an hour catching small waves and paddling to the beaches farther down the shore. Then I went for a swim; the water was much clearer here than in Mazatlan, although it was still pretty dark in comparison to Kauai. The water was also really warm, but if I swam out far enough it got cool, the tradeoff being that it became scary dark and I was far away from the crowd. I don't think anyone worries about sharks here, but I was afraid to ask. This is the ocean, after all, so of course there were sharks somewhere nearby. I just tried not to think about it.

To end my typical day, I went back to the hotel for a shower and more air conditioning, and more cans of tequila. I stocked my refrigerator with them, another recent addiction. Sometime around sunset I would walk around town to see who was out and wanted to chat and buy me a drink, and find somewhere new for dinner. Fish tacos and margaritas were usually the way to go. The final stop of the night was at the cake lady's corner stand, a dangerous thing to have a block from my room.

I spent another day on Darrin's boat, against my better judgment. We went to the Marieta Islands to snorkel. There was a newly married young couple from San Francisco and a family from Belgium. No matter what type of crowd, Darrin always ran his boat the same; rum and joints all day long. It was pretty clear that not everyone liked this, another item I'd have to mention if I ever agreed to write him a business plan. The highlight of this trip was snorkeling through a cave system to a hidden beach with three passengers who couldn't swim. But that didn't stop Darrin. He wanted everyone to see the beach, so he tied giant floats to the women and threw them in the water. They couldn't hang on to his safety surfboard, though, because that was where his dogs rode to get towed to the beach. There was a lot of surge in the water that day and the tide was high, so as we were swimming through the cave the water would rush in and those who couldn't swim, tied to floats, kept hitting their heads on the rock ceiling as they were held underwater. Not drowning your passengers is another essential component of a good business plan. Death does not bring repeat business.

I'd been on the road for seven weeks now, and I can't say I'd learned many new skills. I was still a poor planner and got lost wherever I went, thank God for my iPhone map app. Just follow the blue dot.

I've always been afraid of public transportation. I remember my first time taking a bus across town in Cleveland by myself as a freshman in high school. I got completely lost and ended up getting home hours after I was expected. This was before cell phones; my mom was worried sick and I was in tears. I simply wasn't capable of getting where I needed to go, even with a schedule and a map. That experience kept me from learning how it's supposed to work because the next time I tried to ride a bus was

15 years later. I got an extra job at Christmas at the Barnes and Noble in downtown Seattle, and I didn't want to sit through rush-hour traffic and pay $15 to park every night. I stressed out thinking that I was going to miss my stop, even though the bus stopped on almost every corner. Every night I'd stand by the driver, bugging him about where I was supposed to get off; he was continuously annoyed, and I never got the hang of it.

When I was in Mexico, I had that same fear multiplied. Each bus had seven or eight town names written in chalk on the windows, and the bus stops were just benches in the middle of nowhere with no signs.

I was forced to find the bus stop one day because my niece, Pam, flew to Puerto Vallarta to meet me, and I can't tell you how envious I was that she was able to catch a bus from the airport to get to Sayulita. It doesn't seem like such a hard task, but I was unable to do it and ended up paying about 10 times as much for a taxi to get there. Public transportation is a skill, and I was hoping that I wasn't too old to learn.

I did ride the cross-country buses, but those are more like going to an airport, although easier since there's no security. My longest bus ride was nine hours from Mazatlan to Sayulita, and the other three hours from San Miguel to Mexico City. But both times I was outrageously nervous and got to the station so early I thought I had missed my bus. Yay, anxiety.

I don't know why local buses make me run in fear; if I get lost I can just take the opposite bus back to where I started. And if I arrive late, so what? It's not like I had a job at the moment. I planned to recruit Pam and her fearless bus-riding abilities to teach me the necessary skills for the rest of my trip.

We spent three more days in Sayulita together; I had intended on showing her all the fun places I found, but we mostly sat on the beach and drank Coronas under an umbrella, or margaritas at the beach bars. When in Rome, I guess. I didn't want to subject her to Darrin's boat, so instead our big adventure was to Playa Los Muertos, a beach that can be found only by hiking through an old graveyard.

Our plan was to spend Pam's birthday in Puerto Vallarta, so we packed up our gear, downed the last cans of tequila, and walked to the dreaded bus stop. It was noon, we were dripping with sweat, and we sat with the locals on benches to wait. To Pam's chagrin, I had insisted on being early, just in case. When we finally boarded, the driver was blaring mariachi music with all the doors and windows open, and nothing bad happened. A good start to more friendly bus-riding memories.

PUERTO VALLARTA

Pam's birthday dinner was at an Americanized Mexican restaurant, which mostly meant that it cost more than the others, but it had air conditioning and cute Mexican waiters bringing her free margaritas and singing. We tried to go to a pool hall, but we were told they were all *muy peligroso*, so we ended up at a rooftop bar watching the world go by. A pretty pleasant birthday, all-in-all.

The next morning, we headed to the airport for our flight to Cancun, on our way to Isla Mujeres, to swim with whale sharks. I've never felt quite so violated as at the airport in Puerto Vallarta. I'd been having to sit on my backpack lately to get it to zip, so I was pretty disturbed when the security woman unzipped my bag and started removing everything for everyone in line to see. I was completely mortified when she found my tampon stash. I had no idea what it would be like to buy feminine products in Mexico, or any of Central America, so I filled one entire pocket of my backpack in case I couldn't find any. Lonely Planet didn't tell me anything about tampon shopping in other countries. But the security woman's main concern seemed to be the bottle of tequila that I had wrapped in paper, and once she had ripped it all apart like a child on Christmas, she wadded up my clothes around it and stuffed it back in my bag. And then I had to sit on my bag in the airport to close it again. Thanks.

The rest of the way was much the same: "Please turn off all your electronics." Ignored. "Please take your seat and fasten your seat belt." People got up to run to the bathroom or rummage through the overhead compartments. Everyone just did what they felt like doing and no one seemed to care. But there was free booze the entire way.

CANCUN

We were mobbed by cab drivers leaving the airport and bartered for a good price to our hotel. We must have gotten a great price, because when we told our driver we were staying at El Sol, he tried to leave us at an abandoned building with a sun painted next to the door; he had no idea where he was going. We picked this hotel from Lonely Planet because of the price, and it was close to the beach. But Lonely Planet failed to mention that it was in front of the docks and there was no water access to swim within half an hour's walk. Or any grocery stores nearby. Or open restaurants. Our first night was spent with chips and salsa from the Oxxo and watching awesomely bad Mexican TV.

The next morning we figured out exactly where we had chosen to stay, which was not a place we would have picked given a well thought-out decision. It possibly had something to do with the number of beers we drank before sitting down to make our arrangements. But we were leaving the next day for Isla Mujeres, so we decided to make the best of it. We took a taxi to Playa Linda in the hotel district. We walked through a resort to the beach, only to find that all the resorts have large guests-only areas with no bars or beach chairs accessible to regular people. We walked until we found a hotel bar near the water that would let us in, and that's where we spent our day, drinking on the beach.

Cancun gets a lot of great reviews, but I wasn't terribly impressed. The water was pretty, but there was too much gunk floating in it to swim very long, and not many fish. The resorts all had boats and jet skis, so when I did get in I could only swim in the small roped off squares anyway. Twenty strokes across, hit a rope, twenty strokes back, pull the seaweed out of my goggles. There were very few local families since all the resorts made all the beaches private; it wasn't a very friendly place.

We had a nice margarita buzz working, so we decided to take the bus into the city. As we climbed aboard, the driver asked if we were lost. We may have been the first gringos ever to ride this bus. It was air-conditioned and blaring mariachi music videos, packed with blue-collar Mexicans and now two white chicks. Not for your average all-inclusive resort guests.

I had previously thought central Cancun would be a tourist area, which again goes to prove the point that I may be the worst travel researcher ever. It was much more like the Mexico I saw in San Miguel and the back streets of Sayulita, with great family-style restaurants, cheap food, good beer, and a fantastic taco stand with a super-hot Mexican guy with whom I totally failed to communicate. There was traffic and garbage, and eventually, a part of town where we really didn't want to be. We were the only tourists around.

After almost eight weeks of travel, I was trying to think of the last day I hadn't drank some sort of alcohol. Beers, margaritas, tequila shots, I even tried some bootleg tequila at the Sayulita Public House, called *raicilla*. My curiosity was satisfied; I don't think I ever need to spend a night drinking that again. But as each day began, I considered that maybe it was time to take a day or two off. I was starting to feel my clothes getting a bit tighter, and each day had been starting a tiny bit later than the previous one. Pam was going to be with me for another two weeks, and Andy was visiting in a couple days, but I thought I'd sober up for a bit after they left, if for no reason than just to make sure I still could.

ISLA MUJERES

The ferry from Cancun to Isla Mujeres, or just "Isla," as the locals call it, was about 30 minutes of plush seats and air conditioning and left Pam and me at the main dock on the north side. Suddenly we were surrounded by bars, restaurants, and hundreds of people hawking the same merchandise sold in every part of Mexico, just with a different city name embroidered on it. Everyone was driving golf carts or riding mopeds, with a few cars here and there. The water was the perfect blue of a Caribbean postcard, and it was incredibly hot.

Pam and I walked with our luggage about five blocks to Hotel Posada Del Mar, right across the street from the beach. It was a pretty decent place with Wi-Fi and air-conditioning, which were really the only must-haves for a place to stay. There was a pool with warm, murky green water and a bar with a pool table. There was a large group of annoying, loud young adults, but the air conditioner was so loud we could barely hear ourselves speak, so all was well.

Most people take the ferry here for a day trip, so it was really only crowded from 9 a.m. to sunset. The first morning I went running on the beach and it was nearly deserted, just some guys out setting up rental chairs and umbrellas and some women raking garbage from the sand. No stores were open; no one pestered me to buy things I'd seen every day for the past seven weeks. It was so nice. By the time I was done swimming, the first ferry was arriving. By breakfast, all the stalls were set up and the island was in full swing. The main street got crazy busy for several hours, then as the tourists got too sunburned and drunk, it slowly subsided back to the relatively few people staying there overnight.

The main part of the island is the north shore, comprising about seven streets of stores, restaurants, laundromats and hotels. It's very touristy, but quite charming as well. I would have loved it more if I could walk five feet without someone trying to get me to go into their store or eat at their café. In Sayulita, the boldest salespeople were roving the beach; here it was the people standing in front of their stores.

"Please, ladies, pass inside to the air conditioning and look at my jewelry."

"Ladies, please look at my menu and eat here," as a large plastic card was shoved in our faces.

"You need a golf cart; come right this way."

"Book your whale shark trip with me, the best boat on the Isla."

Enough already. Please stop.

The north shore is where all the action is, then there's a thin strip of land going south to a point on the shore with a lighthouse and some Mayan ruins. The whole island is about four miles long. If I had been running with any regularity, I could run to the end and back. But I hadn't, so we took a golf cart.

We visited the south shore and the Mayan ruins. They were fairly uninspiring after seeing Teotihuacan and Cañada de la Virgen, but the giant lizards roving the rocks were impressive. We also stopped at a turtle farm with tanks full of hundreds of newly hatched babies – possibly the cutest things I've ever seen. The locals didn't seem to think anything about grabbing them by the handful to give to their children to pose for pictures.

By far the greatest activity of my trip up to that point was swimming with whale sharks. We were picked up at our hotel by Willy, a local guide and salesman, along with a woman who had been going there for years and her granddaughter. This woman, Joanne, was pretty funny. She was about 65, smoked constantly, acted exactly how she wanted to, and didn't care what anyone thought. That's how I want to be when I get older. She also knew everyone who needed knowing on the island.

It was just the four of us on the boat, plus Willy and two crew members. By law, one crew member had to be in the water with tourists at all times, and only two tourists per boat could swim with the sharks at a time. We had to wear awful orange life vests from the moment we got on the boat and had to swim in them as well, which made it hard to get any good underwater pictures.

We motored an hour and a half northeast and could see about a dozen other boats converging in the same general area. The first boat to spot a shark radioed the coordinates. The ride was a little bumpy but not too bad, and Pam and I spent the time learning Spanish words for aquatic life. Then suddenly, in the middle of nowhere, we saw dozens of shark fins and it was time to swim.

I volunteered to swim in the first group and the boat dropped us a few feet in front of a whale shark's head. I swam as fast as I could with a camera and bulky life vest, and slowly the shark made its way past me, mouth opening and closing, gills fluttering, tail whooshing back and forth, remoras stuck to its sides. It was enormous and beautiful. We got back on the boat to let Joanne and her granddaughter swim, then traded back and forth for about an hour with the giant fish. I got too close taking pictures and was smacked a few times, but it was more exciting than scary; even though the whale sharks were more than 30 feet long, they weren't interested in eating me.

I was so enthralled by the sharks that I hadn't noticed Willy had been vomiting over the side all morning. Too much tequila last night. He came back to life as we were coming home, so we stopped at a reef to snorkel while the crew made us ceviche and sandwiches with interestingly colored mystery meat. When we got back I booked a second trip to take Andy; I knew this was on his bucket list, and well worth the money. To be honest, swimming with whale sharks was his idea. I just got here first.

Pam and I spent the next day by the pool ordering fried food and Coronas, to recover from a night of playing pool with a couple local guys. We learned new Spanish words to use in a bar, which I quickly forgot due to the amount of alcohol I had consumed. Andy was due to arrive and we scouted out a hotel with a hot tub. I was preparing to abandon Pam for a few days.

It was great to see Andy again when I picked him up on my golf cart the next day. We had been talking now and again over Skype and he was a wealth of knowledge about Mexico and where I should go next. He'd been all through Central America and swimming with the sharks was one thing he hadn't done, so I was happy I could be there for that. We went with Willy and his crew again and had another amazing trip. This time, though, I paid extra for the guys to "overlook" the fact that we weren't going to wear the giant orange life vests. Instead we wore full wetsuits, so we were able to get under water easier for better pictures. There were just as many whale sharks and we swam all day again. It was well worth Andy's trip to Isla. Our hot tub, however, wasn't so great. It was on a balcony overlooking Half Moon Bay, a gorgeous spot on the northern tip of the island, but we couldn't make it either hot or cold, just lukewarm. As we were walking home from the beach, Andy had a great idea to buy as many bags of ice as we could carry, totaling about eight giant bags, and we made an ice bath. We got a bottle of Don Julio, some snacks, and sat in the coldest water to watch the sunset. The guy's a genius.

We picked up Pam the next day to travel to Playa del Carmen, where Andy would spend a couple days with me before he had to get back to work. Andy and I had a room at the Alhambra hotel on the beach. What seemed like the most serene location was actually surrounded by all-night discos. Of course, this wasn't mentioned in any of the online advertisements. After a day of travel and wandering the streets and searching for the best margaritas, Andy was sleeping peacefully. I, however, was disturbingly awake at 4 a.m., wondering when the thumping music would become bearable. Then the power went out, which meant no air conditioning or fans. It didn't stop the music, though; the bars wouldn't let a little thing like no power stop the all-night parties. I was so miserable, lying in bed dripping sweat.

I went downstairs to find out what was going on and found an older woman working the night crew, unable to answer any questions, like "Why is it hotter than hell in my room?" or, "Do you have free earplugs?"

She went sort of Zen on me and asked me to calm down, even though I had asked my questions in a whisper so as not to wake up anyone else and include them in the horrible, hot, loud night. In fact, she had to ask me three times to calm down because I couldn't believe she was saying that to me. I kept making her repeat it. I made sure to smile when I told her how much her hotel sucked. Instead of telling me when the power might come back on, or when the music might turn off, her only answer was that I should take this opportunity to learn something about myself. Well, I know that I'm pretty fucking miserable when I pay for a nice room and the air conditioner doesn't work and it's hotter than hell and the bar next door keeps me up all night. But I already knew that, and that's why I paid for a nice room. I guess I learned that I hadn't changed. I'm ok with that.

At 5:30 the power came back on, at 6 the music stopped, and at 7:30 Andy was up and ready to see the world. Ugh. This might be a good day for margaritas on the beach and maybe a massage. As we walked down the beach, we were accosted by multiple women asking if we wanted a beach massage. At $25 for an hour, I thought it was worth a try, and Andy was up for it. We were led to some massage tables by a bar, behind the rental chairs and umbrellas filled with tourists. I'm not sure what I expected for $25, but I ended up with an old Mexican man who rubbed my shoulders for half an hour, then turned me over and rubbed my stomach. He made me peel off my bikini before he started, and towards the end I was wondering if maybe he should be paying me for all the free feels he was taking. When the hour was up, he left me to try to shimmy back into my bikini and that just ended up with me naked in front of the crowd. Andy had the opposite experience; what guy doesn't like getting rubbed down by a cute Mexican girl? I felt like he got a way better deal.

Andy and I spent the rest of the day drinking margaritas and napping on the beach, then went to find some night life. We asked the taxi driver for a club, and got dropped off at a bar called Chillie Willie's outside of town, very exclusive-looking with a cover charge. It was a strip club. The drinks were outrageously expensive for Mexico and the women looked very sad. It certainly wasn't the kind of strip club you see in music videos, athletic women with fake boobs doing gymnastic moves on the poles. These women were slowly walking around in g-strings and high heels and obviously thinking about how horrible their lives were.

At this late hour, after no sleep, bad bar food and margaritas all day, then a guy rubbing my stomach, I had begun to have some digestive issues. I was too embarrassed to tell Andy that I wasn't feeling well and needed to go home, but the cab ride was about half an hour so I wasn't sure I could make it there anyway. I excused myself and found the women's room and proceeded to have a painful 10 minutes. And then, of course, Mexican plumbing being what it is, I had to leave the evidence after three completely ineffectual flushes. Since I was the only woman in the bar, I was more than happy when I got back to the table and Andy suggested we go home. For all I knew, someone would bring me a bucket and make me fix the toilet.

TULUM

After six days, Andy had to get back to work; his taxi picked him up for the airport and I met up with Pam again and we caught a bus to Tulum, about an hour south. As we were packing to go, I felt the first of some back pain and couldn't figure out what I had done to hurt myself. The giant backpack was not comfortable.

Tulum is a much smaller town than Playa del Carmen, but still mobbed with tourists. There are two areas where you can stay: by the beach with nothing else around you or in town, far from the beach. We were worried that we'd end up in the same situation as in Puerto Vallarta, where we thought we were near the beach and ended up with no restaurants or stores nearby, so we decided to stay in the town. There was one main street, which was actually the highway, and nothing much on the side streets. There were the usual bars and restaurants, and locals selling the same stuff we still didn't want to buy. We spent our first night in a bar catching up on the Olympics and learning more Spanish words for all the sports we normally don't care about.

Pam had to get back to Seattle for school, so we only had one full day in Tulum together and we were determined to do everything we could. After this last day I would be back on my own, but it was so nice having friendly faces around after six weeks by myself. We woke up early and did a scuba dive at Casa Cenote. It was Pam's first scuba experience and my first at a *cenote*, a natural well made by the collapse of a limestone surface. Gina was our guide and she was great; she was Swiss and spoke German, French, Spanish and English. I was pretty jealous of her languages. I keep learning languages almost to the point of being fluent, then I stop using them and forget everything. It probably won't be long until I can't remember a word of Spanish.

Gina taught Pam the basics of scuba, how to clear her mask, find her regulator – all the safety basics – then off we went in the hotel's rusty old pickup. This *cenote* was a mix of salt and fresh water, which made the visibility a little fuzzy, but it was a great place for a beginning diver. Most *cenotes* are full caves where there's a danger of hitting your head on a stalactite if you surface too quickly; this one was open-air and wasn't as dramatic, but still worthwhile. There were some fish, a lot of interesting algae-covered formations, and a rock tunnel to swim through. Pam had a bit of trouble with buoyancy control and Gina ended up dragging her around by her tank to keep her off the bottom or down from the surface. Overall she did great – much better than my first dive on Kauai when my mind kept telling me I couldn't breathe underwater, forcing me to surface repeatedly in a panic. Back then, I ended up having to hold my instructor's hand for the first 20 minutes, mortifying for a water girl. He wasn't even cute, which made it worse.

After the dive we took a *collectivo* to the famous Tulum ruins. It was our first trip in a *collectivo*, which is basically a van that gets crammed with as many people as the driver can find, as long as they're going in the same general direction. It only ended up being 10 pesos cheaper than a cab; the big advantage with *collectivos* probably comes with the longer trips.

The ruins were breathtaking. They weren't as dramatic as the pyramids, but they were on the coast and the background of Caribbean crystal-clear blue water made the trip well worth the smelly, sweaty drive. Every picture turned out to be the greatest picture I'd ever taken – it was that beautiful.

The downside of the Mayan ruins in Tulum was the extreme tourism. In Teotihuacan, the vast majority of the tourists were Mexican, but in Tulum we encountered the first significant amount of Americans. We were stuck on a path behind one obviously American couple with a video camera, and the husband thought he would narrate as he walked. "This was the ancient Mayan Waffle House." "This was the ancient Mayan police department."

For all I knew it might have been true, but still, how embarrassing.

Pam was thoughtful enough to book her flight home out of Cozumel so I could accompany her there then check out the diving. We backtracked to Playa del Carmen to catch a ferry, and while waiting there we met an English traveler going home after three months in South and Central America. He described himself as "a broken man," and couldn't wait to get home and eat gravy. I had signed myself up for a year of solo travel, so if this savvy-looking chap wearing handmade Guatemalan shoes was broken so quickly, I started to have doubts about how long I might last.

COZUMEL

The ferry to Cozumel was 35 minutes on another plush, air-conditioned boat. Mexico really knows how to do public transportation. A couple of very loud, annoying young women, obviously Americans, kept yelling for beer service, and when one of the crew finally walked over to direct them to the bar, where they can pay for and pick up drinks, they were disproportionately upset. No free beer, and they had to leave their seats? What kind of ferry is this? I love watching Mexicans deal with asshole Americans – they just pretend they don't speak English. *"Lo siento, no comprendo."* They were trying to describe their father to the woman, demanding that the crew member go find him, get money, then bring them beer. No Spanish, no money, they got *nada*. It was fun to watch.

The moment we got off the ferry, Pam and I were mobbed by pushy men trying to get us in a taxi, buy their trinkets, or come into their shops. I found myself becoming a bit rude to them; I just couldn't handle it anymore. I didn't want to buy something for my boyfriend or my mother, I didn't want to go into your store, I didn't need a taxi, and I didn't care if your jewelry was nicer than anyone else's. At least in Playa del Carmen there were so many other people that we could walk for a couple minutes without being harassed by salesmen, but it was nonstop in Cozumel. During our stay, when we needed to walk somewhere we'd go out of our way, crossing streets over and over again, just so we could pass the fewest stalls and stores. I had been to too many touristy places in the past couple weeks, and my tolerance was depleted.

We got to our hotel after about 20 minutes of constant sales pitches and our room wasn't ready. "Maybe half an hour," the receptionist said, which in Mexican time would be about an hour and a half. Sitting at the bar, we encountered what may have been the biggest loser American tourist yet. We sat there to watch more Olympics, and of course drink away some spare time, and an overweight, bald, loud, completely obnoxious man was complaining continuously to his Mexican "friends" about how much he hates gringos. Really? After listening for a while and refusing to take part in his conversation when he tried to chat us up, I was able to assess the situation. Americans won't put up with his crap, and Mexicans are too polite to tell him to shut up. He spoke fluent Spanish, so they were stuck.

The next day Pam left for Seattle. Her summer break was over and she was back to earning her Master's degree in Viola Performance and Orchestral Conducting at Kent State University. I missed her instantly. She was not only a great companion, but better with directions and Spanish. It was also nice to have someone to share the decision-making. That's one of the hardest things I've found – deciding where to go, where to stay, and how to get there. Having that second opinion was a nice relief. I don't always like to be in charge of myself. Too much responsibility.

As the days progressed since Andy left, I felt more and more pain in my back, and almost couldn't carry my backpack from the ferry to the hotel. I thought I might have to follow Pam back to the States. It hurt that much, and I had no idea why. If I couldn't carry my pack, I was a useless traveler. The night Pam left, it finally occurred to me why I was in so much pain. I was Skyping with Andy and he was complaining of a sore back as well. I think we had so much sex that we hurt ourselves. That's what happens being a lonely girl traveling solo, I guess. Find something good and do it over and over while it lasts.

I wandered around town and booked a scuba trip for the next day, and spent much of my first day alone in three weeks lazing in my room and watching the Olympics. I think I ordered a pizza. Downtime is necessary, just not too much.

I did two beautiful dives off Cozumel. The reefs were amazingly well-preserved despite all the tourism; there were corals and fans of every color, incredible fish diversity, visibility to about 100 feet, and comfortably warm water. We dove to 70 feet and it was like swimming in Dr. Seuss's fish tank. I did my open water course on Kauai in brownish cold water, and it didn't prepare me for what I saw on my first real Caribbean dive. There was a good current, so mostly I just kept still and watched as I floated past everything. I was afraid I'd miss the tiniest fish, so I concentrated hard to see small things and was completely surprised when a four-foot grouper snuck up on me. There were eels, rockfish, filefish, and everything that you might see in picture books of places you dream of diving. The first dive was at Palancar Gardens and the second, shallower dive was at La Francesa. There is a famous wall to dive there, but I was told there weren't enough experienced people to go, so it's still on my list of things to do. I'd definitely go back there to dive.

I caught a taxi to the dock for the dives because in Cozumel it's illegal for locals to give tourists a ride in a private car. Our dive guide, Francisco, told us that the taxi union is pretty much like the mafia – the drivers have an enormous amount of influence and are able to get locals fined thousands of dollars for taking away their business. After the dive, though, all the taxis got filled and left the harbor before we could grab one, so Francisco snuck us in his truck. Anna, a tourist from Mexico City, told me I could only speak Spanish until I was dropped off, and if we were stopped by the police, I was a cousin visiting from the States. Francisco also had a cooler of beer. Bonus.

Francisco was great on our dives, very professional. He led us through tunnels and pointed out hidden animals, as a good guide would do. He sat next to me on our way back to the dock and told me all about the reefs, and asked me if I'd been to the east side of the island where the locals go to surf. I hadn't. There was only one hotel, one restaurant, and one road, so of course I had to see it.

As Francisco dropped me off at my hotel, he told me to meet him at the dive shop in half an hour and he'd show me the other side of the island. I walked back, got my dive book stamped, had another beer, and he led me outside to his dune buggy. I've never been in a dune buggy; it was the best way to see the island. We drove about 25 minutes, first on the one road that goes east-west, then south to the bottom of the island. He pointed out all the surf spots, none being bigger than two feet and crumbly, but there was more surf than the west side, which was like a lake. He parked and we walked the beach to an open spot in the reef and we sat in the sandy, shallow water. All of a sudden he had octopus arms; I hadn't realized this was a date. I must have lost that in translation.

I had trouble with the men in Mexico from the beginning; it was a huge problem that I wasn't sure how to get around. A six foot "blonde" seemed to get a lot of attention. At first in San

Miguel I avoided eye contact with any man, but the women avoided eye contact with me, so I didn't get to talk to any locals there. Then gradually, I started saying *"hola,"* or *"buenos dias"* to everyone, and found people to chat with, but a lot of unfriendly attention came with that. Then came the tourist areas, where I had to be careful who I looked at because they'd immediately try to sell me things, so I could only look at people who weren't working. But through it all, being nice or chatty with guys there was taken as interest in them and led to mostly uncomfortable situations. Nothing yet that I couldn't handle, but I hate to hurt people's feelings. Or their fingers.

So I was at an isolated beach, far from my hotel with Francisco, and he was having trouble keeping his arms and hands and fingers off me. I turned to find more space in the sand and saw about 20 cars stopped on the side of the road nearby, a great reason to run that way and check out what was happening. And it was a good thing he took me here to get friendly; otherwise, I never would have seen baby turtles hatching. The crowd was an environmental group marking turtle nests at a nesting site with the purpose of making sure that every hatched turtle made it into the water. In the wild, only one turtle from a nest of 120 lives to adulthood, so the nests are monitored. During hatching they dig out the turtles on the very bottom, smooth the sand down to the water, and keep the predatory birds away. There were about a dozen vulture-looking birds circling overhead.

We got to watch all of the newly hatched turtles claw their way to the ocean. Sometimes they'd get confused and go the wrong way and the people crowded around would turn them in the right direction. One man was in charge of digging out the bottom turtles to make sure none were buried alive so they all lived to make it to the ocean.

At that point it was getting dark, so I suggested that we head back to town. Clouds were rolling in, the dune buggy had no roof, and Francisco had mentioned that his laundry was hanging outside. We headed to his house, took in his laundry, and I told him that I had a previous engagement at the No Name Bar, which was true. That was where the guys from the dive boat were headed. He was nice enough to drive me to the bar, but when he suggested that he meet me at my hotel in an hour I had to hurt his feelings a bit. I was free for the night.

I spent a nice night drinking with some new friends, got caught up on the real world, and found out a hurricane was headed our way, just in time for my boat trip to Belize. And just when my peso math got good, it was time to move on to a new country.

CHETUMAL

My transportation to Belize showed me I really hadn't learned anything new about planning, and if I was never going to learn, maybe I wasn't qualified to take myself around the world. I had to check out of my room in Cozumel at 2 p.m. I figured I'd take the first ferry back to Playa Del Carmen, hang out in a bar all day, then grab an overnight bus to Chetumal, get some sleep, then board the morning boat to Ambergris Caye, Belize. It was a good plan. But when I arrived in Playa, I went to buy my bus ticket and found a bus leaving at 6 p.m. I panicked, thinking if I didn't take it, maybe the night bus would be canceled or very late, and I'd be stuck in Mexico for another night. I should have known by then that the buses in Mexico are never canceled or late. So I got on. That put me in Chetumal at 11 p.m. and none of the motels were open. Not a good place to be stuck. The first boat to Belize was at 3 p.m. the next day. So I had a late dinner at a taco stand; I had to beg them not to close, then slept in the bus station with all the homeless local guys. My bed was a grated metal bench, my pillows were backpacks, and I managed to get about six hours of sleep. I woke up feeling every day of my 40 years.

I walked around the station at sunrise and there was nothing there, so I took a taxi to the dock in a part of town listed online as "the heart of Chetumal." The heart actually meant government offices. I had eight hours to kill before my boat left and I was sitting in a giant treeless grassy square surrounded by offices. No restaurants, nothing to do. No one spoke English, and their Spanish was very fast and garbled to me, and it took me an hour to locate a public bathroom in a gas station. Don't get stuck in Chetumal.

Finally, the boat offices opened and I was able to buy a ticket and check in. I paid some sort of tax to leave the country, then was directed to the office next door to pay even more for an exit stamp on my passport. I had now paid enough people that I was allowed to leave Mexico. I killed a few more hours sitting in a cramped office reading the Kindle that Andy had brought me.

I had been hearing about a hurricane coming this way, but no one thought it would hit Belize, so I didn't bother to change my plans. I actually didn't even bother to look at a weather map. About half an hour before the boat departed, the storm started rolling in. There was lightning, thunder, pouring rain and some serious wind bending the palm trees as 30 people and I were boarding the boat. No one had any seasickness medication and a large group of college students were making bets on who was going to vomit first. The boat was small with no windows that open and no air-conditioning. It really didn't look like a good way to spend the next two hours. I don't get sick on boats, but if I have to watch people vomit, I know I'll do it too.

BELIZE
AUGUST 7ᵀᴴ, 2012

AMBERGRIS CAYE

It didn't turn out to be as bad as I had anticipated; the crew opened a rear hatch for the sick people. The boat was incredibly fast; I fell asleep in Chetumel, Mexico and woke up in sunny Ambergris Caye, Belize. Immigration and customs were a bit of a joke; we lined up in a shack and waited for a couple guys in uniforms to arrive in their golf cart. They asked if I had anything in my bag that shouldn't be there and I said no. Welcome to Belize.

I had heard so many great things about the scuba diving in Belize, with the second largest barrier reef in the world, that I reserved an oceanfront condo, Tradewinds Paradise Villas, with a discounted 11-dive scuba package included. It was a good amount over my budget, but sometimes I have a little trouble remembering I have one. My reasoning was that there would be plenty of cheap hostels in Guatemala to make up the money, so why not live it up a little? It was a decent place with a full kitchen, air-conditioning, Wi-Fi, and a swimming pool. I went for a quick swim to erase the past 24 hours of travel misery and bus station smell. I found a grocery store with outrageously priced food due to the hurricane warning and stocked up on Belikin beer and vegetables. They accepted either American dollars, just double the price marked, or Belizean dollars. And no one spoke Spanish. I thought "now is when I'll probably start forgetting everything I learned in Mexico."

I spent my first night in Belize recovering from a horrible day of travel, drinking beer on my balcony, and watching workers hammering plywood over the hotel windows. My scuba dives for the next day had already been canceled due to Hurricane Ernesto, and I was hoping there wouldn't be a mandatory evacuation. I wasn't ready for more boats and buses just yet. I tried to Google the weather and kept coming up with anything but Belize; hopefully someone would remember to tell me if I needed to leave.

The hurricane winds hit sometime during my first night. I woke up to a scary downpour and wind with occasional moments of sunshine. It looked like it was going to pass to the north and it was moving pretty quickly, so no one here was seriously worried. The town was slowly boarding up, but plenty of people were still cruising the streets. The surf out at the reef was pumping and the streets and beaches were starting to flood. I ran into the hotel manager and he informed me that if I want to evacuate the last boat leaves at 5 p.m., then all transportation gets cut off. I went to the store for more supplies, talked to some locals, and decided to stay and check it out. I was hoping to find someone having a hurricane party. All my electronics were charged; I dug out my headlamp and water purifier and discovered a large pack of candles in a drawer. I had several cans of tuna, veggies, corn tortillas, and cans of beans. I boiled a dozen eggs in anticipation of the power going out and filled all my pots and pans with water.

I went out again around 12:30 when my beer supply got disturbingly low. I can't say for certain how that happened, but after running to town through the rain I made a devastating discovery: all alcohol sales were cut off at noon. The first store I went to made me put all the beer back in the cooler. The second store was manned by a cute young guy at the register and I begged and flirted until he sold me four beers, which brought my total ownership to five beers. Sad. If the hurricane hit and broke windows, I'd be out looting alcohol like everyone else.

The storm was a disappointment all day. Just enough to keep me inside, but not enough to be exciting. It was the first day in a long time that I wasn't melting from the heat, which was nice. Hurricane landfall was supposed to take place around 1 a.m., so I set my alarm for midnight. Nothing. I sat outside for a while then set my alarm for 4:30 a.m. and again, nothing. I could hear the ocean boiling, but the lights on the piers didn't reach out far enough to see the reef. I woke up again at 8:30 a.m. when my windows were rattling, and saw that my entire living room floor had flooded; the maintenance guys had boarded up the windows on the wrong sides of the buildings. I was on the second floor of the hotel right on the ocean, which was a stupid place to be, but at least I had a great view of everything that was going on. Heavy rain, lightning and thunder, winds so strong that the palm trees looked like they might snap in half, and still some random people were walking around outside. Ambergris Caye had been demolished by Hurricane Keith a few years before, but Ernesto was passing far enough away to simply ruin the diving for a while.

Ernesto had passed, but the weather was still unpleasant enough to make me want to sit on my lanai and be lazy. I ventured out long enough to walk the entire town and not feel like I was missing much. There wasn't anything to do in bad weather except drink, and with the wind kicking a steady 30 knots or so, an outdoor bar was not appealing.

In a few hours of wandering, I covered all of the main streets and some of the smaller far-off ones. The town itself was run-down and dirty, with garbage on the streets; it was not the charming burg the guidebooks had promised. The people were a mix of Latin, creole and Mayan, and for the most part very nice. I did get followed down the street a few times by older Rasta guys wanting to "get to know me," but I'm not into the stalker types, so I had to decline.

The beaches weren't great; they were mostly hard-packed for golf carts and covered with debris from the storm. This wasn't a place for a beach towel and a drink on the sand. There weren't any swimming areas, due both to the storm and that boats were the main activity, and there were warnings posted everywhere that they won't look for you in the water. The wind was too strong to even think about renting a paddle board, and the yoga studios cost more than I cared to spend. What to do?

I opted to try some Belizean tacos at the local favorite, Elvi's. Whenever I'm wondering what there is to do, food or booze usually makes an appearance. I tried my first "fry jack," a fried corn thing that seemed to replace the taco shell here. It was puffy, slightly hard, and very awkward to eat. Not a winner. The local rum punch was so sweet I think it made my dentist cry from thousands of miles away. By then, I had ceased to wonder why I had been gaining weight.

Around 7 p.m., I walked to a bar called "Fido's," known for its huge tourist attraction, "The Chicken Drop." The bar was a 10-minute walk from my condo. Pass the public square and you couldn't miss it – no street names necessary, one of the things I love about small islands. There were more bars along the way with a few people; from a distance I heard a live band blaring and saw dozens of people in one spot. This must be the place. There was a giant white square on the sand with a mesh fence around it. The giant square was divided into smaller squares with the numbers 1-100 in random order. I went into the bar and bought five squares for $1 each. They play the game 10 times every night, so there are plenty of chances to win. The idea is that they put a chicken in the square and it wanders around until it poops, then whatever number it poops on wins $100.

It was entertaining, but not something that I ever need to see again. Mostly, the chicken just stood there and stared at the crowd. The fun part was the announcer; I've never heard so many cock or poop jokes at one time in my life. When it was time to start, he'd yell into his microphone, "Chicken security! Bring me a chicken!" and some young boys wearing chicken security shirts came out of the bar with a chicken. The band struck up its funky song "Sexy Chicken" and played it in the background the entire time. There was no need to buy the band's CD; I will never be able to get "Sexy Chicken" out of my head until I die. That's how many times I heard it in the two hours I was there.

If the chicken was in the ring for too long without pooping, "Chicken security! Bring me a cock!" and a bigger chicken was added to the ring.

My squares never got pooped on, but it was good fun and something new to watch. I only stayed a couple hours, even though I had planned to stay out a good bit of the night after being cooped up in the hurricane. The local guys at the bar were making me crazy; they saw a girl by herself and it was a feeding frenzy.

"Hey girl, why don't you come back to my place? I got something for you?"

"Hey girl, where's your husband?"

"Hey girl, I'm the one you came here looking for."

"Hey girl, let's you and me go make our own party."

And on and on, in an almost Jamaican-sounding patois. It was pathetic and horrible. One guy grabbed my arm; I told him to let go and pulled and pulled, still trying to be nice. He kept sweet-talking, and I finally told him that he was going to spend the rest of the night digging his severed fingers out of his asshole if he didn't let go. That worked.

There seemed to be three types of guys who lived on that island. The first were the landsharks, as noted earlier; they are easily identifiable from a distance because they're seedy-looking, don't usually have a full set of teeth, and shout things that only seem sweet as I walked by. They are doing their very best to find not only a woman, but one who would pay for their drinks, buy them cigarettes or anything else they wanted. I told one that if he was really serious about finding a sugar mama, he should consider an occasional shower. With soap. Needless to say, I didn't spend any money on these guys.

The second type of guy was the one who saw how horrible the first type was acting toward me and came to tell me what jerks they were – no manners, no class. "They're giving all us guys a bad name, but if you were my girl I'd treat you way better," they'd say. So he was the same basic guy, just going for the soft sell, like he was the knight in shining armor protecting me from the first type.

The third type was the actual nice guy. They didn't hang out at the tourist bars, so I hadn't met any of them yet.

I spent most of my time at the bar chatting up random tourist guys since the local guys didn't bother with them, therefore leaving me alone. I met a guy wearing a Cleveland firefighter's shirt and the same white velcro sneakers as my father. For a second, I thought my dad had come for a visit. I also attached myself to a giant bearded biker-type guy from Texas smoking a cigar. I didn't tell either of them I was using them as cockblockers. I couldn't stop with the chicken jokes either.

Every time I got up for another beer, I'd get waylaid by another local: "Baby, why you got no man? You must be looking for one. I got something you like." So after my numbers didn't get pooped on I gave up and left. I had to run the gauntlet of locals on my way home, too: "Honey you don't gotta be alone tonight," and I was pretty happy when I was back in my air conditioning.

I hate being rude to people, but the guys there were more annoying than the shopkeepers in Mexico. I really would have liked to talk to some local guys, but it was impossible without eventually having to tell them to fuck off. If I was dying to talk to someone, I'd have to go to the grocery store and chat up the women.

I did do that the next evening; I decided to practice my Spanish while buying sandwich at the deli and asked that they don't add any skin disease. After a moment of laughter, the cashier wondered if I had meant "onion."

The weather finally cleared enough to do my first dives on the second-largest barrier reef in the world, and they were wonderful. There were seven of us plus our dive master and crew;

we boarded a 25-foot panga and headed out. There was a small break in the reef that all the boats use, the only place nearby where a boat can cross to the outer ocean. The reef system there was incredible; it went as far as I could see. The weather had calmed down considerably – sunny, with a perfect breeze.

Our first stop was "The Mermaid's Lair" just outside the reef, and we went down to about 90 feet. Almost at the bottom, the first thing I saw was about a dozen sharks below me, nurse sharks maybe five feet long. They were beautiful, swimming peacefully, and they came up pretty close to check us out. We saw many types of fish and turtles, and the fans and corals were large and healthy. The visibility was only about 40 feet, which was good considering the two days of storms that had just passed.

The second dive was at "Tuffy's," again just outside the reef, and it was good as well. The groupers were huge. The colors weren't as vibrant as in Cozumel, but still, both dives were excellent. The group I dove with was very pleasant, and it turned out that only one person on the boat wasn't originally from Ohio. A woman about my age grew up in a town five minutes from where I grew up; I imagined the number of times we were probably in the same grocery store in Ohio, but never met until we went to Belize. Such a small world.

I was supposed to dive the famous "Blue Hole" the next day. A boat came to pick up me and John, my dive buddy from the first dives, at 5:30 a.m., and like an idiot, I set my alarm for 4:30 p.m. Miraculously, I woke up at 5:19, jumped into a bikini, grabbed a pareo and a banana and ran out the door. I made it with a minute to spare. We got to the pier where the big dive boat was docked, and thankfully the crew had coffee and breakfast waiting. We got our gear ready and took off for a two-and-a-half hour ride to the dive site. After about half an hour, the boat did a u-turn and stopped dead. The deck hands were running around opening hatches and messing with the engine, and we had to go home. It took almost an hour for the return trip and I rescheduled for the next day, provided I could stay out of the bars and wake up on time. Only a handful of diesel mechanics lived on the island, even with so many boats, and they had to fly in all the parts they needed so we were crossing our fingers we'd get to go.

Only a couple boats on the island are big enough to go as far as the Blue Hole. Each individual dive shop signs up passengers, and when there are enough people, everyone goes with one company on a 50-foot boat. It's a three-dive day, totaling about 10 hours of riding and diving.

We got back in time to sign up for a regular day of dives with our original company; the first was at "Sandy Bottom" near the Hol Chan Marine Preserve. We went down to 90 feet and saw more of everything – lion fish, huge groupers, little crabs that look like leggy spiders. A nurse shark kept bumping Rubin, our dive master, and eventually he had to punch it in the head. A remora swam with us for the entire dive. We spent our surface interval at "Shark & Ray Alley" with snorkel gear. The crew dangled a chum-filled white container poked with holes over the side of the boat, and dozens of nurse sharks and rays fought over it. We dove down to pet them; they didn't care at all. It was strange the first time I touched a shark – I knew it wasn't going to bite me, but it kept staring at me with those crazy yellow eyes. My mind kept telling me I should be swimming away as fast as I could. The rays were fun and slimy and kept trying to eat my camera; they'd swim at me and at the last moment glide upward and open their cute little mouths and suck. It made for some great movies. Second-best snorkel trip ever, after the whale shark dive a couple weeks before in Mexico.

Our second dive was at "Esmereldas," and Rubin carried a long line with chum and we had nurse sharks and giant groupers fighting over it. This was my favorite dive so far – every kind of fish and marine life, as in the other dives but with an incredible underwater landscape. My favorite fish was the filefish, regaled in a neon purple color with kissy lips. I was staring at one as I was floating on the current, and I must have drifted through a patch of fire coral. It felt like my entire left leg caught on fire. Lesson learned: when diving in only a bikini, pay attention to what you might run into. One of the crew prodded a puffer fish and I watched it try to swim off, its teensy little fins not making much difference with an enormous engorged body. Adorable.

John and I made plans to do a night snorkel; he brought some dive lights from home. But as I was making lunch, I sliced a chunk out of my thumb. At least that made the fire coral sting stop burning so much. I ran to the medical center; I was gushing blood and thought some stitches might be a good idea, but it was closed. I did find an open pharmacy and bought some tape. I figured I'd get to see a lot of sharks on my dives the next day.

I spent the evening sitting on my second-floor porch about 50 feet from the ocean, people-watching. A man in thigh-length dreads spent half an hour breaking coconuts, and two 8-year-old boys were cleaning and gutting fish, throwing the pieces into the ocean for the birds to dive at and eat. Some rays wandered by to see what the commotion was. It was far more entertaining than watching TV.

I did manage to set my alarm correctly and met John at the dock for our second try at the Blue Hole with the Amigos del Mar dive company. We had coffee and fruit and spent two and a half hours on possibly the most intense boat ride ever. We traveled inside the reef for almost half an hour, nice and smooth, then crossed a channel to open ocean and spent two hours catching air on a 50-foot boat. The captain was going to get us to our destination in his time frame, no matter how strong the winds or how big the waves. There was nothing to do but brace my feet and hold on with both hands the entire way.

I was a little nervous going out to the Blue Hole. I had met some people on Cozumel that did it and they were telling stories about people who got loopy with nitrogen narcosis, or narced, at that depth, 130 feet, and floated around doing crazy, unsafe things like trying to take off their masks or swimming away from the group. Someone even mentioned a friend who thought she was playing violin instead of scuba diving. My deepest dive to date was 90 feet, and that was only yesterday. Add to that the brand new gash on my hand that was oozing blood the previous night and that this was only my 12th dive ever, and I was questioning whether I had any business doing this dive. But there I was, so how could I not?

The plan was to slowly descend to 40 feet, wait a bit, then go to 100 feet, then bottom out at 130 feet. The actual bottom of the hole is somewhere around 400 feet, but we wouldn't be getting anywhere near that depth. The first 40 feet was nice – decent visibility, some fish, everyone ok. Looking down, all I saw was black, and that was when my nerves started going crazy. It didn't help that one of the dive masters was already coming up fast, holding onto an obviously disoriented woman from the first group. We kicked off the ledge and slowly descended, and were surrounded by suspended particles, maybe big chunks of sand, and it reminded me of outer space, like floating in the stars. There weren't any fish and just a handful of plants, mostly algae, on the rocks. The stalactites began as the ceiling of the cave opened up like a giant hourglass. The stalactites were huge, resembling the columns on the Parthenon. Everything was great until I looked at my depth gauge and realized that I was at 135 feet.

I don't know exactly what it's like to be narced, but some crazy thoughts started to run through my head. The first thing I did was hold my regulator against my face, because I thought maybe I might try to breathe without it. And then I thought of Star Wars. I'm in dark, dark water, there are white particles floating all around me, my breathing sounded like Darth Vader, and I vaguely recall a fuzzy Death Star mind trip. I remember wondering how I was going to write about the experience, so I couldn't have been narced too badly.

I started talking to myself to get back into reality; I knew we were only going to be at this depth for eight minutes before our slow ascent. Breathe. Look at stuff. Breathe. Breathe. Everything's ok. Breathe.

The next thing I remember was seeing John waving at me and pointing down at giant reef sharks that were circling underneath us. They were grey figures against the black bottom, so I couldn't guess what depth they were at. John was frantically signaling me to rip the tape off of my bloody thumb and squeeze so he could get a better look at the sharks up close. John's a funny guy. At least he thinks so.

We started the ascent very slowly; we stopped on the shelf at 100 feet for a few minutes to make sure we had everyone in our group. We went up to 40 feet and stopped at the sandy bottom; it was good to see marine life again. We continued to 25 feet and stayed there for a while – a safety stop and a reality check. The dive boat had a couple air tanks with regulators suspended 20 feet into the water in case someone ran out of air. We continued to the surface for a total dive time of 40 minutes. That was a bucket-list dive for sure.

Back on the boat for a 10-minute ride and we arrived at Half Moon Caye to dive Half Moon Wall. First we had a surface interval, drinking water, eating fruit, blurting out our individual "Oh my god that was so awesome" stories to everyone else. Our depth was 65 feet and I saw plenty of fish and sea life. One of the big problems out there was the lion fish; they are incredibly beautiful, but devastatingly invasive. Hurricane Katrina did a lot of damage there, one aspect being the release of lion fish from private aquariums. Since then, they've killed off a large amount of the native species, and being poisonous, they have no predators. All of the dive masters carried spears; anytime someone spotted a lion fish, they killed it.

We were followed by giant groupers and a huge barracuda. This dive was a little over an hour, then we headed to the beach for lunch and our next surface interval. Half Moon Caye is a small tropical island, all coconut palms, sand, and every shade of blue in the water. There were some small shacks that rent for $20 per night, or travelers could pitch a tent for $10 per night if they could find a way to get there. The island was declared a natural monument and has a red-footed booby rookery. A great place for lunch.

The third and final dive of the day was at Aquariums off Long Caye. It was aptly named, because it truly seemed that I was the little diver in the fish tank. Every fish I'd previously seen was here in giant schools: grouper, tarpon, lobsters, eels, turtles, rays, sharks, filefish, angels, butterflies, and so many more whose names I still hadn't learned. The fans and corals were unblemished and every color of the rainbow. The diversity was astounding, and huge schools of fish swam through me like they didn't even know I was there. Thinking back on the 85 dives I did on my trip, the perfection of this reef was never equaled. It was far enough away from land that only one boat was there each day, sometimes two. There weren't enough tourists to pollute it or break off pieces of coral with their clumsy fins.

We had to surface after an hour, then sadly, it was time to head home. We had a two hour ride back and the crew showered us with Snickers bars and rum. Suddenly, we were all discussing strippers and English literature. There's nothing better than fun people when you're stuck on a boat.

John and I decided to go crocodile hunting instead of diving the next day. He had been to a hotel near the big lagoon to inquire about renting a kayak, and they told him there had to be two people or he couldn't have one. They couldn't understand why anyone would want to paddle in the lagoon. I was recruited as his second; we got in his golf cart and went to the north side of the island for our red plastic boat. The lagoon was huge, full of mangroves and lots of places to get lost. We started paddling around the edges looking for spots that could hide crocodiles. I kept expecting to see eyes staring at me from the surface of the water and was somewhat disappointed that they weren't there waiting for us. All the hotels in this area had "crocodile crossing" signs and there was a bar called "Crocs," so of course they should have been everywhere.

When we didn't see any right off, we started paddling into the trees, pulling the boat over roots, getting stuck, backing out, trying again – still no crocs. We made our way like that for about an hour; it was sticky hot and we were soaking wet, looking for land. It was possible that it was so hot the crocs were resting under some trees on shore. We paddled until we found land – a few palm trees mixed in with the mangroves – so we pulled up and tried to get out. Our feet sunk into the awful sulfur-smelling mud and we lost our shoes. It took some time to dig them out, and still no crocodiles. After a few hours we paddled back to the dock, trying to take shortcuts through the trees and failing. We went to the nearest bar, had a beer, and asked for directions to anywhere nearby where we could find crocs. We walked and walked and found nothing. A very disappointing day of crocodile hunting.

My next set of dives was at Tackle Box and Rubin's Reef, but the second is only called Rubin's Reef because it doesn't have a name and Rubin was our dive master again. It was just John and I, with Chuckie driving the boat, and when I dove in I was instantly circled by five sharks. I knew they were just nurse sharks and wouldn't hurt me, but it was hard to get used to the idea that I could ignore a shark. One in particular followed me throughout the dive; there was a spot of broken skin about halfway down its body, and he stayed with us the entire day. So beautiful, yet so creepy. As we were finishing up the early dive, Rubin signaled to look up. Six bottlenose dolphins were headed our way. Rubin took his regulator out of his mouth and blew bubbles and the dolphins began swimming in and out of them, gliding between us, bumping each other, I hadn't realized bubbles could be so much fun since I was about seven. We had to end our dive when the dolphins left since Rubin blew out all of his air to entertain them and us.

We spent our surface interval talking about life in Belize and I found out that neither of the crew had ever been to the United States, although both of them had tried to get there. Rubin applied for a visa multiple times but was always denied, each time paying the $300 non-returnable application fee. To apply for a visa as a Belizean citizen, they had to pay the fee and show proof of employment, bank statements, travel arrangements and have a sponsor. Only about 20% of the applicants eventually get to go, which surprised me considering how closely tied Belize is to the U.S. I assumed they could just come and go like I did. But the Belizean government was caught selling passports to Liberians some years ago, and all States-bound travel was terminated. Now it's just severely restricted. Rubin's children were going to

Disneyland without him, and he was determined that one day he'd go, too.

Our second dive was full of more great sea life; I can't say enough about how worthwhile it was to stay on Ambergris Caye when I was going to leave after the hurricane. The nurse shark from our first dive tracked us down and swam with us again; I could tell it was him by the scar on his skin. Rubin caught his fin and held him upside down to pet his belly, then passed him to John, then to me. I couldn't believe I was holding a shark. Normally I don't touch anything I see underwater – I hate diving with people who have to pick up every living thing and disturb its day – but I couldn't resist holding the shark. That might never happen again.

We did a night dive at Hol Chan Marina, my first scuba after dark. I'd been lobster-diving at night before, and of course skinny dipping after the bars, but night diving was spectacular. The corals were feeding, lobsters and crabs were on the march, and giant fish were hiding out in the rocks. Shrimp were guarding their territory, conchs were digging holes; clams, eels and slugs were waking up, turtles were going to sleep, and so many weird things were crawling around that I don't have names for. Any hole I shone my light into had eyes staring back at me, and the giant parrotfish sleeping in their bubbles startled me every time I spotted one. It was a little disturbing every time I caught a glimpse of a 5-foot fish eyeballing me; there's no telling what else was out there beyond my narrow beam of light – maybe things that wanted to eat me.

I went to Willie's, a bar on the dock, with Chuckie afterward. We watched Shark Week on the Discovery Channel. I'm happy to say it didn't keep me from going back in the water, as my time on Ambergris Caye was coming to an end.

On my final day, John and I went on a last crocodile expedition, this time to the south side of the island. We heard there was a place to see them just off the side of the road, so we jogged to the water tower. I was dying; that was the farthest I'd run in weeks, and in the blazing sun as well. We took the side roads by the lagoon, and knew we were in the right place when we saw the "do not feed the crocodiles" sign and saw a croc briefly before he went under. Feeding the crocs carried a $1000 fine or six months of jail time, according to the sign.

We didn't spot any others, so we kept walking until we found a store to get some drinks. I asked where the best place to see them was, and apparently it was right where we were. The store had frozen chicken legs, so we bought a couple pounds and headed back. It was so hot I carried the ice-cold bag of drumsticks on the back of my neck; it was worth the purchase even if we didn't get to feed the crocs. Police presence on the island was pretty minimal, so we weren't too worried.

Our plan was to thaw the chicken in the water near the edge so we could break it up, tie the individual legs on long pieces of vine that were growing nearby, and go "fishing" for crocs. We made sure to get off the main road so we wouldn't be spotted. As we were waiting for the chicken to thaw, a monster crocodile swam up and sat there, staring at us. He was inches from the floating chicken but didn't seem to know exactly where it was since it was in a patch of sea grass. John picked up a short stick and pushed the chicken legs toward the big crocodile and instantly it lunged and swallowed the legs whole. Probably the scariest thing I've ever seen in my life was how fast this thing moved and how many teeth it had. I was a little nervous when it swam up, but after seeing him move I was terrified.

I really hadn't considered what would happen if we saw one since we had such bad luck on our first attempt, nor had I considered how frightening they might be. The chicken wrappers and John's water bottle were sitting on the ground where we left them a few feet from the water, and the croc could smell it. Slowly, he climbed out of the water to investigate the possibility of more chicken, and that was when I got to see his claws. It was a thousand times more terrifying than when he was just sitting in the water. His eyes were tracking every move we made; as we walked around, he shifted his body to keep us in sight. No wonder the authorities didn't want us to feed them.

The crocodile moved to check out the chicken wrapper but picked up John's water bottle instead, mashing it several times in his jaws before spitting it out. My level of terror spiked. Terror for me, anyway. I wasn't sure John was bothered at all. He'd done a lot of crazy things in his life; he was an adrenaline junkie who looked like a school teacher. I'm still not sure exactly how he convinced me crocodile hunting was a good idea, but traveling solo meant making friends where I could. All I could think about at that time was that moments before, I was holding a partially defrosted chicken and trying to tear the pieces apart, and how much I smelled like the croc's last snack. I slowly began backing away.

I recovered enough of my wits to turn on my video camera, thinking that if the croc charged John, I'd have some great footage for his Darwin Award. The footage is funny only because it's completely unwatchable from my hands shaking so badly. The croc finally swam off, and as we were walking home I asked John what he would have thought if a crocodile that size had approached us in the kayak the other day. He shrugged, not at all disturbed. I'm glad I didn't think this idea through very well, or I would have missed a great experience.

SAN IGNACIO

The days of my expensive condo and pampering myself with scuba diving had to come to an end. I booked a bungalow in San

Ignacio, Belize, and made my travel arrangements. It turned out that John and his wife Linda were booked at the same place, just a couple days behind me. It was so nice hanging out with John, diving and adventuring while his wife was reading at the pool; none of the annoying men on the island bothered me when he was around.

I caught the 9:30 a.m. boat to Belize City and took a cab to the bus station, driving through some gritty inner-city decay, garbage everywhere. I was glad I hadn't booked a night there. When we started driving, I thought the driver was taking me to a bad neighborhood to mug me, but that's just the way the city looked.

We boarded an old school bus, my first chicken bus experience. A woman had a giant TV on her lap but there weren't any live animals; I think it still qualifies, though. I had some grade-school flashbacks of a mean driver and bullies. It was the same type of bus with the long green seats. I took the bus to Belmopan, then another to San Ignacio. It was supposed to be an express bus, but all that meant was that it would only stop to pick people up on the side of the road if there was an open seat. I sat with a nice girl, born and raised in Belize, and she pointed out some interesting things in my Lonely Planet book that I shouldn't miss. Her dream was to travel through Central America in a bus with her boyfriend, selling her art. At Belmopan I changed buses and got my own seat. I bought some banana chips with hot sauce from a local and they were delicious. Packing food in my backpack at all times was a lesson I was beginning to learn; I was starving. We left the station in a crazy broken school bus with ripped seats and cracked windows that didn't open, flying down the highway.

I had been noticing a seedy-looking man with cornrows going from seat to seat, cigarette tucked behind his ear, whispering to all the local women. They ignored him and he eventually went away. When he got near the back, he plopped down onto my seat, even though it was clear that my backpack was taking up that space. "Baby, I gonna sit witchu now."

"Thanks, but I just want to listen to my music." I knew I'd have to deal with guys, so I was wearing my headphones, but they weren't on so I could listen to everyone; I dressed in a very conservative shirt, long pants and a shawl in the broiling heat.

"But I wanna get to know ya."

"I have a boyfriend, but thank you anyway."

"Don't be like that, baby."

Then he actually reached out to touch my boobs. I had dealt with plenty of touchy guys, but this was the first to try to grope me. I slapped him, yelled "Get away from me!" and tried to slide him off my seat with my feet. I was surrounded by people, most notably two English guys traveling together, and no one even looked my way to help. He climbed back into my seat, leaned over at breast height and started making disgusting sucking noises with his tongue out; I started yelling again, and still not a single guy looked to see if they could be of assistance. I ended up pushing him out of my seat again, punching him and laying him out in the aisle of the bus. All other eyes were averted as if nothing was going on. Cowards. It wasn't as if I really needed their help, but it would have been nice to know that someone would have helped if I did need it.

He didn't bother me again, but he ruined my first day of chicken bus riding. I got to my bungalow at the edge of the jungle and laid in the hammock until the mosquitoes found me. The way my day went, I wouldn't have been surprised if I had contracted malaria.

The next morning, I thought I'd go running to try to work out some aches and ended up getting chased by a couple guys in town. I was wearing a shirt from my local Kauai gym and the back says

"Take it OFF;" OFF is short for Organic Functional Fitness. They took that to mean I was a stripper and they should run and yell at me until I realized I wanted to take my clothes off for them. They were enthusiastic; it seemed like they thought it would work. I ran to my room and went back to bed.

After a day of recovering from travel, John and his wife showed up and we signed up for spelunking at Actun Tunichil Muknal, or the "ATM" cave. John's wife hadn't gone on any adventures with us due to health reasons, so it was just John and I again. We joined a tour group in a minivan and drove an hour and a half on mostly unpaved, pot-holed roads. We were given a list of things to bring, but no one told me I couldn't wear my backpack in the cave, so of course I had my wallet, iPhone, camera – all the things I would have locked in my room. We were also told to bring bug spray, but when we arrived we weren't allowed to use it because the water we were going to trek through was the town's drinking water. Poor instructions.

No cameras were allowed either. I didn't get that memo. I take my camera everywhere. Apparently there are sacrificial remains in the top of the cave that have been left intact, and not long ago an idiot tourist was leaning over a skeleton taking a picture, dropped his camera, and punched a hole in a skull, so no cameras anymore. But they let John take his giant dive light, which probably weighed 10 times as much as my camera. I couldn't figure out how that was ok.

We arrived at the site and there was a mile hike with three river crossings. My poor running shoes hadn't yet been underwater, but at least they were getting used. At the end of the hike I found out that I had to leave my backpack, and again, poor instructions, as it could have been locked in our van. I was uncomfortable leaving it in the open, so I wandered a bit into the jungle and hid it. This is a pretty busy cave with multiple tours per day, and I didn't want to take a chance that everyone was honest.

The mouth of the cave was a swim-through with overhead water. It was cold but not icy and felt nice after the hike. We all wore swimsuits with light clothes on top, helmets and headlamps that for some reason weren't waterproof. Most of the cave was wet and we walked or climbed through anything from overhead to ankle-deep water, mostly about shin level.

The natural formations were incredible; there were wide open chambers and tight passages that we had to squeeze through. I don't know the technical terms for caves, but according to our guide it had everything we'd want to see. ATM is a few miles long, but we only hiked a small portion - about an hour and a half of climbing and wading through water. Towards the end we climbed up several feet and had to leave our shoes, doing the rest of the hike in our socks. There was broken pottery on all sides of us, containers for water and food offerings and blood sacrifices. They were roped off with bright orange tape so no one could trample them. After a little more walking, all dry now, we found a creaky ladder that led to a chamber with the sacrificial remains. There were five skeletons, one with a camera-shaped hole in the skull, and there were more that weren't accessible to the public. The major skeleton was the Crystal Maiden, laid out as perfectly as she had been around 900 A.D. Next to her was a young boy who had his arms and legs broken and tied behind his back.

There wasn't much wildlife in the cave - some bats, a crab that seemed really out of place, and a single white ant. Thankfully, no need for the bug spray. The hike back was much quicker without the constant narration; we put on dry clothes, sucked down some rum punch and were on our way home. I was able to return with my stashed bag of electronics, I'm happy to say.

The next adventure for John and me was tubing on the Caves Branch River. Linda was going to join us, but she had sprained her ankle nearly the first moment she arrived in San Ignacio. Our tour guide, Edwin, picked us up at the bungalows and we drove out of town for about an hour, almost back to Belize City. We spotted a toucan along the way, and although it is Belize's national bird, it had been easier to find a crocodile; we'd been looking for days. We got to the river and hiked for 40 minutes, stopping several times to learn about the poisonous plants and poisonous insects that seemed to be all we saw. Each poisonous plant had a built-in antidote if you knew how to harvest it, and one of the trees had a compound in the bark that would slow down reactions to ant and snake bites, allowing enough time to get to a hospital. Edwin knew his stuff.

We ate some plants along the way – tart begonias, palm kernels like small, hard coconuts, and craboo, like ... I'm not sure what craboo is like. I had a craboo colada at a bar the night before and it was really good. John asked about a giant black lump on a tree that turned out to be a termite nest. Edwin stuck his finger in it and his hand was instantly crawling with them; he said they are mostly protein and tasted like mint with a carrot aftertaste. He asked if we'd like to try; my first reaction was cringe and back away. Gross. But then I thought, "I'm standing in a jungle in Belize and someone wants me to eat a termite; when will this moment ever happen again?"

So I ate a termite. A few actually; they were swarming too heavily to pick out just one. They crunched in my teeth and they really did taste minty. After a few minutes, they tasted carroty. The world is so bizarre.

We finished our walk and ended up near a cave on the Caves Branch River. We were the first group to get to the water that day and it was just John, me and our guide. We jumped onto the inner tubes we had lugged along the trail, strapped on headlamps and away we went. We floated about 100 feet in the cold water to the entrance of the first cave and it was full of stalactites, stalagmites, bats fluttering overhead – all the great things about caves. John used to belong to a spelunking club, so of course he had his super-bright light so we could look into every hole and around every corner. After 20 minutes, we got to the end of the first cave and into the open, and Edwin stopped us for a swim. This was the halfway point of the tube ride and there were other people getting into the water here from the trail. Some guides only take people half-way up the trail, hurry them down the river, then grab another group of tourists and double their money for the day. As we were coming down the river, a man was looking at us asking where we were coming from; he thought he was at the beginning. We spent 15 minutes playing in the water and checking out the rock for-mations on the outside of the cave while watching other groups speed by.

It was time to continue; back on the tubes, and we entered the next cave. This one opened up into a huge cavern, or a cathe-dral as Edwin called it. There was a waterfall and a cave-in toward the back, so there was a bit of sunlight shining through. It was a beautiful sight; everything was pitch-black, then sud-denly there was a bright spot full of old-growth trees and a wooden staircase winding upward out of the cave. We stopped our inner tubes under the waterfall and started to climb. It was only a few feet tall, but it was dark and the rocks were sharp and slippery, yet another one of those things that you would never be allowed to do in the United States. Completely sketchy and dangerous. Behind the waterfall was a 25-foot-deep pool that we jumped into from a height of seven feet. It doesn't sound like much, but it was almost black inside the cave and the water was so clear that we could make out the boulders at the bottom. But if Edwin said it was ok, then it was ok, just jump. It turned out to be ok. Finally, we walked up the old staircase and checked out the scenery while the other tour groups kept sailing by; none of the other groups got to jump off the rocks or see the waterfall. John and I apparently got the deluxe tour. We tubed through more caves and finished with some rapids. It was quite an enjoyable trip.

Since we had an hour to get home, John and I wracked our brains for every question we could think to ask Edwin. We saw a lot of cyclists on the roads. The roads were very narrow with no berm, and people drove insanely fast there. I was terrified for them every time we passed one. According to Edwin, the cyclists training for races on actual road bikes buy permits to use the road. He said if a car hits a cyclist with a permit, the driver is fined and would probably lose the car, so they go out of their way to avoid collisions.

Edwin also told us that the Belizean government sold a lot of passports to Taiwan, not just Liberia, to encourage immigration. I had noticed a huge Asian population, from storekeepers to restaurants to crop science centers flying the Taiwanese flag. At first, no one could understand them, and no one got along, but eventually the new generation was born and the kids learned both Taiwanese and Creole and all was well.

Belize also has a large population of both Amish and Mennonites. Horses and buggies share the roads; the men have long beards and everyone wears formal-looking clothes. They look more out of place here than in Ohio, where I grew up. But they have carved out their niche and now they get along fine with the locals. There is a third similar group, the Mechanites, who look similar to the Mennonites but use heavy-duty equipment on their farms.

The wages paid to a lower-level worker such as the women who cooked me breakfast or cleaned my room was around $30 Belizean per day, or $15 U.S., for an eight to 10 hour day. It's a good thing the locals don't have to pay the prices they charge tourists.

The nickname for San Ignacio is "Cayo." When the founders of this area travelled inland, they came across two rivers that met and thought they were on an island. They weren't, but Cayo stuck. Now the junction of these rivers is where the locals drive their trucks to the edge to wash them. Can't use bug spray or you'll pollute the drinking supply, but you can drive an oil-leaking truck into the water. Edwin filled our trip home with a lot interesting information.

After dinner with John and Linda, getting lost along the way since neither of our guidebooks had a current map of the town, we found a footbridge over the river in the middle of nowhere. I had a headlamp, so John and I had to explore. The bridge was missing some boards, others were loose, and perhaps it was so dark out that we missed the "Bridge Out" sign, which reminded me I hadn't expressed my wishes to my family should I have a horrible accident or fall through the wooden slats of a bridge into leech- and crocodile-infested waters and disappear. I should have at least emailed them what I want on my tombstone, or my final Facebook post from beyond.

For my final day in Belize, I hopped in John and Linda's rental truck and we covered a couple hundred miles of sights. Our first stop was the Mayan ruins at Caracol, about 50 miles from San Ignacio, mostly on unpaved roads again, and it took us three hours to get there. The ruins were fascinating – a lot of unsafe things to climb, holes to fall into – another great example of things we'd never be allowed to do in the States. By now I'd seen so many Mayan ruins that I kept saying I've been to too many and couldn't possibly go to another, but they were awe-inspiring and I was always glad I went. Seriously, though, I was done with ruins.

There were no personnel or guides at Caracol, so we wandered around and climbed everything that looked fun. Mostly John and I climbed; Linda was still nursing her sprained ankle. This site contains more than 200 separate structures, stone slabs called stelae and altars hidden in old-growth trees, and covers more acreage than present-day Belize City.

After Caracol, which is really the end of the road, we backtracked to the Mountain Pine Ridge Forest Reserve and stopped at the Rio On Pools. We tried to stop at the Rio On Caves but couldn't seem to find them in the maze of dirt roads. To go through the reserve usually requires a military escort, but when we checked in at the gate their truck was broken and they sent us along by ourselves. The natural carved rock pools were refreshing after a morning of climbing ruins, although we only stuck our feet in. We opted to scramble up the boulders to the waterfalls instead. I found the biggest grasshopper I had ever seen – it was half the size of my foot, which is not small. I knew there must be other giant creatures with so much jungle nearby, and I was surprised I hadn't seen more. They were probably all waiting to scare me in Guatemala.

After the pools, we stopped at any trail on the side of the road that looked interesting and hiked into the jungle. We found an old army training center rotting away, made of tree branches and rough-cut wood for benches. The frame was still standing, with laminated "Jungle Rules" attached. The first rule was "Don't antagonize the scorpions and snakes." Something that you really do have to tell boys. We also found a homemade snare, an intricately hand-woven palm frond cage with a small opening on one side and scary sharp spikes inside, baited with a chicken bone. There wasn't much in the way of wildlife sightings besides the giant grasshopper earlier in the day. I was almost planning on getting bitten by a snake in the jungle, but no snakes, no jaguars, no monkeys.

The coolest wildlife I saw in Belize was the Leaf Cutter ant. They walk single-file with triangle-shaped leaf parts that they've chewed off leaves – so many of them you can see them from far away. They spend so much time walking from the trees to their nests that they carve little trails into the dirt, an inch deep and wide. They must walk the same path for months to make such a deep impression in the ground. An inch might not seem very deep, but they're only tiny ants; it probably feels like the Grand Canyon to them.

We kept driving and spotted a giant sign on the side of the road that said "Look," with a smiley face in one of the o's. Of course we had to stop and look. Peeking into the trees I saw a cave at the bottom of a small hill, straight down. I went first down the trail, which turned out to be comprised of mud and slimy, wet rocks, and I started sliding right toward the hole in the ground. Slightly out of control, I grabbed the first tree I could find so I wouldn't fall into what looked like a bottomless hole, and just my luck, it was covered in 2-inch thorns. A lot of other people must have fallen into the same situation, because most of the spikes at the sliding-on-your-ass level were broken off.

Why would anyone put up a sign that would lead you to slide down rocks into a black hole in the ground? After regaining his footing, John inspected the cave with a headlamp and decided that since we didn't have any rope, we probably shouldn't climb down. A literal tourist trap.

Back in the truck, we took the road leading to 1,000 Foot Falls. There was a nice, smooth dirt road leading up to a resort, the sign on the road telling us that the bathroom, restaurant, bar and waterfalls were for resort guests only; no one else was welcome. That must be where the rich and famous go to recover from nose and boob jobs. Right past the resort entrance, the road was a pot-holed mess again.

1,000 Foot Falls is actually 1,600 feet tall, and gorgeous. The valley is immense – you can see the tree-covered mountains all the way into Guatemala. John and I hiked around a bit and found the trails to be perfectly unsafe; it featured plenty of places to fall to a nasty death. I wouldn't have expected anything less.

There was an old Mayan couple that ran the store and lived above the viewing platform. They collected our $2 bz to see the falls. They've lived there for 23 years in almost total isolation, taking care of the grounds, selling handmade jewelry and clothing, and collecting tourist money. They have a bumpy two-hour ride to get to town every other month to buy supplies. The store had no electricity; the soda in the refrigerator was almost as hot as the air outside.

This was my last day in Belize. Overall, I thought it was a gorgeous place with endless activities, but culturally it was lacking. A local told me they've gotten their cultures so mixed up that they don't have anything that particularly represents the Belizean people; they copy things from Mexico and Guatemala since they've forgotten their own roots. The food wasn't anything I'll miss: beans and rice and fried plantains, and with everyone speaking English, it didn't seem as exotic as Mexico. I think I'll probably come back someday, but it was time to shake the ants out of my belongings and move on.

GUATEMALA
AUGUST 25ᵀᴴ, 2012

LAGO DE ATITLAN

It took me 22 hours to get to my next destination in Lago de Atitlan, Guatemala. I left Belize in a taxi to get to the town of Benque. It cost a few more dollars than the bus, but I just couldn't get myself to get back on another bus in San Ignacio after the first disaster. My driver dropped me off a few feet from the Guatemalan border and I walked into the office to check out of Belize and left the customs officials my final gift of tourist money for the exit stamp. I still haven't figured out why every country

charges you money to enter and again to leave; it should be sufficient that they charge tourists twice as much as locals in-coun-
try. The next several feet of walking toward the border held a
cluster of men with huge wads of cash offering to change my U.S.
or Belize dollars to Quetzals, necessary if I wanted to get on the
bus or enter the country. A few feet after that was immigration;
stamp my passport and *"Bienvenido."* Pretty easy.

The walk from Belize into Guatemala was a night-and-day
change of scenery. I left English-speaking, run-down, rock-and-
roll playing towns and entered a colorful wonderland of handmade clothes, mariachi music and Spanish. I wasn't actually
sure what they called the music there, but it sounded more like
Mexico than anything I heard in Belize. I instantly felt better, so
happy to be back in a Hispanic country where the men were less
likely to openly harass me. I'm so much better at handling the
ones that just stare, but I still couldn't figure out why I looked so
out of place everywhere. It was like I left home without pants on
every day.

I caught a taxi to the nearest bus station and hopped a bus to
Flores. The worst part of traveling for me, so far, was getting out
of a bus or taxi and immediately being swarmed by half a dozen
men, all trying to take me somewhere in whatever mode of transportation they had, speaking so fast that I couldn't figure out what
any of them were actually saying. In Flores, I was let off outside
a large abandoned-looking building, but I had no idea it was the
bus terminal. My Spanish was pretty rusty after three weeks of
non-use in Belize, and I made it known to the group that I needed
to get to Guatemala City. If I had better Spanish I would have
known I didn't need any of these guys and just walked through
a couple doors and found a ticket counter; instead, there were no
signs and no buses, just a group of men intentionally trying to

confuse me, and I let myself be led into an office. The man filled out a voucher slip for a nine-hour bus ride to the city, I gave him money, and he produced a ticket. At the moment I was proud of myself for once again navigating the crazy world of transportation, and seconds later I felt like the biggest fool ever. He pointed my way out and I went through two more doors, where I found myself in a room with ticket windows and multiple bus lines to choose from. Duh. I paid a few extra dollars for a man to buy a ticket for me; I just had to look at it as a fairly inexpensive lesson: be patient and understand my surroundings better before making decisions. I thought I had learned that lesson earlier, but apparently not. Maybe this time it would stick.

Unfortunately, as I look back through all of my travel notes, this was one of many lessons I failed to learn over and over.

I now had a ticket to Guatemala City and five hours to kill in a tiny town that consisted of little more than the bus terminal. The benches were concrete and not a fun place to sit. A soccer game was on a 20" TV surrounded by 30 men chain-smoking and yelling.

The bus ride was fairly uncomplicated; my seat mate, Rudy, was born in Guatemala but worked in construction in New York for 17 years, so we had no problems with conversation. I managed to forget my coat and since all overnight first class buses are air-conditioned to the point of frostbite, I ended up sharing Rudy's blanket and sleeping for most of the nine hours, thanks in part to some muscle relaxants I picked up at one of those wonderful Mexican pharmacies.

I was planning on asking Rudy to direct me to the correct connection to Panajachel, much like Felipe did for me in Mexico City, but he got off 10 minutes before the end of the ride. Guatemala has the same policy as Belize and Mexico: "express" doesn't mean there aren't multiple stops for people the driver knows. We pulled into Guatemala City and I was immediately surrounded by men wanting to take me somewhere in their bus, taxi or tuk-tuk, a motorcycle or scooter taxi. My groggy head full of muscle relaxers and a slightly different Spanish dialect didn't help the situation. I mostly stared at everyone and said, *"Necesito ir a Panajachel"* over and over. Eventually that whittled away enough drivers so I chose one and got in his taxi, thinking he was going to take me to another bus station. After five minutes, he pulled to the side of the road to make a phone call and handed me the phone. His son was on the other end speaking English, and he explained that his father didn't know where I wanted to go. Yet he had started driving me anyway. I told the son my travel plan, handed the phone back to my driver, and off we went again.

Five more minutes through crazy, busy, dirty Guatemala City brought us to a stop at a bus and a shuttle. More fast, incoherent Spanish and I was back to repeating my morning's mantra, *"Necesito ir a Panajachel."* I felt bonded to my taxi driver after solving our language barrier, so I asked him which he would choose since now he knew my destination. He said the bus would be more comfortable, but the van would be quicker if I didn't mind being smashed in with as many people and their bags as would fit. I didn't feel like being squished into a van after so many hours of travel, so I chose the bus. This was not the correct choice. It turned out that the bus driver was taking me to another town where I would have to catch two more buses to get where I wanted to go. I missed that part. I really should have stayed in Mexico for another month of language school.

The bus was a converted school bus, my second official chicken bus, and I fell asleep moments after my gear got stashed on top. I was awoken an hour later by a man shouting scripture, singing, and shaking a gourd filled with rattly things. He walked up and down the aisle collecting donations when he was done. I didn't contribute; he seemed far too angry to be preaching about anything compassionate. After him, a man with large pictures of a digestive system explained how important it was to have a healthy gut and he passed out bottles of herbs for people to buy. Next was a man who lost the use of one of his arms and was asking for money for a doctor. I didn't realize that the bus experience included entertainment and panhandling.

The bus was stopping along the highway to pick up hitch-hikers, so I finally got a seatmate, a younger Guatemalan guy. I pulled out my Lonely Planet map of the country and asked where we were; I think I had been on the bus for about two hours at this point. He pointed to a spot where I didn't want to be. We had taken a road away from Panajachel and were now going north straight up into the mountains. This was the point when I finally understood what the guys at the bus stop were saying, and it was way too late to do anything about it. It would be another hour and a half before I'd get to a connecting road to take me back south. There'd better be more preachers and witch doctors to keep me amused, I thought.

I had been on the road for close to 20 hours and was really wishing I had my toothbrush. Or deodorant. Some soap. Coffee. Anything to eat. A bathroom. Someone who wouldn't talk so freaking fast and would use baby words with me. Another lesson learned about things I should keep in my daypack on a travel day.

Desperation made me turn on my cell phone to find the map of Guatemala I had downloaded. I'd made a habit of having a GPS map of every city I went to after Mexico City, so I could follow the little blue dot and never get too lost. It was great that I could drop a pin on my lodging and wander without fear of having to sleep on a bench when I didn't make it home. The only downside was that I needed Wi-Fi once before I could use the map in each new place so my phone could locate approximately where I was and find a signal. After the initial Wi-Fi, I never needed it again until I moved somewhere new. Since I hadn't been to Guatemala before, I had to turn on my phone service to figure out where the hell I was and how I could get back. It was probably the most expensive iPhone blue dot ever. In reality, though, I paid 20 Quetzals, around $3, for a four-hour mountain tour. I tried to adjust my thinking and be happy about the fantastic bargain that was.

Finally, the man from whom I originally bought my ticket came to get me and told me I needed to get off the bus He unloaded my backpack from the roof and gave it to another man standing behind a different chicken bus. They lashed it up top and I got on, hoping they knew where I wanted to go. I had my doubts. And with a smelly, food-deprived determination, I tried to enjoy my next ride.

I had thought I was on my first chicken bus in Belize, but now learned what one truly was. With music blaring, I found a seat near the back, and right before the bus took off, 40 more people crammed onto the already-crowded bus. We sat three to four per seat and the aisle was crushed with people, all wearing beautiful handmade clothing. I was the only white person, which wasn't bad, but what a novelty for the locals. I don't think gringos usually come this far out, wherever I was. As the bus started rolling, more people were getting on and I realized that if I needed to get off somewhere, there was no way I could get out without maiming dozens of small people. I guessed I was going wherever the bus took me, and hopefully the second driver got instructions from the first one and would have pity on the poor lost white girl and tell me when I should get off. I pulled out my phone for another blue-dot check, and another $10 charge from AT&T, and was pleasantly surprised that we were going in the direction I wanted. I had even managed to keep my backpack with me all these hours. I used the next hour of the ride to make peace with the idea of losing all of my belongings, just in case.

The bus stopped in a town that wasn't Panajachel and I got the idea from the driver that I needed to find another bus. Oh, to have better Spanish – what a gift that would be. I thought he said three blocks, so I started walking and hooray, there was a taxi. I absolutely couldn't get on another bus. God only knows where I'd end up. I got a ride into town and walked to the dock – almost to my next destination, Santa Cruz on Lago de Atitlan. I was so happy I almost cried.

A bunch of people piled into a small panga boat and the man behind me, Norman, started talking to me in English. He had lived there for six years, and gave me a guided tour of the lake, which is huge, and pointed out the small towns and the hikes. It was so soothing to hear someone explain where I needed to go with no question about what was said. It took 10 minutes to get to the dock at Santa Cruz, and when we pulled up I saw the sign for my hostel. A shower was in sight. The little things made me so happy.

My hostel was La Iguana Perdida, and it was a nice place. It was very hard to communicate with them while I was in Belize, so I emailed right before I left and said I'd like the $18 room with a bathroom, but if it wasn't available I'd rather be upgraded than downgraded. I hadn't gotten used to the idea of sharing a room with multiple other people at my age. So I was put in the $30 per night room, to be moved to the cheaper one in two days when it became open. There was a restaurant and bar, dinner was communal, and I immediately signed up for yoga to ease my 22 hours of travel pains. There was no Wi-Fi and the cable connections didn't fit my MacBook Air; I hadn't thought about being computer-free for a week and it filled me with extreme anxiety. I would sooner chop off a hand than live without a computer. But I should have been grateful; they had just gotten electricity there a few years ago.

The food at the hostel was amazing. There was a group of Mayan women that did the cooking, and the menu was vast. Every plate, no matter if it was local, Mexican or American, vegan or not, was heaped with food. At the communal dinner, the tables were pushed together and candlelit, and it was impossible to go hungry. And the bar was open till 1 a.m. No need to walk the pathways in the dark to eat anywhere else.

This was my first hostel experience, and it was great. The other travelers were Europeans, mostly English and Australian, and the Americans were here for the weekend from their jobs in Guatemala. The American women lived and worked nearby in the Peace Corps or with the Mayan people to help them improve their daily lives. It was a nice mellow place with a full bar. I needed a couple days to relax and recover from my travel nightmare. Getting old sucks. I walked along a rickety, plywood and two-by-four walkway, nails sticking out everywhere, to a rocky beach to swim; it was pretty cold and I mostly sat on a large rock in the sun. I saw trails all around the lake, and because safety has always been a big concern, I was told to buy a guide for 100 quetzal for the remote areas. That also meant I wouldn't get lost. Even better.

This area was originally a supervolcano, a giant plateau. It erupted, the sides blew out, and the plateau collapsed; silt washed down from the surrounding volcanoes and it formed a giant lake at 5,500 feet elevation. While walking or boating you could see palapas, docks and walkways sunk a few feet beneath the water's edge. Most of the walkways around the lake were either carved into the dirt or you had to walk over the water on the death-defying boards and bridges that sagged when they felt my considerable weight. Just a couple feet underwater was a beautiful cobblestone road that ran around the entire lake. Everyone said that the lake was rising, but that's not entirely correct. Several years ago, an earthquake dropped the water level more than 10 feet. People started building on all the new land, but when the lake started returning to its original level, it slowly began engulfing the improvements and washing away new houses.

I did two scuba dives in Lago de Atitlan. I wore a 7-millimeter wetsuit and was so cold – what a change from Belize, where I was diving in just a bikini. The water was green and the visibility was about 15 feet. We checked out the rock formations and saw a lot of crabs, some plants, and a few fish. This was my first altitude dive, as well as my first lake dive. The pressure changes were more extreme and I had to constantly add or release air from my BCD or I'd sink, or worse, have an uncontrolled ascent. It was easy to see how that could happen. The dives weren't anything to get excited about, but it was a good experience, and one day of diving there was enough.

A few years ago, archeologists discovered a Mayan village 50 feet underwater. The government was studying it, so no divers were allowed. I asked if we could sneak in, but my dive master Andrew said it was a popular fishing spot and was always crowded. The government paid the locals to snitch on anyone who might go there, and if you were caught, your dive shop wouldn't be allowed to take tourists there when it opens.

I'd been out of the water for an hour and was still shivering, so it was time for one of the many hammocks in the sun, my Kindle, and a nap.

I was really digging the hostel scene at the Iguana. At one dinner I was seated with a German family, a Spanish couple, and a grumpy American. I wasn't sure whether to classify the American as grumpy or just opinionated, but he lectured several of us about smoking in an outside area – I had slowly started smoking again. He was very angry about it, but then he gave me a glass of wine and ignored me the rest of the night.

The German family was great. Rheinhart was the father and had been living in Honduras for five years. He was fluent in German, English and Spanish, and again I was jealous. He smoked monster cigars and told interesting stories about his years of travel. He would have made an amazing mall Santa. The Spanish couple from Barcelona sat across from me and hadn't spoken to anyone all evening; they had just arrived in Santa Cruz in time for dinner. They only spoke a little English, but we were able to have a good conversation after I explained to them that I can only talk in the present tense. They travel five weeks per year and try to go somewhere new each time.

My scuba buddy and general companion for the day was Kat, a younger woman from southern England. She was a bit Goth and had been tromping around Central America in her Doc Martens. I've always been envious of people who can make a strong fashion statement; I've never had the courage to do that. Maybe I'm just too lazy. Slouch is sort of a fashion, I guess. We were joined by a man who spoke halted English, but I could never figure out what country he was from. We all sat around after dinner with drinks and talked about travel. I learned that not everything is funny in translation. I don't know why I was so afraid of hostels before; La Iguana Perdida was the best place I'd stayed yet. I had heard so many stories about hostels being wild party places and I felt I was too old to want to party every night, so I never tried to stay in one. Sleeping in a room with eight people and sharing a bathroom was not my style at 40; I like to sleep too much. But I learned that hostels have some nice private rooms as well, they're cheaper than hotels, and I could hang out with a crowd all day then have a peaceful night in my own room. At my three-month travel anniversary, I finally learned something useful.

Kat and I decided to hike to San Marcos the next day. It didn't sound that hard: walk the rickety boardwalks, find the mountain trails, pass two small towns, and after three hours, there you are. Or should be. Everything started out very well – we found the trails, got a little direction here and there, no problem. We stopped at a seemingly deserted hotel for strawberry ice cream; they said they had Wi-Fi but it was a lie. We had the choice after that to take a small, winding upward mountain trail or a wide cobblestone road. I was leading at that point, so of course I chose the wrong path. The cobblestone seemed way too easy and no one had mentioned it. Mud, rocks, almost a vertical path. I kept thinking that if I got to the top I could tell if it was the right way, but every turn I took led to more uphill. So I went faster, and that's when the adventure ceased to be so much fun. I jumped onto a rock, slipped, and sliced open my little toe; yes I was hiking in flip-flops. I stood there for that initial moment staring at my toe, seeing that little bit inside my body where I shouldn't be able to see, and thought, "Oh good, I'm not bleeding." Seconds later, gushing blood. In a few seconds I was standing in a puddle.

I found a tissue to wrap up my toe and let Kat know I couldn't hike anymore. She went back down the trail to ask at the hotel where the nearest public boat dock was. Pass the pool, go down the stairs, they told her. Again, it seemed easy. We started down the stairs and it felt like it took hours to get to the bottom. There was a sign on the dock for the guests staying at the hotel, "Only 350 steps to the hotel," so no wonder.

We waited and tried to flag down boats, but it quickly became obvious that this wasn't a dock that anyone ever used regularly, just as a special request. Up we went, all 350 stairs again, leaving a slimy blood trail the whole way. At the top we took the wide cobblestone path that we should have been on to begin with, found the town, found the real public dock – which was partially underwater – and sat and watched the workmen building a new one. There were men all over the lake building new docks and walkways, and they were so fun to watch. There was no such thing as "safety," just as there was no such thing as "work clothes." Half of the men were in their 60s or 70s and wore the same clothing to hammer and saw as they probably wore to church: shined shoes and long-sleeved collared shirts.

The boat arrived after 15 minutes; we boarded, I bled on all the seats I stepped over, and 50 feet from the dock the boat broke down. This day just kept getting better. Since we didn't make it to San Marcos and missed lunch at the hostel, we decided to get off at the hotel one dock away from the Iguana and walk home. That's when the rain began to pour. Then thunder and lightning. Then the power went out. They might need power to cook us a hot lunch, but not to pour tequila. It was time.

I had been on the road for three months and was beginning to feel a little homesick, or maybe just lonely. I had an extreme desire to have a clean place to set my toothbrush and wear different clothes. To have a closet with more than one pair of shoes sounded luxurious. I'm not sure I wanted to go home, but living out of my backpack was getting old; I wasn't even wearing half the things I brought because they were so inappropriate; I thought my travels would take me to colder places. I figured I was halfway done with my trip now; six months is a pretty respectable amount of time for my first trip. But I resolved to spend my vacation time more wisely in the future. Maybe if I'd ever gone anywhere before, I wouldn't have been so crazy for adventure that I packed up my entire life into a $100-per-month storage container and set out with a backpack full of stuff I imagined I'd need.

My new, cheaper room at the Iguana was a freestanding cabana with a bathroom and a tiny porch – very cute. Besides the freezing showers, the only problem was that the room wasn't sealed from the elements. The walls were wood with a large, purposeful gap between them and the roof. The roof was metal with exposed wooden two-by-fours with some giant holes covered in plastic, sort of improvised skylights. The rain made a deafeningly loud noise on the metal during thunderstorms, which happened every day and night. The roof was also 6'1" from the floor, and I was constantly stooping so I wouldn't catch my hair on the protruding nails. One night a giant, hairy spider surprised me in my bathroom; the electricity was out due to a storm and I only spotted him by the faint light of my headlamp as I sat down to pee. Everything is scarier when the power is out. I killed it with my flip-flop, scanned the walls for any other creatures, and all was well.

There was another torrential downpour a few nights later and I saw another giant, hairy spider on the ceiling near my bed. "Hell no," I yelled at him, "you can't stay there, not above my head." When I was about five years old I thought I had swallowed a spider because I stuck my tongue out at it and when I went back later to see it, it was gone. I had nightmares and that had developed into a formidable phobia, so no spiders are allowed above my head, ever. Or in my bedroom. Or anywhere, really, that I might have to interact with them regularly. Some wooden planks separated the roof from the walls and the spider jumped between those and hid as I violently slapped with my flip-flop. I had to obsessively check that spot all night with my headlamp. I looked up a few minutes later and saw movement, grabbed my neglected running shoe for a more solid hit, and saw a scorpion above my bed. It must have sensed me coming and scrambled back into its hole. I tried scaring it away by screaming and repeatedly beating the area with my shoe. Now I had a giant, hairy spider and a scorpion hanging out in the wooden planks above my bed, probably conspiring to kill me.

Needless to say, I didn't get much sleep. Every few minutes I had to shine my headlamp along the ceiling, searching the entire room for activity. I think I finally drifted off at about 2 a.m.

I told my local friend Juan about my wildlife experience and he pulled out a book of indigenous birds and animals of Guatemala. "These are other things you can expect to see in your room while you're here," he said, flipping through pictures of boa constrictors, coral snakes, and rattlesnakes. I was done sleeping in Guatemala.

The next day I signed up for a backstrap weaving class. A Mayan woman named Tomasa, whose Spanish I couldn't understand at all, taught tourists how to make belts, shawls, table runners, anything they'd like to try. I met Tomasa in the village above the hostel, at the end of an almost straight vertical climb. The people there lived in run-down shacks with million-dollar views of the lake and volcanoes. I was told to sit by the basketball court near the church; no one there could give me directions that my GPS map could understand, and since I was early I watched a group of boys playing soccer. Most of them were barefoot, all wearing their ragged school clothes; they seemed so happy. A good life lesson to be instantly forgotten as soon as I found the next fun thing to buy.

Tomasa's house was a shack with an outdoor wood-fired kitchen and several kids and dogs wandering in and out. I picked out the colors for my belt and started winding the threads on a wooden peg board in the pattern she showed me. When it was roughly belt-sized, we hooked it up on the loom. The loom wasn't a standard loom like those used for tapestries or rugs, but a contraption attached to me around my back with a strap so my hands were free to weave, with the far end tied to a post. Tomasa wove thick threads around each strand which would pull every other thread while I weaved.

I was never clear on how long my lesson would be because I couldn't understand anything Tomasa was trying to tell me, and after an hour she started hanging laundry above my head. I refused to take the hint.

My belt didn't turn out to be the wondrous, colorful, intricately patterned creation typically associated with Mayan clothing. I wasn't told, or at least I didn't understand, how the colors I picked or the pattern I weaved would result in something I'd like to wear. When I finally finished, my belt looked like a third-grade art project. Special Ed third grade, at that.

Tomasa had some examples of things she had made and I got suckered into buying a beautiful table runner I had absolutely no need for. It was destined to be someone's Christmas present, but until then I'd have to tote it around in my already-full-of-useless-things backpack. I spent close to three hours with Tomasa at about $2 per hour for what she charged, so I didn't regret buying the table runner. It was really pretty. Maybe someday I'll buy weaving supplies and make everyone ugly belts for Christmas.

My next adventure was the market at Chichicastenango. I caught the 7 a.m. boat to Panajachel, then a shuttle to Chichi, about an hour and a half northeast through the mountains. By then I was in love with the chicken buses. Not so much the aspect of riding on them with everything I own, but their appearance and general attitude. They must get the buses from the U.S., because I'd seen a few that weren't repainted and had "Your tax dollars for such-and-such county at work" stenciled on them. The best ones were completely blinged-out with flashy paint jobs in every color and pattern, pristine exteriors, mounted decorations like bull horns or antlers on the front, and when they blared their horns it sounded like a barge going by. And they drove fast, almost up on two wheels when they took the hairpin turns through the mountains. They all had names like boats do, splashed across the sides and the back, usually sexy girl names. The road to Chichi was full of great-looking buses.

Chichi has the biggest open air market in Central America, and it was insane. It's held on Thursdays and Sundays, and there are hundreds of stalls on the streets, plus the regular stores. If I thought I knew what aggressive sales people were like from Mexico, I was utterly wrong. Mayan women followed me around shouting and pushing their items in my face, following me for several blocks. The further I walked from their stalls, the cheaper the price became, but I had to listen to progressively sadder stories about how their kids couldn't eat unless I bought something, how no one in her family had shoes, and about husbands who couldn't work; it was my job to personally save their families from ruin by buying a wall-hanging.

I did buy a few things for my family; as annoying as the women were with their sales pitches, the clothing and tapestries were quite beautiful; bright colors and perfectly designed repeating patterns. I was honing my haggling skills, and usually when I was followed by a woman for a few minutes I could get the price down to half of what was originally asked. As long as I'd started my Christmas shopping, I might as well buy enough to justify mailing a package home. I finally bought a tapestry for my niece after three blocks of sob stories, and moments later another woman offered me the same one for 20 q less, about $3. I wasn't the best haggler but I was learning.

The market was something everyone should experience. I still can't get over how crazy it was. Never-ending aisles of stalls that lead in no direction whatsoever. I rode the shuttle with an Australian couple; the man was 6 feet, 5 inches, so I thought he was a good person to follow. I'd just have to look over the heads of the 5-foot Guatemalan folk to find my way.

Everything you could imagine was for sale, from handmade clothing to used nuts and bolts and buckets of shrimp. I was looking for a good folding knife and found some at a table, but they were switchblades and I couldn't imagine trying to get one home through customs. I do regret not buying one. Gotta be safe.

There were times at the market when we were in a traffic jam between stalls; people everywhere were trying to go somewhere else, and no one could move. The tiny Guatemalan women would use me as a battering ram to get through the crowd; I felt four or five hands on my back and ass, pushing me so I would trample through. Sometimes it was fun; other times I stopped dead and braced myself, forcing the little women to make their way around me, which was more fun. I like being big. One tiny old woman didn't appreciate my refusal to move and started punching me. It was impossible to get mad, though, because she was so small she was punching my thighs and I barely felt it.

Back at the hostel I heard a story that made me decide I wasn't going to mail anything home, even though I could barely close my backpack by then. Molly and Daniel had come a few months ago and had been working at the hostel. Molly's mom sent them a care package with Oreos and peanut butter, things that are hard to find here. After waiting for weeks, they finally went to the post office to check on their package. They found a letter from someone in Guatemala City telling them that if they wanted their box, they could bring $200 to the post office to retrieve it. The contents of the package weren't worth that much over and above the postage that had already been paid, so they never got it.

Apparently Guatemala's postal service is a bit of a lottery. Anything from the States that looks good gets taken hostage and there isn't anyone to complain to about it; the police are as bad as the muggers. I worried about sending a package home, but in reality, who would want to steal things I bought there? But God forbid I got my wallet stolen and had to get a new ATM card mailed; there wasn't a chance I'd see it.

I had met dozens of people at the Iguana, and after hearing all of their stories I realized that getting mugged at some point was inevitable. I was the only person without a robbery tale. It was going to happen at least once while I was in Central America, and

I resigned myself to that fact. Wallets and day bags were the only things that got taken, and no one I had talked to had been hurt. Up until then I had kept all of my most valuable things – iPhone, camera, computer, credit cards, Kindle and iPod – in my day pack while on the road. The general advice from everyone was to keep the things I'm most worried about in my giant backpack that gets strapped to the roof of buses, which was a horrifying thought. But thieves don't want to carry off a giant bag. I'd have to remember to buy online storage to upload the thousands of pictures I took when I got to a place with Wi-Fi, and to have a goodbye party for the possessions I loved the most, just in case.

As my time at Lago de Atitlan drew to a close, I found that I was beginning to get used to the wildlife in my cabana. Little spiders didn't bother me anymore; I probably had one stuck in my hair at any given time. After doing an initial wall and ceiling check – bugs don't ever seem to be on the floor – I didn't obsessively keep rechecking. That was improvement.

My last big adventure in Lago was climbing the big volcano. I meant to get up at 6 a.m., catch the boat to San Pedro by 7 to have breakfast, and start climbing Volcan San Pedro by 8. But I didn't get out of bed until 7, so I decided to have breakfast at the Iguana. The women had just started a major cleaning project and didn't want to stop to make breakfast, so I went to the dock to start my day and the guys were fixing the boat that was supposed to go to San Pedro. I finally left at 9, grumpy, coffee-less, and of course that was the day everyone at every stop had a gazillion things to load onto the boat. At Tzunana, two girls were taking flat tires to get fixed; most towns on the lake don't have roads to the other side of the mountain. Those tires took forever to load onto the boat. At San Marcos, some boys had a load of lumber to put on the boat. Then seemingly every old person who could barely walk had somewhere to go. I was irritated because the last boat back to San Pedro left at 5 p.m. and I still needed to have breakfast, climb the volcano, and get back before then. Shawna told me there was a guy staying there that missed the last boat, talked a tuk-tuk driver into driving him to San Marcos, then tried to walk the trail back to Santa Cruz without a flashlight or shoes. He ended up sleeping in a barn. So I wanted to get back before the last boat, but I packed my headlamp just in case.

I finally got to San Pedro and found a place for breakfast; the owners said there was Wi-Fi, but I couldn't connect. I had only had Wi-Fi for two days in the past two weeks and I was suffering withdrawals from my tech addiction; it was really starting to hurt. This day needed to start getting better.

I found a tuk-tuk up to the volcano park; it was 100 q to enter and the price included a guide. With very little ceremony, I started up the mountain with Benito. It was great at first – I wanted to run all the way up. That lasted for about 20 uphill minutes. Breathing hard, going slower and slower, I was no longer on his ass trying to make better time. There was a *mirador* about 40 minutes up and I was so happy, I could have sat there and stared at the amazing view and just concentrated on breathing for the rest of the day. And drinking water. And trying not to breathe in the water. I'd been smoking way too many cigarettes.

Shortly after the *mirador*, the climb went from uphill paths to steps, either carved into the volcano or built with logs. We were still making good time, but it was almost two hours of steps. I went from slightly slow walking to super-slow walking, gasping for air, then coughing up the hundred bugs I had just breathed in, to needing regular breaks. My competitive ego didn't want Benito to know what a hard time I was having, so I would pretend to be fascinated by a tree or a bug and stop to take a picture and breathe. I have a hundred pictures of random plants, insects, whatever. For anyone interested in an extremely detailed documentation of the local environment of Volcan San Pedro, I could write another book.

One fascinating aspect of the mountain is that the local people farm most of the land on the way up the volcano. We passed acres of coffee and maize. I saw men chopping trees at elevations way above 5,500 feet and carrying loads of firewood back down. I can't imagine the work it would take to harvest crops up there. The men had giant crates filled with wood attached to themselves by a thick belt, which they looped over their foreheads to carry down the trail. During one of my Spanish classes in Santa Cruz, Pedro had me reading local stories, and one was written by a man who wished he could stop carrying crops with his forehead, in hopes that he'd grow a little taller.

Back on the trail, I wanted to tell Benito several times that I had to stop and go back down. We were so high that I lost feeling in my hands, my fingers were swollen, and my head was spinning. But I just couldn't get the words out. Always finish what you start. So up I trudged, barely walking up the steps, Benito waiting for me every couple of minutes. One tourist, obviously a long-distance trail runner who didn't take up smoking on his vacation, flew past me and I really wanted to stop. It turned into a battle, though. There was no way I would stop until I got to the top.

Two and a half hours from the start, I finally made it to the summit. Two and a half hours of uphill, mostly straight up on stairs. I sat at the pinnacle and thought I might sit there until I died. But the view was amazing; I could see almost the entire lake, the other volcanoes, and the mountains in every direction. I found a pack of energy chews in my backpack and was so happy to sit there and soak up the peacefulness.

After almost half an hour it was time to go back down. I was feeling pretty good again, so Benito let me lead and I started at a run. Shot Blocs, my energy chews, are amazing. Down was way more fun than up; it was like a barely controlled free-fall. The fun lasted for about 40 minutes before my "down" muscles started getting upset with me. Then I began to notice that my newly acquired beer belly was jiggling way more than I was comfortable with. I couldn't stop thinking of the Simpsons episode when Homer gets hit in the stomach with a bowling ball and his fat jiggles in slow motion. For once my boobs didn't hurt while I ran, since they'd obviously gained beer weight too, but my bras hadn't gotten any bigger. I made an immediate resolution to drink less, which lasted about three hours; I have a hard time writing sober.

We still made good time down, about an hour. Benito stopped about three quarters of the way and called a tuk-tuk, so my ride was waiting when I got to the base. When I got to the dock it was almost 3 p.m. and a boat was waiting for me. I got excited and jumped on, forgetting that I had to get to an ATM while I was in town. So instead of paying cash for my 12 days in Lago, I got to pay by credit card with a 7% fee.

My final night in Lago de Atitlan was spent buying beers and shots for the hostel staff. The women who clean and cook get paid, but the hostel staff works for room and board. I felt that getting everyone drunk was a good tip.

A family of 17 checked in that night. Fifteen kids? Fifteen redheaded kids? Really? I was morally outraged about that, but I was drunk and a little Mayan girl was combing my hair and talking to me in Spanish, asking why my hair was so short and blond and why I have a tattoo on my arm, so my outrage was temporarily forgotten.

My plan was to go to Antigua the next day to check out the local attractions, hikes, maybe get some Salsa lessons. There was going to be a huge party on September 15, lasting for days. I thought it was Independence Day, but I didn't have all of my facts straight because Benito was talking about it and I wouldn't let him speak in English. Then I planned to head to Semuc Champey, and yes, that would be travelling south, then north, then south again. I've already mentioned that directions aren't my thing.

My childhood nightmare came true on my last night at the Iguana: I swallowed a spider in my sleep. At least I hope it was a spider. It must have been kind of big since it woke me up, coughing, at 2 a.m., and I swallowed whatever was in my throat. I couldn't stop thinking about how gross it was. I know that a lot goes on while we sleep; I'm sure it's like Toy Story, but I try not to think of these things. Six to eight hours is a long time to be unconscious. To think something was crawling on me – maybe it found my arm and worked its way up, or my hair, or webbed directly onto my face – that's the thing. It was on my face. Then in my mouth. I had a hard time thinking about anything else for hours.

When I got to the dining room for breakfast, I saw the father of the 15 kids sitting on the porch drinking coffee. And what do you think his wife was doing? Running from dorm to dorm getting all the kids ready for the day. My outrage totally came back, even with the distraction of the spider. I was absolutely astounded by this family. Why is there a need to have 15 kids? Did they think they were homesteading the Wild West? Does our population's survival depend upon having as many offspring as possible? These people were missionaries from the U.S., living in Guatemala to teach the local people how to use their resources more efficiently, while this brood was blazing through them like a swarm of ginger locusts.

And I was still thinking about the spider.

Molly told me she remembered a Ripley's Believe It Or Not fact from when she was younger stating that the average American swallows three spiders per year in their sleep. I guess I'm OK with that, as long as they don't wake me up again.

ANTIGUA

I took a bus to Antigua, Guatemala and it was fairly uneventful. I found an old couple on the street by the bus stop that pointed me to a cheap, pleasant hotel. My initial walk made me think Antigua would be nice, kind of like San Miguel de Allende in Mexico, but a bit more touristy. I couldn't find a grocery store, but there were 12 travel agencies. I walked just enough to find an ATM; my legs were still screaming from the volcano hike the day before. The city was beautiful and the people very colorful; bright, loud chicken buses screamed through the streets and I was still thinking about that spider.

A volcano nearby had erupted the day before I got there, and lava would have been visible if the low clouds had cleared. Since I'd started my trip I had witnessed Hurricane Ernesto, an earthquake, and a volcano eruption. I tried not to take it personally.

A Google search told me it's almost impossible to swallow a spider while you're sleeping, and that the stories are urban myth. An article I couldn't believe said spiders view humans as giant predators and they don't want to come near us. I call bullshit. I can't count the number of times a random spider has webbed onto me unprovoked. And how can anyone prove a myth is only a myth? I don't think "Mythbusters" would want to tackle this one; there's nothing to blow up. I actually got onto my computer to start researching my next destination, but that stupid spider just wouldn't get out of my head. No pun intended.

Antigua was a strange place. Its old-time cobblestone streets weren't remotely even or easy to walk on; most of the streets were one-way, with lots of back alleys and no street signs. It was like a circle of hell for the directionally impaired. The city is surrounded by volcanoes. I made a point of going to the rooftop of my hotel with my compass to figure out which volcano is north and which is south. I hoped with that information I'd be able to find my way within at least a couple of blocks back home, but it was rainy season and all the volcanoes' peaks were covered in clouds, so it really didn't help at all.

I continued to be grateful for the iPhone app "Citymaps2go." It didn't need Wi-Fi, and as soon as it figured out where I was I got a blue dot showing the direction I was walking. For about $2, I have maps for every country in the world. I bookmarked my hotel, my new Spanish school, the yoga place and the street with the ATMs. I honestly don't think I could have traveled by myself without this app.

While I was unpacking my backpack in my room, I found a pair of shorts that I forgot were in there and figured I'd try them on. Suffice it to say, it was time to start working out again. Eat better. Stop drinking so much. Quit sneaking cigarettes. I immediately set my alarm for 6 a.m. to go running.

I hit the snooze button a couple of times, but my new resolve stuck and I managed to drag my ass out of bed at 6:15. Shoes on, iPhone map queued up, off I went. A few blocks into my run, over those horrible cobblestones that required me to watch my feet constantly, I saw a couple running and decided to follow them. They looked like they had a route. After a few more blocks, I was checking my phone to see which direction I was going when I heard both the guy and the girl screaming about 20 feet in front of me. When I looked up I saw a man jump onto the back of an idling motorcycle and two guys quickly drove off.

The running guy chased for a few feet but turned back to the girl, who was crying hysterically. I ran up to see what happened, but they were talking Spanish so fast I couldn't understand anything. All I could figure out was that one of the men on the motorcycle did something to the woman. Maybe he grabbed her iPod. Maybe he grabbed her.

All I knew was that I was a few feet away from some sort of assault in full daylight with all kinds of people in the street. It pretty much killed my resolve to get up and go running again.

I was already out, though, so I kept running for another 20 minutes before I headed back home. I was trying to keep my iPhone hidden, but I ended up getting completely lost and had to consult my map anyway.

It was weird being witness to something I couldn't understand; I wasn't sure if I should be worried or not. I had been constantly wandering around towns with my phone in my hand; otherwise I'd never find my way back anywhere. There were cops with machine guns at all the ATMs and internet cafés, so Antigua seemed pretty safe. And why would these guys choose a couple to rob when there were plenty of single women like me walking around?

I was still operating on my presumption that these tiny Guatemalan guys weren't going to bother with a girl my size. I didn't want to get too paranoid and kill all the fun of my trip.

I went to the first day of my new Spanish class and the most memorable part was a spider dropping down and attacking my teacher and me. Possibly not attacking, but now I truly believe that Guatemalan spiders are out to get me. That scared me more than the morning's drive-by mugging.

My first weekend in Antigua I joined a group to climb Volcan Pacaya, which was rumbling and smoking at the time. It was a vastly different experience than Volcan San Pedro. A van picked me up at 6 a.m., then spent 20 minutes driving around gathering 15 other tourists. We had a truckload of Germans, Britons, Spaniards and a Korean, who kept walking away when I tried to talk to him. He was kind of cute. For once I was the only American. We drove for an hour and a half away from Antigua, over crazy highways and through small, run-down towns.

Our driver was determined to get there in good time, and since I was the first pickup he made me sit in the front with him and witness every moment of his scary driving. There's nothing like flying down a curvy, two-lane mountain highway at top speed trying to pass every motorcycle and chicken bus on the wrong side of the road. I felt like I was starting to get used to everyone's way of driving here, and maybe even picking up some tricks for when I got home. They're probably not as legal at home, though.

The final town we drove through was so poor it looked like a patchwork of rusty corrugated metal. People were hanging out laundry or returning from the woods with their day's supply of firewood. It was one of the poorest places I'd seen yet, but the people there had million-dollar views of the volcanoes, and you could see all the way to the Pacific Ocean.

Each house had a cooking fire with smoke pouring out the roof, and combined with the hour and a half of diesel fumes from the highway, my eyes were burning. It was incredible that the air was still so clear.

We finally got out of the van and were instantly surrounded by children trying to rent walking sticks for 5 q (about 70 cents), painfully thin dogs, and men on horses wanting to sell us a ride.

The crowd was so thick it was difficult to walk three steps. Our guide found us and off we went, followed by the caravan of children and horses and dogs.

This volcano hike was much easier and shorter than San Pedro. It was a wide, winding path of loose volcanic rock, never too steep. We took breaks every 20 minutes of so for the slower people in the group. It was hard to believe that with smoking, drinking and general laziness, I wasn't one of them.

The views were breathtaking as we climbed higher; we could see multiple volcanoes, mountains, and all of Guatemala to the ocean. The boys with the sticks turned around after about 10 minutes, but the men on horses followed for a while, watching for signs of fatigue and a wallet emerging. They were funny at first, yelling "Taxi," but after a while 10 men yelling it every few seconds got on everyone's nerves. One guy rode up to me to tell me that his horse was bigger and he was pretty sure it could hold me. Great boost to the self-confidence.

After a final plea for rides, the men turned around and we had some quiet in which to enjoy the panoramas. We kept climbing another 30 minutes and were surprised by two women selling cold sodas and bags of chips on the side of the trail. That was another reason I was gaining so much weight there – soda, chips, and pastries were the only foods that the *tiendas* sold; I really had to seek out fruits and vegetables, and no one even knew what "organic" meant when I asked. Instead I was directed to a plant nursery.

The wide path eventually turned into a skinny volcanic trail across an old lava field with smoking vents on all sides. No lava was flowing, though – very disappointing. This was the volcano that had been erupting, but there was no sign of lava yet. I don't think I'm destined to ever see actual lava. The one time I went to the Big Island of Hawaii to see its erupting volcano, it had stopped a couple days before I arrived, then started again after I left. It will have to remain on the bucket list.

We went into a cool cave with dripping water everywhere, then over more funky rock formations to the base of Pacaya. No one was allowed to climb to the summit, but we had a great view from where we were. The peak was split and bits of smoke were drifting out, with more smoke pouring from countless vents all the way down. Our final stop was at a giant vent that smelled like a sauna, and we stood there and roasted marshmallows.

It was another good experience and great sightseeing, but just like the ruins, I was done with volcano climbs. It felt like it was time to get back to the ocean, scuba diving, and margaritas.

The next morning, I tried to beat the street traffic and I left my room at 6:15 a.m. for a run. The roads were jammed with people trying to get the best spots for the Sunday street markets. The mornings there were always gorgeous before they turned to rain at around 3 p.m., and it was nice to listen to the different bells from the competing churches. Even getting out at 6:15, I couldn't catch a sunrise. It was way too early for me. I couldn't see one from the other end because I'm just too old to stay out till 5 a.m. The problems of approaching middle age.

I had a long day of shopping ahead of me that I wasn't looking forward to; it was time to buy gifts for the family and figure out the postal system. I don't know why I hate shopping so much, but whether I'm at a mall or arguing with a 4-foot-tall woman, shopping is all the same to me. Evil.

I put on my happy face and worst looking clothes to get ready for the markets. I had to remember that every starting price was more than twice as much as the merchants will sell for, no matter how many starving kids and lazy husbands they have at home.

I emailed my parents when I returned from the markets; I am indeed a girl. I shopped all day. I completed my mission. My feet were killing me, but I had gifts for all of my loved ones. And myself, of course, and much more than I could stuff in my already-jammed backpack, so I could not avoid the post office any longer. I was pretty proud of myself, though; I've done a lot of cool things on this trip so far, but perhaps this was the biggest actual accomplishment, given how much I abhor shopping.

I didn't buy any "guy" gifts. Guatemala didn't seem like the place to buy things for the men in my life. I don't know a lot of hippies anymore who would wear the bright woven colors, and the t-shirt quality was pretty poor. Honduras sounded manlier; I'd have to try there.

I did find my knife, which was definitely a manly gift, but sending a box of switchblades home seemed like a bad idea. The one I bought for myself had a shiny, stainless-steel blade with a faux-wood handle, and for some reason, a small fold-out flashlight. I could see myself messing with the flashlight and accidentally hitting the button to open the blade and cutting off my finger. I talked the vendor down to 30 q, about $3.50.

I had also been eyeing a blanket since I got there. I didn't know why I wanted the blanket so badly since I didn't even own a bed, but it was so beautiful, made out of different patches from the different districts around Guatemala. I finally went to that store to look at it more closely and decide in advance on a price I'd be willing to pay. The woman's opening offer was 600 q or $75, and it was worth every bit of that. You could probably find it at some trendy online store for $500. My first bid was 300 q, $37, and we finally settled somewhere in the middle. I knew that was a lot of money here, but for some reason I just had to have that blanket. It weighed so much it would probably cost me $200 to mail home.

I did get into a groove with my haggling style; the half of a Valium pill I took helped steady my nerves for negotiating, thank God for the pharmacies there. I would find something I liked, the woman would give me a price, I'd make a super-low counteroffer, we'd exchange prices until I found her best price, then I'd drop everything I was bargaining for, saying how expensive this stall was and that I thought I saw something similar down the street. At that point, her best price would get better as she ran after me, then we haggled something even lower than her new best price and I'd accept. I kept feeling a tiny bit guilty, but it seemed like such a fun game. The only place this didn't work was the blanket store, because that woman knew she had the best stuff around. And, all of my haggling was in Spanish. Even better.

But haggling or not, I probably blew a week's budget shopping, and another week's budget on shipping.

That brought up the new task of where to get boxes; there weren't any at the post office and I hadn't found a shipping store like they had in Mexico.

I struck up a friendship with Carlos, the night watchman at my hotel. He helped me with my Spanish and patiently answered all of my questions and put up with me waking him at all hours of the night; the only way to get into the hotel is by ringing the bell. I thought I'd ask him to be my shipping guy; he works six nights a week at the hotel and I doubted he made enough to live on. I figured he'd box all of my stuff and take it to the post office for $10, or $20. Worth it for both of us. If shipping was cheaper for a local than a tourist, better yet.

With my plan ready, I had a veggie burger on a toasted wheat bagel with guacamole, lettuce and tomato, and I settled down for some Guatemalan TV. I wished I could get the Browns game.

Plan A didn't work. Turned out Carlos had never mailed a package before; that was probably his wife's job. He also worked two full-time jobs – six nights a week as the night watchman at this hotel, and six days as the day guy at another. Crazy. He slept on a cot in the hotel office and woke up when someone rang the bell. Even if he did know his way around the post office, I couldn't ask him.

I did finally manage to get my packages sent with the help of "Super Julia," my Spanish teacher. I was asking her about the post office in class, whether or not there was a more secure place to use, and where to buy boxes and packing tape. She decided we'd take a mini field trip to mail my stuff. But we had to do it all in Spanish, because it was during school hours.

We picked up my gifts, bought supplies, and walked to three different places to get quotes. I would never have known those stores existed, they were so hidden. We didn't even go to the post office. Two hours and $150 later, my gifts were in the mail. I thought when I get home I would need to get a good job; I really like paying people to do things for me.

I was so happy to get my packages mailed that I signed up for a Salsa lesson. And that's all I'm going to say about that experience.

Julia also looked up my Mayan *nawal*, like a Hawaiian *'aumakua*, my spirit animal. It's a hummingbird. It was somewhat disappointing; I always thought I'd be something ferocious. It also said that I'm impulsive. That part wasn't surprising.

While I was still in a fairly large town, I took advantage of resupplying my tampon stash, just in case I was unexpectedly in need, in the middle of nowhere. I found a pharmacy, but couldn't spot anything useful. I walked to the counter and asked the man, in Spanish, "Can you help me find the things that a woman uses every month." I never learned any words for these things, but he understood.

I did go on a real field trip with my Spanish class. We got on a chicken bus and rode to Old Antigua, the site of the first capital of Guatemala. Antigua became the capital in 1527, then in 1541 a massive volcanic eruption, coupled with several days of torrential rains, destroyed the old capital. While the lava was consuming the city, it blocked off all the drainage and caused a flood as well. Only one church remains from that time, the rest of Old Antigua is relatively new. There was a cemetery that was very New Orleans-ish, but the chicken bus was probably the best part of the trip.

I still felt bad for Carlos and his nearly 24/7 work schedule, so after the trip I bought us pizzas to eat in the hotel lobby. It was two-for-one Tuesday. We watched TV and spoke Spanish. I ate my entire pizza and was a little embarrassed, but I couldn't help it. More reason for him to think that Americans are pigs, I guess. I realized at this point that I was bored in Antigua. I liked it, the school was great, the markets were entertaining, there were endless bars and restaurants, but I wished I had left yesterday. I needed some outdoor adventure.

I made plans for my departure, a van ticket to Semuc Champey, and I decided to try to beat the Guatemalan Independence Day craziness. I was done with Antigua and had no desire to stay for some kids in parades and more fireworks. I had enough of fireworks after San Miguel. There were also too many people flocking to the city to see the erupting volcano; it was a nice sight, smoke in the day and lava glowing red at night, but it wasn't scary and after some pictures, there was no need to see more. Nice but not exciting.

SEMUC CHAMPEY

The trip in the van was supposed to be five hours, but due to the parades starting a day early, the traffic was insane. Half of the two-lane freeway was taken up by groups of children jogging through the mountains with torches. Actually, the torches were coffee cans roped to sticks with something smoky on fire inside. That set us back about an hour.

With so much time to kill, I started the basic chitchat. It was the same thing every time I met someone new: "My name is Melissa, I live in Hawaii, yes it's cool, I'm traveling for a year or until I run out of money, I've been here and here and want to go here, blah blah blah." I did pick up a lot of good information every time I spoke to someone new, but after four months of introducing myself, it would have been nice to hang out with people who already knew me.

I discovered that my seatmate, Bobby, was a fellow Ohio State grad. Funny how many people from Ohio I met. I didn't mention that I graduated about 10 years before him, which is a generous number; I was consistently the oldest person around, but for some reason I didn't want to let him know how much older I was. We reminisced about Ohio; he still lives there and we made plans to meet up in a scenic location and make one of those O-H-I-O pictures that people post on Ohio State's Facebook page.

After being so far behind schedule so early into the trip, our van driver was determined to make up time any way he could. Speeding, passing multiple cars on blind curves, driving on the wrong side of the road, whatever it took. We had to stop when a construction truck was backing off the highway, and since there was no way around, our driver laid on the horn and yelled curses out the window. It wasn't as if we were a pizza that had to be delivered hot, so we weren't sure why he was so mad. When he could finally sneak around the truck into the other lane to pass, he was still yelling at the truck driver and hit the car coming the other way. The car had a "For Sale" sign in the window so I figured we'd be there another hour haggling over the damages, but our driver just yelled at him and drove on.

And then we were back on the road again doing twice the speed limit until we got pulled over by armed policemen for a random stop. Our driver was in so much of a hurry that he didn't bring the proper paperwork, so all eight of us had to get out of the van to wait. I thought we could just pay them and be on our way, but no, many phone calls had to be made. We had a lot of time to kill, so a few of us ran across the highway to pee in the bushes with a chicken bus full of young boys half-climbing out the windows trying to get a peek.

Bobby and I had a great idea to make our O-H-I-O picture here, spelled out with Bobby and I being the O's and the policemen being the H and the I, but using their rifles to make the letters. Neither of us had the courage to ask.

After another hour wasted standing in the sun on the side of the highway, we were back on the road, until we were run off it by a chicken bus. But that only resulted in a minor waste of time.

Two hours late and way too many dirt roads later, I was at my hostel in Semuc Champey, Guatemala, and I headed straight to the bar. I got so hammered that Kimberly, the bartender, had to navigate me back to my bed.

I woke up with a pretty vicious hangover, really only my second one of the trip, so I was proud of that. I should have stuck with tequila, but the beers were in such huge bottles I couldn't resist.

I had made arrangements for a full-day tour of Semuc Champey, leaving at 9 a.m. At 9:15 we had to start walking, because it was Independence Day and our van couldn't get through. The parades had started and my group had to thread its way between throngs of children in traditional dress, bands, and groups from the schools – basically everyone in this tiny town. It was close to 10 a.m. before we found our way to the van and the road, and wow, my head hurt.

The trip to Semuc Champey was approximately half an hour of rocky dirt roads, and again behind schedule, the driver was making better time than my head wanted him to. Our group was three Israeli couples plus me. The next day was Israeli New Year and everyone was on holiday.

Our first stop was the cave Las Marias K'an-ba, a wet cave that required some degree of swimming most of the way, holding candles over our heads. The first bit of icy water over my head wiped out my hangover and that was a relief. We were climbing rocks, swimming, crawling up rickety ladders, and going over waterfalls. It was a fun cave. Our guide singled me out to do the "advanced" tour: when everyone else got to climb a ladder, I had to climb up by rope. When everyone else jumped off a rock, I got to climb eight feet higher to jump from there. I wasn't sure why he felt I needed extra adventure, but I can never back down from a challenge.

Surprisingly, no one died in the cave because of the lack of any type of safety precautions, and our next task was tubing the river. Easy and relaxing.

At the end of the river there was a rope to swing from and a bridge to jump off. Somewhat scary, but fun. Just like in Mexico and Belize, a lot of things you can do here would be illegal in the States.

Our next stop was lunch; we all brought sandwiches from the hostel, but I wanted to try some local cooking so I bought a plate at a stand. Not great. So I tried my sandwich. Not great. I was going to throw everything away when a Guatemalan girl walked up and asked if she could have my leftovers. Poor girl. I gave her my plate and all the fruit I had in my backpack.

In Antigua, I learned from my Spanish teacher that the children start getting coffee in their bottles at eight months. They call it "baby coffee." After that, the kids mostly drink Pepsi, which has a huge monopoly in Guatemala, with signs every five feet advertising it. And like the girl I gave my food to, the children who sell food and fruit aren't allowed to eat it; they mainly get corn tortillas. With a diet comprising mostly corn and coffee, more than half of the population is malnourished.

A group of local girls was selling trinkets in the booths, so we bought them each a lunch plate. I'd never seen happier children in my life.

After lunch, we went to the *mirador* above the pools to get a look at everything. It was a 30-minute walk up the mountain, mostly on carved steps. The top was amazing; it was the view that everyone comes to Semuc Champey to see. The river flows strong at the entrance to the valley until its midpoint, when it goes underground, leaving clear blue pools to swim and relax in. The valley is narrow and covered with jungle, mountains rising up on either side. The only word for it is "breathtaking."

When I first approached the *mirador,* I heard something strange but familiar; it was Bobby trying to organize his O-H-I-O picture with an amazing background view. He wasn't at my hostel, so it was a pretty big coincidence to run into him on top of a mountain. We took our pictures and headed down to the pools.

Clear, cold blue water with islands of tropical plants and waterfalls were exactly what I needed after a day of caving and climbing that started off with a bad hangover. We floated for a while, then loaded into the back of a pickup truck for the bumpy ride home.

I avoided another hangover by going to bed shortly after dinner and drinks. I arranged for a shuttle to Rio Dulce at 8 a.m., it being the only transportation going in the general direction of Roatan, where I decided my next stop would be. I'd been in Guatemala way too long and it was time for the ocean.

The group on this ride included two different Israeli couples, not nearly as pleasant as the couples on the cave trip. We piled into the van and started back up the bumpy, pot-holed roads.

This driver didn't seem to realize that he was driving a shuttle and kept stopping to pick up people on the side of the road to make a little extra money. Every time he stopped, one of the Israelis yelled at him; they were a pretty angry bunch. We took a detour and pulled off next to what looked like a prison, where the driver got out and unloaded crates of bananas at the gate. While he waited there, the biggest Israeli, maybe 6 feet, 2 inches and 275 pounds, got out to yell at him. They obviously had somewhere to be, although I learned months ago that when travelling in Central America, a schedule is only a suggestion. The Israelis were all fluent in Spanish, so I don't know why they were surprised.

From what I understood, the driver was waiting for food in return for the bananas, and two more Israelis got out of the van to yell at him, as if it was going to do any good. After another 15 minutes, the food was delivered and we were on our way.

After another hour we were stopped at a construction roadblock, and we weren't allowed to go through. I took this time to find a place to pee on the side of the road. The Israelis used their time to yell at the man in the orange vest.

There was an old road and a new road. The new road was half-blocked with large boulders, but the old road was clear. Everyone was speaking too fast for me to understand exactly what the problem was. And suddenly, after waiting half an hour, we got cleared to take the old road for no apparent reason. There wasn't any construction, nothing blocking it; I never figured out what was going on.

Finally, after seven hours with no paved roads, we arrived in Rio Dulce. I was quite happy to say goodbye to my vanmates. I made a reservation for the morning boat to Livingston, the only place I swore I would never go. Too many bad stories. I thought I could get a direct ride to the dock in Honduras from Livingston, according to my Lonely Planet, so that was my only choice. If I had travelled through Guatemala in anything like one direction I would have had more options from other towns.

I got on the 9 a.m. boat to Livingston and went straight to the travel agency, where they told me that they couldn't take me to Honduras. They needed six people to make the trip pay and I was the only one signed up – another wonderful aspect of travelling solo. Instead, the agent gave me a map with a route of two boats and three buses, and said, "If you're lucky, you can make it in a day." There was no way that would happen on my own.

I checked into a hostel, and just to prove how lucky I was, the Israeli couples were checking in there, too – the bad ones, not the nice ones. The first thing they did was argue with the cleaning woman about their rooms. After lunch and a couple beers to restore my patience, I went to a couple other travel agencies and found one that ran the same direct trip to Honduras and only required four people to sign up. I was incredibly anxious to leave Guatemala and get to the ocean, so I bought four tickets.

HONDURAS
SEPTEMBER 19ᵀᴴ, 2012

Thirteen hours of boat, van, and ferry got me to Roatan. The trip was better than expected. I paid $200, the fare for four people, and it might have been the best money spent so far; that was how badly I wanted to get out of Guatemala. I left my hostel at 6 a.m. for the docks and took an hour-long boat ride to Puerto Barrios, where a man was waiting for me. I hopped in his van, just me, and we sped through miles and miles of country.

The border crossing was easy, but it would have taken hours if I was by myself. Samuel, my driver, knew everyone along the way, buddy to all the guys and flirting with all the women. At the Guatemalan checkpoint they stamped my passport, then we found the money-changers. After a 10-minute drive to enter Honduras, Samuel was different, and he told me to put my seat belt on and behave. There were two lines at immigration with dozens of people waiting, but Samuel took me to a third window that was closed, shouted, "Hey, *hermano!*" grabbed my passport and some cash and we were done in five minutes. The guy never even looked at me. Samuel probably saved me an hour of waiting in line.

After police searched the van, but not my enormous backpack, we got sprayed down with an antibacterial solution and went through Corintos, San Pedro Sula (with a Wendy's and Burger King every 50 feet) and a lot of other small towns all the way to La Ceiba for the ferry. Outside San Pedro, Samuel pointed out the poorest town in Honduras – miles of corrugated metal cobbled together into shacks. It was a sad sight.

The ride featured a rambutan stand every mile or so, acres and acres of banana plantations, and semi-trucks sharing the two-lane highway with horse-drawn carts and bicycles.

Without Samuel and his van, I don't think this trip would have been possible in a single day, at least for me. Besides the time saved at immigration, I didn't have to walk the mile between leaving Guatemala and entering Honduras with my heavy backpack, and there was no sitting at bus stations wondering if I was at the right place, or going the right way. Also, Samuel knew where the good food was along the way.

At the ferry station in La Ceiba, I had a couple hours to kill and found the only café nearby. When I asked for a menu, the big woman chuckled a bit and told me they only served one dish for lunch and one for dinner, so you get what you get. It was fried chicken, spaghetti, avocado, rice, beans, and fried plantain. I found a newspaper with the latest crime statistics for Honduras and wondered whether I should just keep moving.

At the ferry station, I encountered the first security I'd seen in my travels. They actually scanned my bags and walked me through a metal detector, where they took my switchblade. I was pretty upset; I'd become pretty fond of that knife. But after puzzling through Honduran Spanish, which is slightly different than Guatemalan or Mexican Spanish, I found out I could reclaim my knife at the end of the trip.

The ferry was great – one of those gigantic boats with air conditioning, TVs and comfy reclining seats. It could probably hold a few hundred people, but it was pretty empty. The ride to Roatan took about an hour and a half.

The cab ride into Roatan to my hotel cost nearly as much as the ferry, and it was so dark I couldn't see anything. I found dinner at a bar filled with American expats, watched a Garifune group doing a tribal dance in the street, and called it a night. I made it.

ROATAN

I had booked a cabana online; the hotel advertised Wi-Fi and a dive shop. My general rule was to book in advance for a night or two, see if I liked the place, then if not, use my day to find a better place to stay. I learned this in Mazatlan, where I booked a week and left after three days and couldn't get a refund.

My cabana was cute and my first mission was to shower. All I got was a couple weak trickles of ice-cold water. I had a ceiling fan that didn't move any air, and it was incredibly hot. And no Wi-Fi. That is what really makes or breaks a place in my addicted-to-technology opinion. Actually, there was Wi-Fi, but it wasn't working when I arrived. I only know because I was recruited to do tech support for a man sitting by the front office; he couldn't figure out how to connect. He was French but bought his computer in Germany, so navigating through the network options took a bit of effort. All the words were several inches long with lots of h's and z's. When I finally unpacked my computer to check the connection, there was none. I didn't have enough Spanish to explain to the Honduran girl at the desk that she should reboot the modem, but it was finally understood that the phones were all down, therefore no internet. I also learned that the hotel cut off the Wi-Fi at 8 p.m. and didn't turn it back on until 8 a.m. Totally unacceptable.

I spent the morning looking around Roatan while searching for coffee, and it was a beautiful place. Dirt roads, docks, clear blue water, but hotter than hell. I considered trading in my cute cabana for a hotel room with air conditioning. I found several places that offered yoga, Spanish classes and paddleboard rentals, and there were dive shops every 20 feet. As I was walking past the dive shop at my hotel they were writing the day's trips on a white board, and the 11 a.m. dive was at "Melissa's Reef." I took that as a sign that I was at the right place and that I should start scuba diving immediately.

I was completely wrong. The dive masters were ok, but the group I dove with was super annoying – people who have to touch everything they see, bouncing up and down and kicking me. The new dive boat that was advertised online wasn't used; we went in a half-broken-down panga. We didn't even go to "Melissa's Reef."

Add bad Wi-Fi and unfriendly people at the hotel to that, and it was time to search for my new home on Roatan.

Less than a block away I found a different cabana with air conditioning, refrigerator and microwave, a dive shop with friendly people, and 24-hour Wi-Fi. All for $10 more per night. Even better, it had an attached restaurant with real football. Not just soccer, but NFL and college games. I reserved a week.

The first question everyone asked there was, "How long are you staying?" Most of the people I met on Roatan came for vacation and never left. The island is surrounded by spectacular reefs and a huge population of fish, so it was no surprise that the island contained more dive shops than restaurants and hotels combined. I heard that there were so many that they passed a law to stop any new shops from opening.

I dived a few times with Coconut Tree Divers and they took me to some great spots. They were also fun to hang out with; the front porch of the shop was constantly filled with people drinking coffee and beer, eating lunch, talking about diving, and just passing the time. Anytime I wanted to find someone to talk to, I only needed to walk half a block from my room.

I hung out mostly with John and Tree; they both worked at the shop but I hadn't dove with them. John spent 35 years working as a host for parties and nightclubs, and Tree spent almost as many years working as a carnival barker, or so he said, so they both made excellent companions for hanging out and talking story.

Tree and I rented paddleboards and paddled to West Bay, about a mile and a half away. The water was calm, which is good since this was only the fourth time Tree had been on a standup board. We made it to our destination, a bar where we could watch football and drink banana rum cocktails. As the time to head home approached, the wind picked up, against us, of course, so we had to stop at another bar about halfway back for more rum. Some exercise, booze, and a tour guide – what more could I want? We made it home in time to hit the bars with all the locals. I don't think I had seen this many bars in one place since college. Roatan is definitely the place to go to if you like to party.

David, from Switzerland, was my dive buddy. He had a round-the-world dive trip planned. His next stop was a live-aboard in Galapagos. One afternoon we swam out to a boat with a purposely slanted mast moored in the middle of West End Bay; the boat used to be in service, but someone owed some-one money and used the boat as payment, and the new owner thought it would make a good playground for the local kids. So he parked it out front of his restaurant, fixed the mast at a good angle and attached a rope swing. Anyone can swim out and play. There were people, probably just expats, who thought it was an eyesore and wanted it removed, but like most things on Roatan, if you can pay the right people you can pretty much do what you want.

Since David was leaving, I started thinking about where I was headed next. I had absolutely no plan. Every day, the people at the shop and hotel asked me how long I was staying, and every day I told them I didn't know. A week passed, diving and drink-ing and the occasional joint, yoga, eating at all the local stands, and I didn't feel a pressing need to make a plan. Maybe I'd leave tomorrow, maybe next month, maybe I'd wait till I found a seahorse.

I didn't spend a lot of time keeping my journal on Roatan; each day was fairly similar to the last. I really started to feel I needed a purpose, something to accomplish. That probably came from only talking to dive masters, tour guides and Spanish teachers, people who are paid to know everything about something. I surrounded myself with people who seemed to know way more than me. Honestly, I was beginning to feel a bit dumb. Contemplating what I want to do when I grow up seemed like a good way to pass a few days in between dives.

The only thing that didn't make me feel dumb was talking to other Americans. I met an American woman at the bar one night and instantly disliked her. She interrupted a very important conversation about strippers and pole-dancing, normal bar topics; sometimes you just have to have a non-PC talk with the guys. She butted in and started spewing women's rights; not that I'm against them, but past 10 p.m., after drinking for several hours, no one wanted to be serious.

I originally thought she was dumb because she insisted I'd been diving with her for days, despite the fact I had never been on a boat with her. I was quite surprised when we were on the next morning dive together, as she was bragging in the bar about her scuba prowess. What turned out to be the most amusing thing about her was how bad she was underwater – riding her invisible unicycle, waving her arms around, getting so out of control that she had to keep grabbing the dive master for help. Sometimes laughing at someone is necessary for mental health.

I began keeping a list of topics on my iPhone that would provoke her into angry rants for the next time I saw her at the bar.

My cabana was situated on the exact crossroads of the main section of the new road; it had a porch raised about six feet so I could sit and people-watch. I was awakened one morning by a booming voice on a loudspeaker; the President of Honduras had come to town for the official road-opening ceremony. I meant to be up and watch the procession, but I had been at the bar with John and Jay, another friend, and didn't remember a whole lot of the night. Except for a giant bruise on my butt, I vaguely remembered sliding down my stairs. I had wandered into Jay's cabana, woke him up, and made him clean all the mud off of me, but don't ask me why I did that. Who knows. So I was pretty hung-over when the voice started screaming in Spanish.

The new road was a gift from the Canadian government, which pledged $40 million to pave and build sewers. Instead of sending the money here, they actually sent Canadian workers and materials and did the work themselves. Smart people, those Canadians. If they had sent a check for $40 million, they would have bought a $20 million road and a couple of rich Honduran guys.

I had planned to wander down to the ceremony to try to meet the President, but in my state of extreme hangover, battered and bruised, I was in no condition to speak to anyone, much less try to impress someone important. I wished I had thought of that the night before.

I put off leaving again and decided to get my Advanced Open Water scuba certification. I couldn't beat the price, and I might need it if I went to Australia, where they're much stricter about the PADI regulations. I hadn't needed it for all of the deep dives I did in Honduras and Belize; no one seems to care in Central America. I went down 135 feet on my eighth dive ever. You go, Belize.

I picked my five dives: deep, wreck, search and recovery, fish ID and navigation. Yes, navigation. It couldn't hurt. It was fun to have something to do while diving besides following someone around. Since I was the only one in the class, Marco was essentially my private tour guide.

The deep dive was first; Marco and I went down to 130 feet and saw a shipwreck. It was too deep to explore. Instead, we did puzzles to test how slow my reactions were, or if I had any reactions left at all. I didn't fare too badly. Everyone fails the color test at that depth.

Navigation was next, the one I was dreading. It's hard enough navigating with my iPhone telling me where to turn. Swimming straight lines back and forth while holding a compass was ok, very hard to get lost. Swimming in squares wasn't even bad, even way out in the ocean with no reference points. But finding the boat again? No chance.

The following dive was my first real wreck dive. Marco and I went to El Aguila, a ship that was sunk purposely for the benefit of divers. It had tight corridors, sideways rooms, and all types of animals growing on the walls and hiding in the nooks and crannies. It was like an underwater fun house.

Search and recovery was the most fun. After El Aguila, Marco and I sat on the rocking boat and practiced tying knots until I thought I'd be seasick. The mission for that dive was to find a scuba tank that Marco had hidden, tie it up and transport it back to the boat. I was allowed to ask him a few questions: in what direction was it last seen, how deep I could expect to go, et cetera. Then my compass and I were off. I had to go about 300 feet south in 45 feet of water and grid-search a big sandy patch. I found the tank without too much trouble, and tying knots underwater was fun, although a bit difficult. I attached a lift bag, blew some air into it with my regulator, and swam everything back.

I put too much air in the bag and shot to the surface, so I emptied some out and the tank hit the reef with a thud. No one was watching, so I didn't feel particularly foolish. The most difficult part, finding the boat, was shockingly easy. Blindly stumbling upon the boat was just as good as knowing where it was in the first place.

My last dive was fish identification. Marco took pictures of fish, coral, and other types of marine life, and I tried to identify them as we swam along. I thought my handwriting while sitting at my desk was bad, but my writing underwater was like a kindergartener's crayon scribble. I didn't find my seahorse, but I did see a peacock flounder, which was almost as weird.

At the conclusion of my dive class, I announced to everyone at the shop that I would be leaving in a few days. I just had to stay sober enough to buy a ticket. No wonder people come here for a month and stay for years.

Instead of planning my departure, I signed up for a shark dive on the opposite side of the island. It was a real shark dive, too – not feeding sweet little nurse sharks or watching from the safety of a cage. I caught a ride across town to another dive shop, and 15 of us jammed into a little panga boat for a 15-minute trip. The dive site was called Cara a Cara, face to face, and we were briefed on all the things we should not do under penalty of losing a limb. Basically, stay completely still at all times and keep our backs against the reef.

We dropped down to 70 feet and the dive master brought out a closed bucket. Suddenly about a dozen large Caribbean reef sharks were circling us.

For the first part of the dive, we stood on the sandy bottom with our backs to a rock ledge and just watched the sharks swim. When the dive master determined that the sharks were playing nicely and the current wasn't too strong, we started swimming with them, which was way more interesting. I turned around and sharks were all around – a shark behind me, above me, under me, staring at me with creepy little black eyes. One had a giant hook attached under his mouth. This was the most nerve-wracking dive I had ever done. I've watched Shark Week too many times.

After 15 minutes of swimming, we went back to our ledge so the dive master could take the lid off of the chum bucket. Three frantic minutes of thrashing sharks fighting for the fish bits, then it was over. Definitely worth the money. I even found a tooth.

I had now been on Roatan for three weeks, the longest I had stayed in any town, with the exception of my Spanish class in San Miguel. I was definitely asking myself why I was still there. I was so comfortable on Roatan; I could speak Spanish or English, there were bars and street food everywhere, to-go booze was perfectly acceptable for walking down the road to the next bar, and the dive shop patio was always filled with fun people who hosted near-constant parties. Every day I swam and practiced yoga, and just sat, watching the beautiful weather pass by. I had found a wonderful comfort zone from which I was having trouble crawling out.

John had the opportunity to house-sit for some friends at a fabulous house on the water, and he invited me to tag along. It felt great to live in a real house with a real kitchen and a real washing machine. I did dishes and swept the floors and realized I'd all but forgotten how to do housework. It was actually nice to clean. Not that I was anxious to get back to the real world, but I knew that when I got back, soon enough I'd be wishing I could go back to the time of daily maids.

I also got to take long showers with hot water. It was luxury beyond belief.

I spent three days at the house smoking pot with John, eating his island-famous lasagna, and watching the dolphin-training pens across the bay. I wasn't really happy about dolphins being held captive, but when you're stoned it's kind of neat. I had a big comfy bed to sleep in and a nice guy to share it with. If the homeowners hadn't returned, I might have stayed indefinitely.

I had been learning a lot about Roatan in the three weeks I'd been slouching there. One man owns the electric company, RECO, and he charges 63 cents per kilowatt-hour. Ouch. Everyone bitches, but there's nothing they can do. The new road also caused some friction since the president came to officially open it. The road was the beginning of mass tourism and what inevitably follows in tourist destinations everywhere, and no one liked that either. For the time being Roatan was perfect, but development plans were already in place; the first corporate hotel chain was starting to build. A Hyatt, of course. The taxi drivers weren't allowed to park on the main road anymore. They could when it was just dirt, and they were angry about losing the privilege. The president told the chief of police that parking laws will be enforced, and it was fun watching the drivers argue in the middle of the road with the newly appointed parking enforcement officers.

It really came down to one thing there though: what John calls "affordable corruption." You might get pulled over for anything, but 100 or 150 lempira would take care of it, depending upon the severity. It cost about $25 for a major infraction if you were nice to the cop and had cash. No problem.

As an example, after Monday Night Football, John got on his motorcycle to go home. And yes, he'd been drinking a bit, but no more than is usual there. Not far down the road, he got caught in a traffic stop. He smelled like booze and his registration was fake. The cop made him get off his bike and began to question him, then decided to confiscate John's bike because he'd been drinking. The cop looked at the registration and told John that it was fake; John argued a bit to make it look good. This wasn't the average Roatan cop – he was from the mainland, so he recognized that the address of the registration office was printed incorrectly. John asked what he could do to get out of the situation; maybe make a prepayment on the fine. The cop said that might work, but he didn't know what the fine would be. John walked back to town to the ATM, walked back to his motorcycle, "shook hands" with the cop – losing 500 lempira ($25) in the process – and even got some tips on making his fake registration better. Roatan business: no paperwork, no hassle. Everyone's happy.

The taxes were outrageous, but everyone had a plan to get around them. The sales tax was 12% on everything, and businesses got charged a flat 25% income tax. All of the businesses had a rate for each service, but paying by credit card meant being prepared to pay an extra 10-20% because they then had to declare that income. Paying with cash meant no one had to pay tax, and they liked you better.

There was also a great way to get around airline baggage fees when flying into Honduras. If you knew you were going to be overweight, you could line the top of your suitcase with school supplies and get a pass on the charges, because you were making a donation to the schools. Then actually donate the school supplies, to be a nice person.

There were multiple stories going around about the heavy cocaine trade on Roatan; it's the first stop on the way out from

Columbia. It was easy to think that these were true, because it was almost faster to buy coke than get a drink in some of the bars.

I saw several abandoned bars on the beach as I walked through town. I asked why no one was running them; you couldn't beat the location. It seemed that they all were once owned by people who tried to rip off the cartels. One day the people here woke up and a heavily armed group of Colombians had virtually taken over the town. They were at every street corner with guns and pictures of the people they were looking for, stopping everyone who went by. The Roatan police fled; they wanted nothing to do with the situation. It would have been like Barney Fife taking on Robocop. The result was a few bars and boats that no longer had owners. These, of course, are stories I couldn't prove, but they were excellent grist for the rumor mill.

There was one crazy woman who lived nearby. I spent one afternoon drinking Salva Vida, the local beer, and watching a drunk man chase her. He was pissed and yelling that he wanted to break her hands. That might sound harsh, but it was a funny situation; not only did no one interfere, but the locals were egging him on, telling him how much more she deserved.

While there were many strange characters on this island, that woman stood far above the rest. She was a bit crazy, but mostly a junkie.

As the story goes, normally she would simply run up and down the road singing and screaming and taking off her clothes, throwing things at passing cars, fairly tolerable. She had been chased by the police many times and would get naked and jump in the ocean until they got bored and left. No one was responsible for her and the mental ward on the mainland wouldn't take her.

One day she was running up and down the road ripping out the flowers the shop and restaurant owners had planted. That was the last straw for a lot of them, because when they yelled at her she waited until nightfall and did horrible things to the property of whoever yelled at her, like unmoor their boats. Nine people called the police while she was terrorizing the flower beds, but they never came.

That evening, after drinking plenty of Salva Vidas, Marco dug out a can of mace and decided that if she kept messing with the dive shop, he was going to mace her. He decided that we needed to practice since no one at the shop had ever used mace before. It was harder than it looks, more so when drunk. We picked a spot on the wall and aimed, not very well. Marco also wanted to test what it would do to a patch of skin, so he sprayed himself. It was way more fun to watch than TV. The biggest consequence of mace practice was coughing for hours after inhaling the fumes where we were sitting. That part wasn't so fun.

Upon reflection, the dive shop owners decided a bucket of water would be kept on hand instead of mace. That was the day that the crazy girl went to the cemetery and stole all of the flowers from the graves. She brought them to the center of town and screamed while shredding them. That was beyond the limit of what these generally laid-back people could deal with. People tried to chase her down, and she picked up a rock and randomly smashed car windows as she ran by. A drunk guy recognized the flowers he had just put on his mother's grave, and that caused him to decide to break her hands. A crazy, screaming drunk chasing a crazy, screaming junkie down the middle of the new road; and when she finally fled into the ocean, he waited there for hours for her to come out, still wanting to break her hands.

In retrospect, it was a shame there was no one to take care of the girl, but she was given chances and destroyed them. Also, no one could ever catch her, so she wasn't in any real danger.

TEGUCIGALPA

The last thing John said to me before I finally left Roatan was, "You're flying into the second-most dangerous airport in the world." I immediately envisioned an airport full of pickpockets and muggers, but he was talking about the safety record. It has the second-highest number of yearly accidents in the world. Why would someone tell me that right before I had to fly there?

I arrived at the Roatan airport, which was only slightly bigger than the smallest airport I've ever seen on Molokai, Hawaii, and saw my plane; not a puddle-jumper, but not very big. There were 30 seats for 8 passengers, which was good since I would get my drink quicker. No way was I going to fly into the second-most dangerous airport in the world sober.

There was a bit of a storm and I was caught off-guard as I was eating my airline lunch. They still serve free meals on flights in Central America. Gross and unhealthy, but free. The next 10 minutes of turbulence actually made me stop eating, and very few things do that. That was the moment I remembered what John said, leaving me with another half an hour to envision all of the ways the plane could break into pieces and catch fire. For the first time ever, I made sure I turned all my electronics off.

When the pilot announced that we needed to prepare for landing, I almost thought I needed a barf bag. I couldn't believe he said that to me before I left.

Needless to say, all went well and no one died. Next, I needed to find my connection for San Salvador, then Panama. I had decided to visit a friend who happened to be in town.

PANAMA
OCTOBER 12ᵀᴴ, 2012

The moment I entered Panama was the moment that the Van Halen song started playing on a continuous loop in my head.

I chose to go to Panama for two reasons. The first was that my friend Mandy and her family were staying there and offered me a place to stay, and second, I had gotten an email from a woman I met in Antigua who was headed to Cuba and wanted to know if I would join her. If I decided to go, the only decent flights I found were through Panama.

PANAMA CITY

With much confusion, and in the middle of the night, I arrived at Mandy and Joe's apartment on Isla Perico, just across the water from Panama City. It's on the Amador Causeway, which was made to connect a few of the nearby islands with the discarded materials from the Panama Canal dig. They had a view of the bay where all the boats dock while waiting to go through the canal, or just to have downtime. The bay was full of boats and ships of every size and type, and I could sit and watch them all day.

Joe was working in Panama for a month, dry-docking a boat he built a couple years previous. He and Mandy and their kids, Makaio and Koa, have wandered around the world building and working on boats. I originally met them on Kauai when Joe was working for Captain Andy's. The apartment they lived in had showers with disco lights and music, something I've never seen, before or since. I also met a Colombian hooker next door. I thought that was quite exciting.

While Joe worked, Mandy and the kids and I took a trip to Isla Contadora, one of the beautiful nearby islands, for the day. It was a two-hour ferry ride on one of the boats Joe had built. The island used to be pretty busy as a stop on the drug routes; a lot of money was invested, but now there was only one hotel open and everything else was slowly rotting away. The water was a beautiful blue, and we spent the day drinking Bloody Marys and building sand castles with the kids.

Contadora means accountant in Spanish. I know this because instead of writing "unemployed" on all of my immigration forms, I wrote *contadora* so they wouldn't be afraid to let me in. I thought that Isla Contadora was a strange name for an island in the middle of nowhere, Panama. At first I thought of "Hitchhiker's Guide to the Galaxy," when they put all of the middle management on a spaceship and stranded them – a planet of accountants, hairdressers and telephone operators.

But really, the island, and all of the others in Las Perlas, was big in the pearl trade and everyone would bring their pearls to Contadora to trade with the Spanish; hence, "Accountant Island."

The most famous pearl that came from Las Perlas was owned by Elizabeth Taylor. Richard Burton bought "La Peregrina" for her for $37,000 in 1969. The pearl was formerly owned by Mary Tudor, Queens Margarita and Isabel, and the Bonapartes. A slave originally found the pearl and was set free after bringing it to the Spanish court.

After we returned home, I nervously bought a ticket to Cuba and started my research. I knew nothing about Cuba, except that they have really cool old cars.

Mandy is the most amazing person. She is a great mother, and totally fearless and outgoing. The adventures she has been on would take me until I'm at least 65, if I started now. She has some great stories.

But surprisingly, we did something together that she had never done: we went to the Panama Canal to watch the boats go through. When I say she's never done it, I mean the tourist part; she's actually worked on boats that crossed the canal. Her 3-year-old son Makaio has already done two crossings. I felt so far behind.

Mandy, Makaio, 1-year-old Koa, her brother-in-law Jimmy, and I went to the Panama Canal Museum and spent the day learning the history and watching boats go through the Miraflores locks.

The Panama Canal is the only thing I absolutely had to do on this trip, although I'm not certain why. I wanted to find a boat on which to cross, but now that I had plans to go to Cuba, I didn't have the time to sit and wait to see if anyone wanted to take me. I wanted to check out Bocas del Toro as well. Crossing the canal would have to stay on the list.

Even with the built-up excitement of seeing the canal, the experience was much better than anticipated. The museum is four floors of old machinery, pictures, geology, small-scale models of the locks that you can open and close – so much amazing historical stuff. The museum also showed a 3-D movie that was loud and almost scary.

We went to the fourth-floor observation deck and watched two ships go through. It's hard to believe century-old concrete and locks still worked so well.

The ships we watched were a tanker and a car transport. The transport was so big it didn't look like it should fit; it had a foot or two of clearance on either side, if that. Four rail cars on shore pulled the ship through with lines, driving back and forth, tightening or slackening the lines to keep the ship straight in the canal. When the giant boat was through the lock it smacked into the wall, and we got to see concrete crumble off the side and into the water. The little rail cars were moving frantically to get the ship back in line.

If I can show up one day in 100 years and watch a boat knock concrete off the canal, I don't know how the walls aren't completely destroyed by now.

We could see the trucks and bulldozers working in the distance on the canal expansion. I guess I have to start planning another trip here to see that, too. Maybe learn to sail and find a boat to cross during the grand opening – that would take a big chunk out of my bucket list.

The only negative experience at the canal was the number of tourists using their iPads as cameras. Ten people with iPads can block 100 people from seeing anything. I have countless photos that are ruined because someone, usually a woman, was holding up an iPad and couldn't be bothered to fold under the cover. Very rude.

I left Joe and Mandy's condo to check out Bocas Del Toro before I flew to Cuba. It was so nice to have some family time, playing with the kids and having a friend to sightsee and shop with. When I left I had the "B-I-N-G-O" song playing in an endless loop in my head, which is a hazard of hanging out with young children, but at least it replaced Van Halen. After 30 years, I still don't know what the song "Panama" is about.

BOCAS DEL TORO

My flight to Bocas del Toro was an hour and a half late, so I didn't get to see the layout of the town; it was too dark and stormy. I spent most of the walk from the airport to my hostel staring at my iPhone map. My hostel of choice was full and the hostel next door only had dorm rooms available. My planning ahead had gotten slightly worse, to the point of nonexistence. I'm too old to sleep in a room with drunk 20-year-olds on eight bunk beds, all sharing one bathroom. Fortunately, though, they had one bunk room empty so I had eight beds all to myself, and the next day I had a reservation for my own room. I really should have done this trip 20 years ago; it would have been so much cheaper if I didn't care about roommates who stay out all night, because I would be there with them. But at 40, I wasn't staying out all night, and had to pay double because I couldn't share anymore. It was still worth it. From the balcony of the hostel I could see bars, stores and restaurants, and hear plenty of loud music. I instantly figured I'd enjoy my week there.

The first thing I did was scuba dive. I had spent my time on Roatan looking for a seahorse, with no luck. The only time anyone supposedly spotted one, it was a ruse to get me to look off the end of the dock. "There's a seahorse attached to the dock! You can see it from here!" And, being obsessed with finding one, I looked, only to get pushed into the water with all my clothes on.

I was told that Bocas has seahorses, so I went to a couple scuba shops until I found someone who would take me to the sites they frequent; and we found two on our second dive.

They were every bit of awesome that I imagined. A tan seahorse was hanging out in a crevice in the reef, and a brown one was grasping a bit of coral with his tail. I've seen some amazing things diving, but this was the best so far – better than the sharks, the rays, the rockfish, peacock flounders, everything. The diving wasn't spectacular, and it was more expensive than I'd gotten used to on Roatan, but the seahorses were worth it.

The dive featured fields of starfish, a wreck, and interesting rock formations, but not a lot of fish or great corals. I was determined to dive in every country I visited, and even though the seahorses were a fantastic find, the visibility was poor and I didn't feel the need to dive there again. I might have been way over budget on lodging and booze, but I was right on track with my dive goal. Gotta prioritize.

I was given a spear on the first dive, as I was in almost every dive since Mexico. I loved that I could show up to a dive shop, talk to them for five minutes and be given a spear. The three-prong spear is known the world over as a "Hawaiian sling," so when I told them I lived in Hawaii, they automatically assumed I knew what I was doing. Plus, carrying a spear made me feel like a badass compared to the other tourists, so I never passed up the opportunity.

Lionfish are out of control throughout the Caribbean, so there is no limit to the amount you can kill, or any restrictions on the way you do it.

I always have a bit of trouble killing with my first shot; I always hit them in the gut and they just hobble away, and I have to chase them down and shoot again. In Belize and Honduras, giant groupers smelled the meat and waited for me to release my lionfish, and dead or not, they would suck them down in a single gulp. But there was nothing to eat them in Bocas; they were the biggest fish I saw. I killed four on my first dive, and with nothing to eat them half-alive, I had to scrape them from my spear with a rock or my fin and try again for the kill. I was a bit careless on my last kill and stabbed myself with one of its venomous spikes while I was scraping it off the spear.

I'd heard a lot of stories about lionfish stings, and none were pleasant. The effects range from those of a bad bee sting to hospital time for a full-on allergic reaction. When I felt the spike enter my thumb I thought, "Oh, great, maybe I'll have cardiac arrest at 50 feet; that'll be a new experience." It was instant, throbbing pain. I swam up to my dive master and used hand signals to try to tell him that I stabbed myself with a poisonous fish but I wasn't dying yet, so no worries. I think he understood.

By the time I finished the first dive, my thumb was almost twice its normal size, bright red, and massively painful. But since we hadn't yet found any seahorses, I refused to be taken back and we went on to our next dive site.

By the end of the second dive, my thumb was almost back to normal, but I still planned on drinking plenty of rum afterward to bully any remaining toxins out of my liver. It helped that a fairly unattractive man was diving in a Speedo in front of me; I was so grossed out every time I looked up that I forgot about the pain.

After the seahorses and the ride back to the dock, it was nap time. Bocas in October is stiflingly hot, like most places I had been to thus far, and the hostel only owned three controllers for its air conditioning units. It was a big production to get a cool room. Every time I left, the desk person cut off the power to my room by a switch in the lobby, then turned it back on when I returned. That's a great way to save money and the environment, but a pain if you come and go a lot like I did. After getting power turned back on, I got an air conditioner remote, went upstairs to my room, turned on the air conditioning, went back downstairs and turned in the controller. Every time. A few times people had locked the remotes in their rooms so other hot people didn't get air conditioning until one was located. It wasn't the best system.

I spent some time exploring Bocas del Toro, checking out the bars, restaurants, and shops crowding the water's edge. I found great Thai and Mexican food, and even though I'd now spent two weeks in Panama, I still wasn't sure what Panamanian food might be. I could spend a couple months in Bocas and not see everything, but that had been true of everywhere I had traveled. There just wasn't enough time, or there were too many bars. Either way, I wished I had the time for another week there. I only spent one day scuba diving, but after Belize and Roatan, I'm not sure that any diving will ever be amazing again. I was looking forward to diving in Cuba; I had heard that the reefs there are pristine.

Toward the end of my week, I did a full-day catamaran trip with two snorkel stops. I had been out drinking the previous night; Andy told me to check out the Riptide, a boat that is permanently anchored and turned into a bar. There were a few locals, actually expats, but they were older and just wanted to watch a truck repair show on TV so I left. I tried the Indian restaurant, but it was so packed with people that I waited forever, couldn't get a drink, and finally left. As I was wandering out, I noticed people drinking downstairs and walked over; it was the town's bookstore with a bar, another local hangout and very friendly. It came complete with Dave, one of the craziest bartenders I've ever met. This was the type of place I like to find anywhere I go. I stayed way too late and did too many shots, and wasn't feeling so great when I woke up for the catamaran trip.

After 10 minutes of motoring, I started feeling really bad. I've never been seasick, but I imagine it's about the same, except for the guilt of knowing that it's self-inflicted. I crawled onto the wooden planks on the back of the boat and let everyone know there was a good possibility that I would be chumming the water soon.

Surprisingly, I didn't, and after an hour everything was good.

The first snorkel site was very clear; we swam on the edge of a mangrove forest. Starfish were everywhere, along with corals, schools of small fish, and dozens of pulsating jellyfish. Mangroves made me nervous ever since crocodile hunting in Belize so I was a bit timid at first, but after a while and with some reassurance from the captain that there were no large animals lurking about, I was able to swim into the trees to look around. It was still creepy, though. The second snorkel wasn't as interesting, but it was still enjoyable. After swimming in cold water, then lunch, I was ready to drink a couple beers as I fished on the way home. I didn't catch anything but a buzz.

The boat's skipper, Captain Hardy, was a nice guy and suggested that I meet up with him for some drinks at the Riptide. He invited me to go fishing on his private boat and purposely left the bar early so I wouldn't have to subject myself to another morning of boat hangover. But The Book Store was on my way home, and I failed miserably at being good. As they say, though, bad decisions make good stories.

After having a couple drinks with the same people I had met the night before, the bartender told me I could drink the rest of the night for free if I went topless for 10 seconds. As a budget traveler, that sounded like a good, money-saving idea. And it was, but again, I woke up before a boat ride uncertain if I could survive the day.

Captain Hardy's fishing boat was much easier on the stomach than the catamaran, but I still couldn't look at a beer until the afternoon. The guys started drinking before we even left the dock.

We ended up catching a 10-pound yellowfin tuna and a 5-pound mackerel. It wasn't much for the hours we spent, but I got to see several of the small islands nearby. On the way home we stopped at Isla Bastimento and tied up to the dock at Los Secretos. Hardy and our other fishing companion, Pete, were friends with the owners. It was possibly one of the most beautiful bars I've ever been in. I had to add it to my mental list of places to come back to, maybe spend a couple of nights. We had dinner, then Pete filleted the tuna and everyone in the bar got sashimi, my favorite thing about fishing.

I wasn't ready to leave Bocas del Toro, but it was time. I had an early flight back to Panama, one more day with Mandy and the kids, then a flight to Cuba for 12 days. I had no itinerary or much of an idea of what Cuba would be like as I never imagined I'd get to go there, but as long as I was bringing cash, everything should be ok. It usually is, anyway.

CUBA
OCTOBER 23ᴿᴰ, 2012

HAVANA

I had met a woman in Antigua who had put the idea of Cuba into my head; we kept in touch, and I was meeting her at the airport to explore the country with her. Gina is a Russian woman who had lived much of her life in Germany, but now resides in New York. We got along well in Guatemala and I was happy to have a travel companion in a country about which I knew next to nothing. The flight from Panama to Havana was great; I found Gina at the airport and we went through immigration together.

She always made me go first in line, just in case I didn't make it through "The Door." We were both a little nervous that I wouldn't be allowed in. I was told that I was required to have health insurance, which I hadn't had the entire trip, and that I would be forced to buy it at the airport if necessary. I couldn't find anyone to sell me anything, which automatically made Cuba different from the other Spanish-speaking countries I had visited. I did get ripped off by the outrageous exchange rate, though, so they all have that in common. But no health insurance. Our taxi driver was blaring Madonna and we made him change it to Cuban music on the ride to our *casa particular*.

Gina had made the initial lodging arrangements for us. A *casa particular* is a family home that has a legal room for rent. The owners register with the government and get a license to operate, and they have a painted symbol above their doorway so you can always find a place to stay by wandering around the neighborhoods.

Ours was in a high-rise complex in New Havana. We had a "mother" and a "father," and I could understand about every seventh word they said. Cuban Spanish was near impossible for me to follow. They didn't say the letter "S" at all, but that didn't stop them from talking to me constantly. Eventually, they started speaking slower and using baby words. Gina was much better at understanding them; she's had more Spanish over the years and hadn't spent the past month surrounded by white folks. Our *casa* was decorated in 1970's fashion, like much of Havana seemed to be.

Gina timed her trip to meet up with a couple German friends; we walked to the Hotel Nacional to have a celebratory mojito and meet them. Claudia and Michael had been in Cuba for 10 days and were about to go home. They rented a car and drove all over the island; they thought it was easy.

For our first night out, we went to Cabaret Parisien for a show at $35 each. It was pricey, but everything in Havana is expensive. The exchange rate is $1 for 1 Convertible Peso, or cuc, then they charge 15% for the service. So actually, everything is 15% more expensive. The cabaret was fun – great music and salsa dancing in crazy, risqué costumes. It was exactly how I imagined a show in Cuba, complete with a giant-bowl-of-fruit hat.

We spent the next day wandering through Old Havana, stopping at all of the famous bars Hemingway frequented, including the Bodega el Media and Floridita. We drank way too many mojitos. I hadn't consumed that much sugar in the entire five months I'd been traveling. All of the bars had Cuban bands, usually a singer and three others playing various instruments and singing backing vocals. We also stopped at a couple museums for early Cuban art. The town was clean and beautiful, with brightly colored buildings and friendly people. At least they seemed to be; they were smiling, but I couldn't understand what they were saying.

Once again, it was time to go on a quest for tampons while in a town. Gina and I wandered into several shops with no luck, until someone pointed out a specialty store. It wasn't exactly a pharmacy, but contained a conglomeration of all types of household items. After looking around, I asked at the counter; the saleswoman unlocked a glass case and presented me with a box of the most utilitarian tampons I've ever seen – straight, thick cardboard tubes stuffed with cotton. Apparently feminine products were still from the 50's, as well as the cars.

The biggest question Gina and I had was whether we should take the buses everywhere or rent a car. Finding a bus schedule proved to be nearly impossible. We would have had to spend $20 to go to the bus station to make a reservation, $20 to come back,

then $20 again with all of our bags, if we didn't want to take the
chance of sitting there all day. None of the tourist information
stands were any help; I couldn't figure out what their purpose
was. Everywhere I turned, there were a dozen men yelling "Taxi,
lady!" but no one knew the bus schedule.

We did finally take a taxi when we were coming home late
one night, a gorgeous black 1955 Chevy in mint condition. The
cars in Havana were amazing – a few were modern cars of makes
I didn't recognize, but what caught my eye were the vast numbers
of American cars made when my parents were young. Some were
beat-up but many were in excellent shape. There were also hundreds of bicycle taxis and horse-drawn buggies to ride.

After talking with the German couple about how easy it was
to drive around Cuba we decided on renting a car. We went to
several rental agencies called Cubicar, all the same but with different pricing. We found the best price at a large hotel in Old
Havana. It was pretty straightforward, but Gina argued about
everything; I thought the salesman was going to kick us out. But
she had spent the day angry about lunch, our host family, basically everything. She wasn't afraid to tell people she was upset,
which I liked about her.

We finally got our car, a generic blue four-seater, but we had
no road map. That was another argument Gina had with the
rental guy, which lasted for quite some time, but didn't help us at
all. Eventually, one of the men drew us a map to the *autopista* and
we went home to collect our things and get on the road.

It was about 4 p.m. at this point, and we had to say goodbye
to the people in our building, which took close to forever. One
woman, Clara, with whom we made arrangements to spend our
last night before flying home, wanted to introduce us to everyone
who was currently staying in her apartment, and after too much

small talk and very little understanding, it was 5:30 before we could leave. Our first destination was Viñales, about four hours away. We had no map and the sun was setting in two hours. I'm not certain why we thought it was a good idea to leave at that point.

But leave we did, with total fanfare from the apartment building. We agreed that I would drive and Gina would navigate. Almost from the start it was "slow down," "watch the bikes," "careful;" she was a classic backseat driver. I was surprised at how well I was driving given that it had been so long, and I finally had to tell her to relax, and just tell me where to go. Driving through Havana was a little crazy, but not nearly as bad as Mexico City or anywhere else where everyone owned a car. The first thing I noticed was that there were no street signs anywhere – no direction, no arrows, nothing. We followed the man's hand-drawn map and everything seemed to be going well. Some roundabouts, a tunnel – we drove and drove and I was quite happy.

We entered a small town with no cars – everyone rode bikes or horses – and that was when I started to wonder where we were. The sun was setting and I thought, "Ok, we're going south, I think that's good." But it turned out that Viñales wasn't south. Then the road turned into a dirt track. "I don't think this is the *autopista*," I said. We drove through a muddy pothole the size of our car. Gina said we needed to follow this road for 24 more kilometers, or until the dead end that was just ahead of us.

It turned out that we weren't on the *autopista* at any time. Gina knew this, she told me later, but didn't tell me an hour earlier when it would have been easy to go back. I just figured that we were in an underdeveloped country and maybe their main highway becomes a dirt road in places. I'd spent months driving on dirt roads.

I turned around and we went back to the small town, and everyone was waving and making signs that we couldn't understand. I wanted to stop, but Gina believed every person wanted to rob us and refused to let me talk to anyone. Our host family in Havana convinced her that this was true, and that we shouldn't talk to anyone or pick up hitchhikers either. But I didn't want to die in the middle of nowhere in Cuba, so I stopped and rolled my window down for the next man yelling at our car. I couldn't understand a word he said. I pulled up to a gigantic black man who scared Gina more than the first guy, and he told me I was driving the wrong way on a one-way road. That explained the yelling. I wish I understood enough to ask why a town with no cars had one-way streets; that will forever be one of life's mysteries to me. He used hand signals to direct us back to the main road.

As we searched for the elusive *autopista,* a gorgeous sunset painted the sky. Unfortunately, that meant darkness soon. We decided to go back to Havana, spend the night, and try again early in the morning. But at night with no signs, we got completely lost. "Have we been past this before?" "Which direction did we come from in the roundabout?" "Where the fuck is the tunnel?!"

After a couple more turnarounds, we found familiar ground – we found the tunnel, we found the glorious ocean on the left-hand side. Gina was almost in tears; I was trying to pretend everything was great, but all the while I was thinking about where a good place to spend the night in a car might be found when we were so lost we couldn't find Cuba's biggest city. I had decided that if worse came to worst, I could pull into someone's driveway and pay them $10 to sleep in the car, but at no point did I find a single place that would be appropriate. I would have settled for slightly sketchy, but we couldn't even find that.

I truly enjoyed my first driving adventure in Cuba, stressful though it was. Never once during my trip did I imagine I'd be driving across Cuba, so it was definitely a mark in the positive adventure column. We got lost, but I didn't freak out even though there were no lights anywhere and I had to dodge bikes, walkers, and swerving oncoming traffic. I thought Gina might have a panic attack, so repeating *"todo esta bien"* over and over helped us both.

We both laughed and cheered and almost cried when we found the Hotel Nacional again; it was directly across the street from our *casa*. The front of our *casa* was a favorite hangout for the locals who were all there when we left several hours earlier, so it was a funny scene when we returned. Our "mother" was sitting on the stoop and instantly needed to know why we were back, wondering if we had been assaulted or had spoken to strangers. Luckily, the woman who had reserved our room didn't show up, so we could spend another night without any hassle, except for that of explaining to everyone why we were back and receiving a lot of "I told you so's" in Spanish. Everyone decided to blame me since I was driving. Whatever. That's what I got for having a stressed-out navigator who wouldn't tell me when she knew we were lost.

We unpacked the car and brought all of our packs back up to our small room with one small bed. I liked Gina a lot in Guatemala, but now I was sharing a bed with her and spending every moment together. It was working so far, but it wasn't my normal way of doing things. We had to take the car to a secure parking space at the hotel, so we had a beer and laughed about all the crazy things that had happened in the past five hours. We also made the decision that if we had a lot of trouble making it to Viñales the next day, we were going to ditch the car and take buses for the rest of the week. Who cares if there was a fee to leave the car some-where? If it was going to be a pain in the ass to get anywhere, it would be worth it. Besides, the rental agency only had Gina's credit card on file. Mine wasn't accepted there.

I tried to write my travel notes in the *casa,* but people wouldn't stop talking to me, mostly asking why we were still there. So I had to sit in the stairwell with a couple beers from the shop next door to get away from everyone. Our driving escapade had been the most adventurous thing I'd done on this trip; I was way out of my comfort zone and I survived. I didn't succeed, but I survived. And I didn't care that the people here thought I was a moron for get-ting so lost. *Todo esta bien.*

Cuba as a whole had been way outside my comfort zone. I could usually sit at a restaurant or bar and plan my travels on the internet, but it wasn't possible here; the only Wi-Fi was at the big hotels, for a hefty fee, and many of my usual sites were blocked. I couldn't even use my VPN to access my blog. We got a guide-book from Gina's friends before they left, but it was in German, so Gina had to translate anything interesting for me. I thought there would be regular buses and tourist agencies like everywhere else, but instead I found nothing but people I couldn't understand and men who wanted to marry me. Gina thought I hit some sort of Latin sweet spot; everywhere I went, men fell over themselves to talk to me and tell me how much they loved me, while ignoring women who I thought were way prettier and younger than I am. Yet amidst all the declarations of love, I still had to pay for my own drinks. I didn't get it.

Gina and I got up early and started our drive to Viñales again. We had a newer, slightly improved hand-drawn map to the *auto-pista,* and we were hopeful there would be signs along the way that we had missed in the dark. As we were leaving, we had to endure more cautions from our "family" about the hurricane heading towards the southeast, road conditions, talking to strangers, hitchhikers, et cetera. While they were hurrying us out, we somehow ended up looking through a book of old pictures. Not to show us places to go, but random pictures of family members in a house. I guess we became family quickly.

With just a couple extra turns out of Havana we found the *autopista*, a giant four-lane highway that bisects the country. We did find a sign hidden behind a tree, but the road itself wasn't obvious from the bridge, so I didn't feel too bad about the night before. It was actually a nice road compared to other countries: wide lanes, well-maintained, and almost no cars in sight. Gina began her backseat driving again, gasping and shrieking when she thought I might hit a hitchhiker in the road, or a horse and buggy. When she thought the windshield was dirtier than acceptable for safety, she reached over the wheel to turn on the wipers. I kept thinking we were going to have to have *that* talk soon.

I let her drive the car to park it at the hotel the previous night, and in the five minutes she was behind the wheel I decided I would never again be her passenger. She was timid and slow, and it took three turns just to pull into a parking spot. To me, that's scarier than fast driving, so I planned on doing all the driving and dealing with her anxiety. I really am a good driver.

We were roughly halfway to Viñales when Gina wanted to pull off the *autopista* to sightsee, then find our way through the back roads. I was more of a mind to get where we were going – make one successful journey, then get more adventurous from there. Yet another sign of my old age. I was having visions of last night, being the only car for miles with dozens of people sitting on the porches wondering how the hell we ended up there. But whatever, we should explore. When we pulled off the highway onto a two-lane road, I asked where we were going and Gina just said, "I don't know." Excellent navigation. But it was a pretty road through the countryside, very similar to Hawaii actually, with small mountains, palm trees, bananas, and sugarcane. And plenty of horses and oxen pulling carts.

We came to a fork in the road with a sign, Las Cuavas de los Portales. These are the caves where Che Guevara hid during the Cuban missile crisis in 1962. This was when I decided it might be a good idea to tell people I was from Russia, too. Gina and I looked like we could be sisters. The first question everyone in Cuba asked was "Where are you from?" Virtually every guy I passed walking on every street asked me that. No one said "hello," or maybe "how are you?" That would have been a nice change. I was a little tired of telling people that I live in Hawaii, but no, I'm not actually Hawaiian, yes, I was born in Ohio but I didn't live there very long. I felt like I should just hand out flyers to new people so I could stop repeating myself. Not that I don't like talking to people, but I'm not a fan of extreme repetition. In Cuba, I thought it might be best to lie a little.

We walked through the cave system; it looked like a great place to hide from Americans. Gina's German guidebook said there were plaques on every bench and table explaining what Che did, but we didn't see any. We just walked around admiring the landscape.

It was starting to rain and we wanted to get back on the road, but a man at the entrance stopped us. He pointed to a sign with entrance fees, 1 cuc per person and 1 cuc per camera. Gina gave him 1 cuc, which I took back to break my 3 cuc note, and she argued that he owed us money. I tried to explain that it was good, but I think she just liked to argue when money was involved. Is that a Russian thing? A German thing? Maybe it started when she moved to New York.

The next town on our route to Viñales was Las Palmas; we stopped there for more directions. I was becoming resigned to the idea that no matter how many times we asked for directions, we would always go the wrong way at some point. No one ever gave us more than enough to get out of their small town; it was almost like they didn't know what was down the road. Given the language difficulties, we always missed a turn somewhere. Gina wanted coffee so we drove into town, through masses of people walking and biking in the streets, looking for a café. We found several *tiendas* selling rum and beer, but no coffee. I let Gina wander off to find some and guarded the car. I needed my five minutes of argument-free personal space.

We never did find coffee, but we got directions to Viñales. We went the wrong way, of course, got different directions, and were back on the road. We were on another scenic country road, and were the only car around. I was beginning to suspect that people didn't leave their towns, especially knowing that most people couldn't afford a car. It was amusing how people stared at us when we drove by, like "what the hell are two women doing driving by themselves, and so fast?" But everyone looked very pleasant. The houses were well-kept, the streets were clean, and there was no garbage blowing in the wind like in Guatemala. People here were proud of what little they had.

After nearly four hours we made it to Viñales, and somehow Gina found our *casa particular* almost instantly; maybe her navigation skills had finally kicked in. Our *casa* had a leak or some other unintelligible problem, so the floor was ripped up. The woman walked us across the street to Mercy's house, and she had a room available. Three beds, air conditioning, and a bathroom for 25 cuc per night. Three cuc for breakfast and seven for dinner, if we wanted to eat with her. We called our Havana "mother" to let her know that she could stop worrying; we had arrived.

Viñales had a bicycle tour that Gina had been talking about, so we set out to find the office. We stopped for lunch on the way and Gina started complaining that the 7 cuc dinner we signed up for was too expensive, but the lunch we were having was 5 cuc and couldn't be nearly as good as a home-cooked meal. She was kind of angry and thought we were getting ripped off by our new mother at the *casa*.

Gina was probably saving money as she went by arguing over every dollar, but I couldn't imagine she made many friends in her travels. I remember her complaining about her host family and teacher in Guatemala, but I hadn't realized that complaining was a way of life for her. At this point, she had been traveling for more than two months, and it was hard to imagine her finding any happiness along the way.

We left lunch for the bike shop to sign up for the tour. The shop was no longer there, so we were sent to find a man on the street, but he only rented bikes. He sent us to someone else, but Gina didn't want anything to do with a man on the street; if he didn't have an office, we couldn't talk to him. We found another office nearby and were told they offered bike tours, but we looked at the routes and Gina's question was "Why should we pay to do this when we can see all of these sights in 10 minutes in a car?" The trip included a cave system, a mural painted on the side of a mountain and a tobacco farm tour. It was only 15 cuc for a three-hour trip. I thought we should do it; who cares if we can drive to these places? We were going to ride bikes in Cuba. That was the point, and I didn't even care if we saw anything. Gina wasn't into athletic things, but she nonetheless insisted that if we had to bike on the road, it was a waste of money.

The man behind the desk was getting frustrated with her. "If it rains tonight, and it *is* rainy season, we will have to bike on the road," he said. He couldn't predict if it was going to rain so he couldn't say for certain where we would go, but he promised we would see all of the sights we paid for. That wasn't good enough for Gina, though, and she continued to argue. She was so excited to ride bikes in Viñales – that was our sole reason for coming here – and she was making everyone in the office hate us, and threatening to walk out. All I could do was pay my money, tell the man I would see him at 9 a.m. and that I preferred to ride off-road, and wait outside. Really, 15 cuc for a guided bike ride through a Cuban tobacco farm, cigars included – how could I possibly pass that up? That is why I'm not rich: I don't mind paying to do interesting things, and I refuse to hurt someone's feelings to save a dollar. Gina would probably have a heart attack if she found out how much it costs to scuba dive. There was no way I was going to let her into the office with me when I found a place to sign up.

Finally, Gina agreed to the bike trip at the same price I paid and we left. I was mentally weighing the pros and cons of finding a bus schedule and sneaking away in the middle of the night without her, but the freedom of the rental car was too great, along with the possibility of so much more to see than a bus could offer. I could stick it out another seven days.

When we got home, Gina decided we should drive an hour to the beach, then almost instantly turn around to make it back for dinner at 7 o'clock. She had no concept of relaxation, she just wanted to see everything possible. I voted to sit on a rocking chair on the porch and watch the tractors and horses go by. I have never found it necessary to be moving every minute of every day, and I would still get to see way more of Cuba than I ever imagined I would. Gina left, and I had two glorious, peaceful hours by myself.

After dinner, which wasn't a rip-off but not quite great, Gina and I went to the only night club in Viñales, an outdoor bar with a stage and a band. The music was great and everyone was dancing salsa like professionals; it was intimidating to even think about going on the dance floor. I turned down offers to dance from a few guys, knowing I'd be awful after my one and only salsa lesson. Graceful is not a word that describes me. One man, Ivan, a giant black man with short dreads, declined my "no" by dragging me out of my chair and giving me no choice. He spent time showing me the basic moves and it turned out to be fun. Or maybe it was just the daiquiris; rum and sugar are the only convincing I need to dance.

During the band's intermission, a man dressed in some sort of tribal wear danced around the audience with fire sticks. Some he put in his mouth, some he kept in his hands, and others he put down the front of his pants and waved them around until the fire went out. It was the strangest thing I have ever seen in a bar. All the men had to cross their legs and look away.

Gina and I woke up early the following morning and had another interesting Cuban breakfast at the *casa*. There was always fresh fruit, but everything else was hit-or-miss. Strange eggs, dry toast, mystery meat – so far, Cuba had not impressed me with culinary prowess.

We walked to the bike shop and were given squeaky old mountain bikes, then stood waiting for the rain to pass. Viñales had weather and terrain as close to Kauai's as I've ever seen. Palms, bananas, coffee, guava, mangos, and red dirt – beautiful – with rain showers that come and go fairly quickly. Our bike group consisted of our Cuban guide, who looked like he'd never ridden a bike in his life, and two women from Holland. Our first stop was a tobacco farm, which had no electricity or running water. The farmer came outside to meet us, said a few words, and led us into the barn where the tobacco hangs to dry; but since it wasn't the season, we didn't actually see that. We sat at a picnic table and watched the farmer hand-roll a cigar, after which he passed one to each of us to smoke while his wife brought us coffee. We sat at his house and smoked for half an hour.

Normally, I wouldn't associate a bike tour with a half-hour cigar break, but since I had long since given up on exercise and was smoking more and more cigarettes, it seemed almost natural.

It had been raining on and off thanks to Hurricane Sandy, and by the time we got back on our bikes and rode for five minutes, the red dirt had turned to mud and we were a mess. I found it amusing, but I'm sure I was the only one. One of the women lost her flip-flop in the mud.

Our next stop was a cave, but we weren't allowed to go in; we were just supposed to climb a ladder and peek inside. When it started raining harder, we broke the rules and explored a little and our guide stayed out in the rain, taking each of our bikes to a giant puddle to wash off the clumps of mud. They were so caked that the other women were having trouble riding and were unhappy, but we were getting our off-road tour as we had all demanded.

The last sight, but not the last stop, was a "prehistoric" painting on the side of a mountain, or that was what our guide told us. And that was what the road sign said: *Mural de la Prehistoria*. I expected something preserved from the time of early man, although I had no idea when the first people settled on the island. In actuality, it was a painting on the side of a mountain, but it looked like it was drawn by a 3-year-old with watercolors. It depicted a couple dinosaurs and a person, and it gets repainted every year. There was nothing historical about it that I could discern, but just the fact that Fidel Castro commissioned such an ugly mural made it worth seeing. Gina didn't find it amusing.

Our final stop was somewhat of a mystery; we waited at a house with a chair full of bananas on the front porch while our guide and a woman from the house washed our bikes. He told us to eat the bananas, then came back when we were done to let us know what they cost. It was a pretty sneaky trick, but they were so cheap as to be nearly free. We stayed there for about half an hour since there wasn't anywhere to wash the bikes in town and we were sure our guide would get in trouble if he brought them back dirty.

It was an interesting but very odd tour that was a worthwhile three and a half hours. I say worthwhile only because I had no expectations. I think "goofy" might be a better way to describe it.

MARIA LA GORDA

Gina and I peeled off the layers of mud, packed our belongings, and started towards Maria La Gorda. This was the destination I had picked for scuba diving, all the way on the southwest point of the island. We drove though small towns that could have been set in the 1950s, and again it seemed that we were the only car among bikes, horses and oxen on the highway. There were some old American cars parked in the towns, and hitchhikers were everywhere. Hitchhiking is an accepted form of travel in Cuba, and everyone does it. People stood on the side of the road and waved at us, and looked mad when we passed by. Both of our house mothers had told us not to stop for anyone, but I really wanted to. Gina wouldn't hear of it. I thought it would make for a more interesting trip. We didn't need to pick up the guys with machetes, but why not ladies and kids and old people?

We got turned around a few times, but pulling over and shouting a town name at someone standing on the side of the road was enough to get us back on track. This was a great day of driving; nothing eventful happened, and we got to see more cows, pigs, horses, and oxen roaming the streets. The only new sights on the road were billboards of socialist propaganda; something I'd never come across before. Several times I started laughing out loud when it kept occurring to me, "Holy shit, I'm driving a car across Cuba!"

We didn't have a reservation for our first night in Maria La Gorda, but we were told there was a *casa* owned by Señor Tomas and Cookie, although they didn't have a phone and would be hard to find. Or there was one hotel. At the three-hour mark of our trip, we arrived at the water, and it was a bluer, clearer Caribbean than I had seen before. Unlike the other towns I'd been to in Central America with bars and shops crowding every square foot of oceanfront, there wasn't a single bar, shop, or hotel for miles, as far as we could see in either direction. We pulled over to take some pictures and an old woman and a little boy walked over to sell us dinner; it turned out that she was friends with Cookie. She stands at this junction every day to find tourists. If we turned right we would enter a tiny run-down pueblo that looked extremely sketchy, or we could turn left, drive nine miles along the deserted beach, and find the only hotel on this part of the island. The old woman stopped cars to look for renters, or people who would like a home cooked Cuban meal with plenty of fresh lobster. We chose the hotel over the *casa* in the run-down town, mainly because I wanted to sign up for a scuba dive.

All the hotels in Cuba are nationalized, meaning all the money goes directly to the government, which in turn pays the workers their miniscule salaries. Actually, that's how every occupation is there – farmers, landlords, gas station attendants, doctors, everyone.

Having a hotel in Maria La Gorda was a big deal since there are very few in the country, mostly in the bigger cities. For $42 we got a room on the beach with two beds and air conditioning, and the aqua-blue hotel was the only building in sight. It was the very picture of a "getaway." The only things to see from our front porch were water and sand – dozens of miles of relaxing nothingness.

As soon as we dropped our bags, I ran to the scuba shop to see if I could get on a boat in the morning. A very handsome Cuban man told me that "maybe we dive tomorrow, maybe not." Handsome, but not very helpful. Hurricane Sandy was still on her way and had brought some strong winds, so they would decide in the morning. "Show up at 8:30 and see," he said. It was reminiscent of the bike tour in Viñales, but that was what we got for showing up during rainy season.

After washing my filthy, mud-stained clothes in the bathroom sink, we went to dinner, a mildly disappointing buffet. I was desperate by then to have just one good meal in Cuba, and I still had a few days to find it. We met some people at dinner, and had Cookie's friend's phone number; we all decided that would be our plan for the following night. We just had to call in advance and she'd send one of her kids to Cookie's house to get the phone. Brilliant.

Gina and I followed our new friends to the hotel bar: a woman from France, one from New Zealand, one from Lithuania and a man from England. We were smoking cigars, drinking rum, and getting to know each other. The French woman said she liked to spend the end of each day thinking of her top 10 travel moments for that day. She asked what ours would be and I came up with two. The first was smoking my first Cuban cigar on the tobacco farm in Viñales – that will always be a favorite memory. The second was while we were driving that day. We were on a two-lane road, and in front of me was an old Soviet-era truck belching stinky black smoke, and I wanted to pass him. There was a giant tractor pulling a trailer in front of him. Coming from the other direction was a team of oxen pulling a cart and a man on a horse. Bicyclists and hitchhikers were on both sides of the road. I couldn't think of a time when I've been in a traffic jam with that many different modes of transportation. I loved that place.

The next morning, I went early to the dive shop and was told by the handsome man that I was too early, to come back later. I'm habitually early; I always have been and can't help it. Time was moving slower than a snail; I had been far too excited about diving in Cuba, something else I never imagined I would get to do in my life. I had heard that the reefs were nearly untouched since so few tourists come here to dive, as compared to Mexico or Belize, and the locals didn't have enough money to do it.

8:30 finally came around and we were going to dive. All I had to do was go to the front desk to pay first, but only for one dive, since the weather might be bad later. I ran all the way to the other end of the hotel, impatiently stood in line, paid, ran back to the shop, got equipment and jumped on the boat. Yay! A uniformed man on the dock watched everything that was going on; I couldn't quite figure out what his job was. I think he was counting people and tanks.

A scuba club from Argentina filled one entire boat and the rest of the tourists were on a second. There I met the first fellow Americans I had seen in the country. They arrived through Mexico and were more nervous about the return trip than I was, going through Panama.

We dove a wall for the first dive; there were a lot of great corals, fans, and colors, but very few fish. My dive buddy, Claude from Belgium, and I did a couple of swim-throughs in rock for-mations. The dive master, Martin, turned to check on us every two or three minutes; the frequency started to get annoying. There are only so many times in a dive I want to be disturbed to let someone know that I'm ok, especially if I don't look like I'm drowning or panicking. Maybe that was a Cuban dive thing, making sure at all times that everyone is ok at every moment. If I got more than four feet away from Claude, Martin would bang on his tank to get our attention and flash the sign to buddy up. It was very annoying.

There was one new piece of life I hadn't seen before: long green corals with black markings. As much as I've Googled since returning home, I haven't found a correct name for it. These cor-als were everywhere, covering everything else like kudzu, waving in the current like snakes. The visibility of the water was probably the best that I had dove in up to that point in my trip.

During the break between dives, I had to pay for my sec-ond dive since they decided to go out again. Gina was out walk-ing the beach and she left our key at the reception desk. I had to run across the hotel complex, get the key, run to my room, grab money, run back to reception to pay and leave the key, then run to the boat to get ready. Not a lot of relaxing between trips.

As we prepared to leave, I spent my time watching the man in uniform again. I was fascinated. He didn't help people onto the boats, he didn't help load tanks, he didn't do anything but watch. My best guess is that he made sure that everyone who goes on a boat comes back. Maybe one of the instructors has a crazy plan to strap six tanks together and scuba dive to Florida. I can't find any record of that being attempted, but I'm sure the Cuban govern-ment wouldn't tell us if it had been. I don't know if it's even pos-sible. Put it on my bucket list.

The second dive wasn't as good as the first. The wind had picked up, so we only took the boat a small distance out and had to swim over a lot of sand before we arrived at the reef. It wasn't a wall like the first dive; we just swam over patches of rock and reef – mildly disappointing. My new dive buddy was Simon, the man I had met at dinner the night before. Again, when we got four feet apart, "tink-tink-tink" from the dive master's tank to scold us for getting so far away from each other. He really needed to relax.

The diving at Maria La Gorda was good, but overall a little disappointing. There weren't many fish anywhere; someone later told me that fishermen have seriously over-fished that site. It was the most expensive diving I'd done yet, and the dives lasted the shortest amount of time, around 40 minutes each, no matter how much air was left. I had over half a tank left after both dives. They charged for equipment rental as well, which was not unusual, but they charged for each dive, not just for the day. I thought that was bullshit. But there was no haggling; the government sets the prices and the employees have to account for every cuc.

I might never dive in Cuba again, but I'm glad I did. It was another thing I hadn't imagined I would get to do in my lifetime.

The next day, the group of us from the hotel decided that the food was too awful to eat another night, and we called the woman Gina and I had met on the roadside. We were eager for some home cooking. The Lithuanian woman, whose name I couldn't begin to spell or pronounce, spent a good amount of time telling us about her supreme negotiating skills, so I let her loose on the family. The original offer was 10 cuc per person. After Lithuania got done with her, it was 40 cuc for six people, a pretty amazing feat negotiating with people who don't like to haggle. We drove the nine miles back to the intersection into the ramshackle town of tin and plywood houses.

The family was gracious and friendly, and we were served as if at a restaurant. The table was covered with bowls of beans, bread, rice, plantain, papaya, cucumbers, and more. We drank local beers. The best dish by far was the enormous platter of lobster, all cut into convenient pieces so we didn't have to mess with the legs and claws; just pick up a piece and scoop the meat out with a spoon. Finally, a good meal in Cuba.

After we stuffed ourselves on more lobster than six healthy-sized people could eat, we leaned back on our chairs recovering and saw the rats walking through the rafters. Definitely time to go.

The last day at the hotel was a lazy day – walking on the beach, reading, planning our next drive. I was stocking up on road food at the hotel store when I noticed juice boxes. I suspected they were chocolate milk for children because they had little cartoon people on the front. I grabbed a pack and discovered they were Piña Colada juice boxes. They were the most amazing things ever. Or, a close second to tequila in a can.

The internet had been down since we arrived, always "try again tomorrow," every time I asked. I felt that with the hurricane coming, and the fact that I had already been in a hurricane and a volcanic eruption, my parents might appreciate hearing from me. I had an international calling card from Pam which of course wouldn't work in Cuba, so I had to go to the desk to buy a card. Five cuc for three minutes to my parents in Ohio. It was also five cuc to call the town nine miles away. Five cuc to anywhere in the world. As Gina put it, in her best sinister Russian voice, "phone call eez phone call."

Even though some of Gina's actions annoyed me, overall it was very interesting to travel with a woman who grew up in a communist country; she could explain so much more than I would have picked up on my own. She pointed out the similarities between present-day Cuba and the Soviet Union when she was a young girl, like the same cement-block architecture in every town. Up to this part of my trip I hadn't considered most of the things I learned in history class, so seeing them first-hand was very eye-opening. The most apparent thing I had never learned in school was that the people live better and are happier there than in most of Central America. It was much cleaner, as well. The propaganda still weirded me out a little, though. Constant reminders to the people that they have a duty to their country. The billboards didn't advertise products; they pointed out the benefits of socialism, education, and guns, accompanied by pictures of Che and quotes from Fidel and Raúl.

Gina and I started back on the road to Jaguey Grande, and stopped partway to see a crocodile farm. We pulled in and the lone man there explained that everyone had gone home for the weekend – we should come back Monday for a tour. We stood around asking him questions, hoping he'd let us wander around by ourselves, when another worker miraculously showed up. We could take our tour after all. The first pens were filled with adorable little crocodiles, two to three feet long, all huddled together in the shade. They were barely moving, mouths wide open, trying to keep cool in the heat. Next we saw the babies, possibly even cuter than the newly hatched turtles in Mexico. They were so tiny and skinny, and they skittered into the water quickly when we approached. Those pens were covered with metal fencing, not so the babies wouldn't escape, but because the giant birds treated it like a buffet. Our guide picked one up and let me pet him; I wanted to take him home more than any kitten or puppy I've ever seen.

The last stop on the tour was a large, enclosed pond where the adult crocodiles lived. We walked out onto a 5-foot-high platform and watched them sleep. It was pretty uneventful. I think I expected something more terrifying, like in Belize, but they were nice to look at anyway. This was the last area where they lived in captivity until they were released into the nearby lagoons. The whole time we were at the farm, we could hear sheep and goats we assumed were there to feed the crocs, but they were actually to feed the workers. If I were a crocodile, I think I would sneak back and eat them once I was set free, but they rarely surprised anyone by coming back from their new home in the lagoon. Our guide showed us some mean-looking scars on his leg. I guess if a croc takes the time to surprise you, he means business. After showing us his scars, our guide offered to take us for a walk through some tall grass along the fence to get a closer look. The scars weren't a great selling point for this walk, but I went; Gina decided she liked her legs exactly as they were and stayed on the platform taking video in case anything interesting happened. A croc blinked a couple of times, and that was the most interesting thing we saw. Lazy.

We made it to Jaguey Grande, and along the way I felt the beginnings of a cold. I hadn't been sick in so long it was a surprise. We went through a fair number of small towns and the driving was more stressful; barely two lanes, people everywhere, bikes with two or three people on them, motorcycles, horses or oxen pulling carts, and giant trucks and tractors pulling trailers full of people – the closest thing I saw to a bus system. Being lost so much, dodging all the people, and now being sick was starting to make me a little cranky.

Our new *casa* was owned by a tiny, cute blonde woman. There wasn't a lot to do in town, so Gina and I went to dinner and wandered through the streets. The only memorable moment from the evening was an encounter with a man as we were walking home around 9 p.m. He did the usual "where are you from?" instead of "hello" or "nice night, huh?" He looked kind of creepy, so we didn't answer him; we just kept walking. He asked again and didn't look like he had any intention of leaving us alone, even though we weren't even acknowledging his presence. I did what Gina did in these situations: I said "Russia" in as sinister a way as I could manage; it usually worked for her. And what did this man do? Of course he started talking to me in Russian. Busted. Gina leaned over to whisper the translation in my ear and I couldn't help but giggle at the situation. Eventually she told him, in Russian, that I didn't want to talk to him and he left us alone. Thinking back, I wouldn't be surprised if Gina had told him, in Russian, that I was an asshole and wasn't worth his time. Maybe she was getting tired of me, too.

We left the next day for Cayo Santa Maria far, far away. The *autopista* would get us there faster, but for anything interesting or scenic we had to take the country roads. There were miles and miles of horrible, pothole-filled dirt roads through some of the most beautiful scenery. I was still doing all the driving and Gina was reading our German Cuban guidebook, finding points of interest to stop at. The first stop was the Bay of Pigs. Thinking about it as we approached, I wondered what it would look like, and all I could think of was a war-torn landscape where the American invasion helped a Cuban militia attempt to overthrow Castro, never quite repaired. But that was more than 50 years ago. The Bay of Pigs in 2012 was like a scene from "Dirty Dancing." Cute little hotel cabanas along a beach, the typical clear blue Caribbean water, loud Cuban music and 50s style everything. Not exactly what I had in mind.

We walked the beach to stretch our legs and started on to our next sight, the Bay of Pigs Museum and the Che Guevara Memorial and Mausoleum.

I've been in places before that I shouldn't have been, but never in my life have I felt so strongly that I was in the wrong place as when I walked into the Bay of Pigs Museum. There were displays of all types of weapons, from guns to canons, and the walls were covered with pictures and newspaper articles with captions and headlines in violently inflammatory propaganda language. Well, propaganda to some; it depends upon which side you're on.

"Yankee imperialist cowards" under a picture of captured men being handcuffed.

"Mercenary Yankee Bombing" read a newspaper headline.

"Victim of yankee shrapnel manages to scrawl a last revolutionary message in his own blood." Come on, really?

"The yankee mercenaries were well-armed but lacked our moral strength."

And on and on until "Victory! The armed wing of the revolution punished the mercenary impudence to invade our socialist country!"

Then there were all the stories about the humane treatment of the captured cowards who wouldn't confess to taking part in the invasion, and the miserable moral condition of the yankee murderers. Another wall was covered in pictures of the martyrs who gave their lives defending their land. I was quite uncomfortable.

Most places in Cuba require a passport; every *casa* and roadside checkpoint. The museums only required a name and nationality. I signed in to all of them as a Russian.

The Che Guevara Memorial and Mausoleum was very cool. It covers about two city blocks, most of it in a park-like setting. A giant statue of Che surrounded by quotes from Fidel, flags and sculptures. The museum had pictures of Che from boyhood until his death, things he owned as a child, and pictures from all of his military campaigns. Historically, it was a treasure. The mausoleum had the remains of everyone he died with, and there was an outdoor cemetery with an eternal flame. No pictures were allowed in any part of this, and that really hurt because I felt like I was missing a limb when I had to leave my camera behind.

The next town in our guidebook was Santa Clara, and it seemed like a good stop for another break on our long drive to Cayo. The lonely country roads on our way had long stretches of a white substance that I thought was sand; what a strange way to repair all the potholes, I thought. There came a time when half of the road was covered in white, and I was driving on my side with oncoming traffic in my lane headed straight at us. Rather than drive on the mystery substance, the other cars and trucks pulled off to my far right and drove on the dirt rather than on the road. We couldn't figure out why. Nothing in the guidebook mentioned this strange behavior. After some time we saw men actively raking the white stuff and we stopped to ask what they were doing. One man dropped his rake, picked up a handful and sprinkled it in my hand through the car window, and it was rice. They were spreading it on the road to dry in the sun before they bagged it and loaded it onto their ox carts. I had driven on some earlier, before I noticed that I was the only one doing that, so I asked the man if driving on it was ok. He stared at me with a look on his face that clearly said "moron," and said it would be better if I didn't do that again.

Santa Clara is a decent-sized town, but I wasn't fond of it. It had the same crowded streets and stressful driving as all of the towns. God, I missed having my GPS maps, so Gina and I parked and walked around the square. We had a horrible lunch. The whole place seemed sinister to me, but I think that was because of the experience at the Bay of Pigs Museum that made me feel like everyone in the country hated me. I made Gina leave.

CAYO SANTA MARIA

After 10 hours on the road, we made it to Cayo Santa Maria, or just "Cayo," as everyone called it. Unlike the Cayo in Belize, though, this was actually named appropriately. The last 30 minutes of driving was on a bridge very much like driving through the Florida Keys – two lanes and nothing but water on either side. An armed checkpoint stood at the start of the bridge, because Cubans aren't allowed unless they are on a bus going to work there.

We picked Cayo over other similar places for a couple reasons, one being that it saved us additional hours in the car. It was a newer place and didn't have many hotels, so we thought that might mean it was less touristy. No one we spoke with had been there, so we relied solely on the guidebook. It listed three hotels, all very pricey in comparison to our *casa particulars*, and we picked the cheapest one to check out first.

The sun was setting as we arrived at the hotel. I was completely frazzled and achy from driving all day; my sole thought was of a couple of beers and a bed. The hotel had one room left, but after looking at it with the desk clerk, Gina didn't like it. "It's too jungly," she said. It was a nice room with an ocean view, but the waves on this side of the island were kicked up from the hurricane winds and there wasn't much beach to walk on. Gina didn't want to stay. I got a beer from the bar to go and we set off in search of the other hotels, knowing in advance that they were double the price.

We got lost almost immediately and ended up in an outdoor plaza, which we shouldn't have been driving in, and asked for directions. We were directed to an all-inclusive resort starting at 250 cuc per night, and without even looking at the room we asked for directions to the third hotel. We ended up in the plaza again. I knew it was the same plaza because there was a giant pirate ship blocking the "road." We got more directions from the same amused man and we found the hotel, another all-inclusive resort for 177 cuc per night. Gina asked to see the room and wasn't happy with this one, either. The first hotel was only 85 cuc, still expensive compared to the *casa* at 20 cuc, so we decided to go back. I was so happy to be done with the day; there weren't any more options, so beer and bed became the plan once again.

While we were driving around lost and viewing the other two hotels, the man at the first hotel had rented out the last room. We drove all the way back across the cayo and paid double for a resort room. Displeased didn't begin to describe my feelings for Gina.

The resort was immense and we needed to be driven to our room by an overly friendly man in a golf cart. It was possible that he wasn't overly friendly, but the final two hours of the day had left me beyond tired, in a foul mood, and my cold was getting increasingly worse. It was already 10 p.m. We had 20 minutes until the dining hall closed, so we grabbed drinks and finally got to eat. The hotel was expensive, but at least it included all of the booze and food. The internet was 12 cuc for half an hour, and incredibly slow. I drank myself back into a good mood as I checked a week's worth of email. Our bartender was a nice, chatty man who took the bus to work with all the other employees on the cayo. He rode the bus two hours, worked for 16 hours, then rode two hours back home. The next day, he spent the same four hours on the bus but only worked an eight-hour day. Then another 16-hour day, with one day off per week. Yet another realization of what a blessed life I have in the U.S.

The morning dawned and we could finally see the view from our room. Now Gina liked it because it was "jungly." Whatever.

The beach was intense from the storm winds; the waves were breaking almost all the way over the sand and we had to walk with care so we didn't get swept out into the angry ocean. We encountered very few other people walking; mostly they were stuck in one spot waiting for the water to subside so they could go back where they came from. There was too much vegetation to walk anywhere on higher ground.

Our one-night stay allowed us to remain on the property until 3 p.m., and I decided on a couple drinks and a nap by one of the many pools, grateful that Gina wanted to walk around more – I liked my alone time. I ate and drank until 2:55, determined to get my money's worth, found Gina, then we sprinted to the room to pack our things and leave.

SANCTI SPIRITUS

We wanted to drive to Trinidad, but we started so late that it would be well after nightfall before we arrived. The only rule I had started following, excepting the previous night, was that I didn't drive anywhere new after dark. Far too many people, bikes, and animals were on the crazy maze of roads; driving day after day, it was just too much. We started picking up hitchhikers – women only – to get information and easier directions, and they agreed that we shouldn't drive into Trinidad at night, so we set our sights on Sancti Spiritus.

Picking up hitchhikers was a fun new experience. We would pick out a specific woman who looked friendly and nonthreatening, someone who wasn't in the middle of the crowd of people looking for a ride, and pull over. We only wanted one rider and focused on a lone woman. The first time we stopped, we learned that was never going to happen. As soon as we pulled over, everyone could see we had an entire car with only two people, and when the back door opened four people darted out to cram themselves inside. They didn't even ask where we were going. It was impossible to pick up only one person, although we did stand firm with our "women and children only" rule.

We had only intended on stopping long enough to look around Sancti Spiritus and hadn't researched anywhere to spend the night. It was a bigger city with the same maze of roads and lack of GPS, so we were instantly lost, driving in circles. I spotted another tourist car with a couple women and started following them, thinking they would know where they were going, but it turned out they were lost too. While we were stopped trying to decide on a route, I saw an old woman on the street corner with business cards; in Cuba, that means she had a *casa particular* and was looking for guests.

Gina and I followed her to her *casa* and it was much the same as all the others; it could have been my grandmother's house when I was a young girl. The outsides of the *casa*s were all different, depending on the town they were in, but the insides were full of "antiques," old school knickknacks that you can probably only find in flea markets now. Someday, some American is going to get the idea to go to Cuba and buy everyone's typical household items, sell them on eBay as antiques, and make a fortune.

We stayed in the house long enough to get a hurricane update. After it smashed its way through Santiago, the locals didn't care anymore and we couldn't track where it was, only that it had entered the States. We did hear that because of flooding there was a dengue fever outbreak a few towns over, but we couldn't confirm that report.

Gina and I wandered through the city; it was late by then and all the restaurants were closed. Our German guidebook listed only one that was open late, but the directions sent us to a dark street with several shady-looking people hanging about. We saw the sign for El Soltano, but there were no lights on anywhere. Gina asked the least shady-looking man why the restaurant was closed and he said it wasn't, we just weren't looking in the proper place. He led us to a doorway next to a house and into a dark hallway. Gina made me go first in case he was taking us to a convenient place to rape us, although after having absolutely no bad experiences with the Cuban people, I had long since given up on thinking anyone on the island was a bad person. We went down some stairs, and wound up in someone's house. Another man took us to the back where three tables were set, and two more were set on an outdoor patio overlooking the river. We found a private underground restaurant and we were the only guests. The family was friendly and served us massive amounts of cheap food. Not great food, but more than we could possibly eat.

There wasn't any real tourist activity in Sancti Spiritus, so Gina and I made it an early night. We awoke, again sharing a room, and ate breakfast at the *casa*, again moderately awful but inexpensive. Those were the two constants of our days in Cuba: sharing rooms and not-great food. Three constants, really, if you add the insane activity on the roads. We started the final leg of our road trip into Trinidad. I was nearing the end of my visit and would be returning to Havana in two days to fly to Nicaragua.

TRINIDAD

We stopped along the way at a few lookout points; one of them had a small café serving fresh-squeezed sugarcane with coconut water. It was quite the production; the café only makes it when someone orders it, and we got to watch two men grinding stalks of sugarcane in a hand-cranked press. After they squeezed out enough juice, they opened the coconuts with a machete and we were served. The entire process took 10 minutes, and the men sang as they worked; it was worth every cuc to watch them. Gina looked at her drink and saw something floating – a piece of cane, a bug, I wasn't sure. After Central America, foreign things in my food and drinks no longer bothered me. I'd simply pick it out and continue. But Gina was upset and took her drink back to the counter. She wanted one without anything floating in it. Out came the men with new stalks of sugar cane, back to the press, hack open another coconut. Several minutes later, Gina had a new drink with something floating in it. I silently prayed she wouldn't return that one, too.

We arrived in Trinidad – a small town, but completely confusing to drive through. The roads point in all directions; some are one-way, some are just closed at the end with no warning and nowhere to turn around. Every time we slowed down to find a new direction, we were swamped with people at our windows trying to direct us to this hotel or that restaurant; it was comical but intimidating. I was driving through hordes of people on cobblestones, dodging horses and dogs, and it had been years since I drove a car with a manual transmission. That day just happened to be the day I hit my limit for driving in a third world country. Dozens of hours over nine days and I wanted to put on the brake in the middle of the street and run away. I was inches away from freaking out. I was looking forward to returning to Central America and taking buses, as much as I dislike them.

Once again, Gina and I were utterly lost. The roads were so narrow that there was nowhere to pull over and get out; we just kept driving in circles. But just like in Sancti Spiritus, we found our small miracle: the two women with whom we did the bike tour in Viñales happened to be walking down the street, and they said there was another room for rent in their *casa*. We loaded the women in our car; they were on their way somewhere, but I begged them to abandon their plan and take us home. The new *casa* was like a museum – there couldn't have been any furniture or decorations newer than 1940, and everything was spotlessly clean and in excellent condition. I was afraid to sit in the chairs. This would be the place to go when the American embargo is lifted, as the Cubans want so badly. Antiques roadshow would never need to go anywhere else.

Gina and I decided we were going to turn in our rental car for the small drop-off fee instead of driving back to Havana, as we had originally intended. I needed to get back, but Gina had a few more days and wanted to continue by bus. She asked me to drive the car back to Havana by myself, her most absurd request yet. No map, no guidebook, no GPS, no sense of direction – I was certain I would never make it out of the country if I had to drive solo.

I bought a bus ticket to Havana on the way to the rental shop, and the grumpy, horrible man at the counter told us it would cost 90 cuc to turn in the car here. We were told that it was only 45 cuc by the man in Havana. Gina refused to accept that, and the man wouldn't budge, saying it was written in our contract. For the first time on this trip, I agreed with Gina's anger. He pointed to a line of illegible handwriting, and wouldn't call Havana to confirm. That was more money than we would willingly throw away; we were going to drive back to Havana tomorrow. I got my money back for the bus ticket on the way to the *casa*. Our mother let me use the phone to call Javier at the agency in Havana; simply because we called to inform them of our change in plans, we got half the fee waived. That must have been the illegible part of the contract. If we returned it immediately we could even get an entire day's fee refunded. Gina and I walked back to the office, confident in our victory over the grumpy, mean man, and he had closed up for the day. So we had one more day with the car, but I was so fed up with driving I didn't even want to look at it. Remembering that it was guaranteed by Gina's credit card, since mine weren't accepted here, I was more than happy to ditch it where it was parked. I bought another bus ticket.

My cold had progressed to the point of constantly coughing up phlegm and a wicked headache, so I was glad to spend the evening at the *casa* by myself. This was the first and only time of sickness in my five months on the road thus far, so I still considered myself lucky. It was annoying but nothing worse. I'd seen some amazing things in the past five months, and missing one night out in Trinidad wasn't going to kill me. I had one more day to recover and check out the music scene there before I had to leave. Gina was mad that I wouldn't go to the bars with her, but I couldn't understand how someone could run around every minute of every day and never relax. After nine days with her, merely watching her contributed to my weariness.

Trinidad is an amazing little city. It's not very big, but it always has a lot going on. People were everywhere working, talking, walking, sitting in cafés, looking at art; there was so much to see that I wished I wasn't sick. I was also worn out with Gina, so I declined her invitation to drive to a waterfall in favor of sitting on the rooftop terrace. I watched men brick up a roof and women hang clothes to dry; I listened to the sounds of the city and just absorbed everything. It was a great way to spend the morning.

When Gina returned, we headed back to the rental agency to deal with the car again. I told the mean, grumpy man about the "report" Javier had submitted, allowing us to drop off the car for 45 cuc. He still demanded 90 cuc and I had to get bossy with him. It was a good thing he understood English, because I was still unable to think in Spanish fast enough to express my anger. I told him we were going to leave the car key and 45 cuc, and there wasn't going to be any further discussion. We argued for a while, he refused to call the agent in Havana, then he finally relented and they yelled at each other for a few minutes. If there was really only one rental car company in the entire country, wouldn't they all have the same rules? The mean man handed me the phone and Javier repeated over and over that the other agent wasn't a liar, which was confusing. I think he was trying to reassure me somehow, but the translation was completely lost.

Everything was worked out in the end, but no one was happy, least of all the Trinidad agent. He had to send emails to various people informing them as to why we weren't paying 90 cuc, and had to have corresponding emails sent from Havana to back his story. I guess that if his money and reports came out wrong, he would have to pay the extra 45 cuc himself, and that is probably three months of his salary.

Paperwork is a huge deal here. In each *casa* the women keep minutely detailed ledgers with the boarders and amounts paid. Every store and restaurant has a notebook of every item sold and the amount charged. In the hotels the women filled out multiple forms for every transaction, and there were people watching everything at all times.

I could understand why the Trinidad agent was upset, but I certainly wasn't going to pay double for a service when I was already quoted a price.

We left the car in front of the agency and tried to slink off quickly. I was worried about all the tar covering the sides and that we would get charged. No one here puts up cautionary signs while doing roadwork, like "wet." They just let drivers drive through fresh tar all over the country. That must be common enough, because no one said a word. I had tar stuck to my legs from leaning against the car that didn't come off for weeks. It wouldn't have surprised me to find bits of rice embedded as well.

After a beer to celebrate the successful negotiation of something we never should have had to negotiate, Gina noticed that her camera was missing. She had to walk back to the rental agency and speak with our angry friend again to see if she left it in the car. They had already driven the car to the mechanic's house and Gina had to spend yet another day dealing with car-related issues. I found out by email a few days later that the camera was never recovered. Gina had picked up a carload of hitchhikers when she used the car solo on one of my "de-stress and recover" afternoons. She was sure she stuffed the camera under the seat, but it must have rolled back and was pocketed by a passenger. The best way to trust people is to use locks, or so I've been told. Even though Gina and I hadn't gotten along perfectly as travel companions, I felt awful about this. She had been through Guatemala, Panama, and Cuba and hadn't uploaded any pictures to a cloud service or even to a computer. Devastating, but not a life-ender.

For my last night in Trinidad, Gina and I went to the steps on the square. It's basically a long, wide stairway that leads to an outdoor stage and a couple of bars. Most everyone ends up sitting on the cement steps because there are so few tables or chairs. Everyone in town, with the exception of non-respectable Cubans, as determined by the bouncers, goes to drink, lounge, and dance. Gina and I got a table, but after a drink we wanted to wander around a bit, and who did we find but the group we hung out with in Maria La Gorda? That's one wonderful aspect of traveling

I hadn't anticipated before my first trip; I frequently ran into people I'd met before in different places. I connected with two groups of people from Lago de Atitlan in Antigua, and seeing the great people from Maria La Gorda made me realize that if I travelled long enough I would start seeing people I knew in many different countries. The prospect was very exciting – almost like running into old friends when you're lonely.

We sat on the steps and drank and caught up on what everyone had done since we'd seen each other last. The band was great; I hadn't yet heard a live Cuban band I didn't love, and there were dancers along the entire front of the stage. And not just regular dancers, but people so talented I never wanted to dance again. It was a great last night in Trinidad.

I had two choices of transportation back to Havana, and just like in Guatemala, I chose exactly wrong. I should have known by then that I need to pick comfort over speed. It's not as if I really needed to be anywhere that an extra hour or two would ruin. I opted for the van and it was a big mistake. I got stuck in the horrible seat in the middle that feels like you're sitting on a rock. I don't think it was even a real seat, but the general rule everywhere I'd been was the more passengers you can cram on one ride, the better. I'm fairly certain no one else minded the van; anyone considering it just needs to be smarter than me and avoid the dreaded middle seat.

The other problem was that I was seated extremely close to a smelly Australian man who could not stop talking to me for the entire five hours. I had stayed out partying on my last night thinking I would sleep all the way to Havana, but that plan was a total failure.

I was able to ignore him for portions of the ride and reflect on my time in Cuba. My first thought was that I would come back any time; it was an amazing adventure. Maybe with a different travel companion, someone I know I'm compatible with, and can sleep in the same bed with, as was necessary for most of the trip. That said, without Gina I may never have gone to Cuba. She was a bit more enthusiastic about seeing every little thing than I was – I do like my lazy days – and somewhat more negative than I felt was appropriate, but we did manage to see almost half of the country. So it was definitely worth it.

When I got to Havana, I needed to plan my days in Nicaragua. Without internet service, planning really became a problem, but my Lonely Planet guide got me started. I had the name of a hostel, a basic map, a rudimentary understanding of the bus system, and a plane ticket. That would be enough for a few days.

HAVANA

I returned to Havana for the night before my flight, which was ridiculously early in the morning. I was staying at Clara's *casa*, and I was definitely regretting the choice. I knew it was a busy place, but I didn't expect that several people would be watching TV in different rooms, all with the volumes turned up enough to drown out the others. I was sharing a bathroom with a very loud couple who didn't seem to understand that I speak Spanish, even though that was the only language I spoke to them. They just pretended to ignore me. But I guess that just shows that my Spanish was still not past a third-grade level. All I wanted to do was sleep; my cold was even worse, and the six people smoking in the house didn't help, although I really wanted to bum a cigarette from one of them. Addiction is so inconvenient. I went out to dinner to escape the crowd and drank multiple mojitos, thinking those, combined with my cold medicine, would allow me to sleep through anything. Wrong.

My last night in Havana was less than perfect. I tried to sleep; it didn't work. I put on my headphones; that didn't work either. I think I drifted off at about midnight, five hours before my alarm, and was awoken by some housemates after two hours. It must have been their honeymoon.

When I finally did give up trying to sleep, I wandered into the shared bathroom and there were several used condoms all over the floor, mostly about two feet from the garbage can. They actually got upset when I knocked on their door and asked if they could please clean up. After some time I was able to use the bathroom, just in time for the woman to bang on the door. I spent the next hour listening to both of them violently throwing up.

Five in the morning arrived soon after and I had to crawl out of bed to pack for the airport. It was time for coffee, but no one was awake as promised and I couldn't get myself to rummage through the cabinets in the dirty kitchen. I started to wonder exactly why I chose this apartment to stay in; there must have been dozens nearby. I guess I figured nothing could be too bad for a single night; I hadn't run into any Cubans who annoyed me that much.

I was getting ready to leave, 5:10. 5:20. 5:30. No coffee. At 5:40, my taxi driver rang the bell, so it was time to wake everyone up. I wandered from room to room yelling *"Hola!"* until I heard someone mumbling. Besides missing my coffee, the woman had my passport, as required by law for a boarder. I was still sick and had gone two days without sleep, and I was in no mood to deal with a grumbly woman who had promised me coffee at 5 a.m. I let the taxi driver talk to her, and he brought me steaming hot, mud-like coffee from the kitchen with my passport.

The taxi driver, Manuel, was a godsend. He took over when my brain shut down. He collected all of my things from my room, helped me finish packing, made sure that I had put my passport and wallet somewhere safe, and took everything to his car.

As we drove to the airport, I started waking up properly and had a pleasant ride with him. Manuel had a classic car, but wanted nothing more than to buy a new one. Cubans weren't allowed to buy new cars unless they were very important people, and even if he could, Manuel couldn't afford one if he saved all his tips for years. He earned exactly what everyone else earned, 15-20 cuc per month. He did get to keep his tips, though.

I ended up giving Manuel all of my extra cucs. I paid almost 15% to change them from dollars, and it would be another 15% to change back. Why give the government even more of my money? This poor kid had to deal with a lot when he came to get me this morning. He definitely earned it.

The airline attendant gave me the third degree as I was checking in. "Where are you going now? What are you doing there? When will you return to the United States? I need all of those itineraries." I couldn't understand what his interest was since I was leaving his country. I was so sick and tired that I answered more questions than I was comfortable with, only later realizing that I should have kept my mouth shut and my plans to myself. Interrogating a sick girl was surprisingly easy. It took several days before I felt like they weren't tracking me anymore.

Emigration was even worse, "Stand in front of the camera. Don't smile." The woman checked my passport picture to my face to the picture on her screen over and over. No one had ever cared that I was leaving their country quite like the Cubans did.

NICARAGUA
NOVEMBER 6ᵀᴴ, 2012

An hour later I was on the plane, looking and feeling seriously unwell. There were two German men sitting next to me who must have been supermodels. Each was around 6'3", thin, completely gorgeous, one blond and one brunette. I was coughing and snot was dripping from my nose, and sadly realized that kissing a German supermodel was not a goal I would accomplish on this leg of my trip. They stood up and moved to seats far away from me.

I flew back to Panama, then on to Nicaragua, where I would have to catch a bus to Grenada. Nicaragua was the first country that made me fill out a health questionnaire, and obviously they had never had a native English-speaker spell-check it.

"Does it have decay?" I wasn't sure how to answer that, but I checked yes. I felt so awful, it could have been decay. I ended up checking yes in every box, but no one even looked at my form. At immigration, posters hung everywhere about who to call if you felt sick, and a woman in a white lab coat with a clipboard stood watching all the passengers go through. I was certain that I had a fever at that point, and I didn't have the energy to find a bus to Grenada, so as I approached this woman I started coughing as loud as I could; maybe she would cart me off to a hospital where I could finally get a good night's sleep.

She didn't even look at me. I was actually disappointed when I wasn't rushed off to quarantine.

I stood outside the airport with my bags, wishing all the men shouting "Taxi!" at me would go away, or at least talk more softly, when I saw a sight so happy I thought I might cry: a giant Best Western sign. I ran across the street and fell into bed for the next 14 hours.

ROATAN PART II
NOVEMBER 7TH, 2012

When I woke up, I knew I had passed the days of a mere cold and was now genuinely sick. I couldn't imagine navigating an unknown country. Being sick and finding the correct bus, my hostel, money, food – none of that sounded like fun. So I walked back across the street to the airport and bought a ticket back to Roatan. It was an easy flight, and within 20 minutes of my arrival I had my old room back, a credit at the grocery store since I didn't have any money yet, and four people at my door to welcome me home.

The store had a wide selection of antibiotics and I bought some of each just to be sure I killed whatever was living inside me. The first three days back I slept nearly continuously, but I didn't go for more than a few hours without someone from the dive shop stopping by to make sure I was still alive and had food. It was the closest thing to a big happy family, and it felt nice.

The antibiotics seemed to be working and I was able to wander out of my room to watch some Monday Night Football before going back to bed. As soon as the intense amount of sugar from 12 days of Cuban daiquiris left my system I thought I would be all good, and I wanted to try to get back to Nicaragua. I had flown over it twice and it looked beautiful.

Four more days in bed and it was time to drag my sad self to the clinic. Amoxicillin and vodka were not working as expected.

Had I known what a great experience the doctor's office would be, I never would have spent a week lying in bed watching CSI reruns. A 10-minute, $2 cab ride got me to the clinic at Anthony's Key Resort. The driver wanted to take me to Dolly's Clinic with the sign on the street covered in rainbows and hearts; I had to adamantly refuse and direct him elsewhere. I was seen by a doctor at the resort clinic in less than a minute after walking in. Five minutes later I was getting blood drawn and peeing in a cup; I received drugs for nausea and pain, and I was told to come back in five hours for my results.

Five hours of awful TV later, I was back at the office with a confirmed bacterial infection, thank you very much Cuba. I got more drugs and a bill for $42. Best doctor experience anywhere. I don't even get taken care of that quickly at home. I learned that I shouldn't be afraid of the doctor's office regardless of the stories I'd heard. Maybe I would come home if I needed major surgery, but anything else seemed like a pleasant day's adventure, except for the sickness part.

There was no fuss about health insurance, which I didn't have; no waiting in long lines, and totally affordable care. I still couldn't eat, but at least I was on the correct drugs and maybe after a couple more days I'd have the desire to do something besides sleep.

In the meantime, I was glad that I was back on Roatan to recover. The usual friends were still making house calls to make sure I was alive, and I even got a few drinks delivered from the bar. I couldn't drink them, but it was nice all the same.

I spent two weeks lying in bed on Roatan, mostly watching horrible crime drama reruns over and over. My world was filled with serial killers and arsonists, all neatly caught at the end of an hour. I had to wander outside every once in a while to make sure that real people still existed. My drugs made me too nauseous to eat, and day by day I could see my beer gut dissipating. Five months of beer, cigarettes and little exercise were almost made right by a two-week bacterial infection diet. I had time to catch up on the emails from home; everyone was wondering if I had died since the last phone call from Cuba.

NICARAGUA PART II

NOVEMBER 18TH, 2012

I made it back to Managua, feeling much better than the last time I was there nearly two weeks before. I couldn't be too angry about being sick, but it was a giant waste of time. I couldn't have asked for a better detox program, though: it was also two weeks since I'd had a drink. My last night on Roatan I went out to celebrate and ordered a "Monkey Lala." After a few sips, John had to practically carry me home. My poor body was defenseless against toxins, so the plan was to ease back into party mode a little at a time.

It was a good time to leave Roatan again. There had been two prominent murders in the last month, one being the day before I left. A Canadian tourist was shot while leaving a bar he had no business being in, and the Canadian government was going nuts. Although a good portion of non-Honduran locals are originally from Canada, the media was portraying the island as a lawless, desperate place that no one should visit. That would only make crime worse, since tourism was the only industry I could see.

Crime had risen the previous summer due to the Olympics, as I was told. The cruise ships came to port and too many people stayed on board to watch TV rather than spend their money at the shops and restaurants. Break-ins were at higher than normal levels.

The previous day's death had been much closer to home for the islanders; the victim was a longtime resident named Vern, the boat owner and captain of the catamaran that did daily runs to Utila. I even watched him loading his boat for the last trip when I was going out for a final scuba dive. Later in the day we heard his catamaran had been found in a bay and he was dead on board, shot and stabbed. His crew had jumped overboard. I never heard if anyone was caught or why it happened, but I did know this was more than the government would tolerate, especially two days before elections. The Cobras, Honduran Special Forces, were going to come from the mainland and kick some ass. Roatan needs tourism badly.

I hoped Honduras would get this all worked out and settled down, because Roatan is an amazing place, the people are fun and the diving is great. Everyone should be able to enjoy it.

UNITED STATES
NOVEMBER 19TH, 2012

CLEVELAND

Yes, Ohio.

I had to skip Nicaragua again and fly to Ohio. It wasn't part of the plan, but that's the beauty of not having a plan.

Since I've always lived so far from my parents I rarely make it home, and the only time my parents ask me to come is at Thanksgiving, when all of my family goes to Cleveland. This year was no exception. It went a little differently, though, as normally I can't take enough time off from work to justify such a long trip;

the flight from Kauai to Cleveland takes 16-18 hours. I was speaking with my father on the phone and he couldn't understand why I couldn't visit this year. "But you don't have a job!" I had no excuse in his eyes.

At first I blew it off; it wasn't even a consideration. But little by little, the Catholic guilt started working on me, the voice in my head telling me that my parents weren't getting any younger. When is the next time I'll have time? When I arrived in Nicaragua again, I bought a ticket to Cleveland and spent the night in my Best Western. I swore I'd get back one day to wander through the country.

On the flight to Ohio, all I could think about was going through customs in Miami. That's a major entry point for several countries, and I was certain customs would be extra thorough going through my backpack. The only things I was worried about were the items from Cuba. All the websites told me to make sure I threw out all receipts, mementos, or anything else that would identify me as coming from Cuba, but I couldn't do it. I'm a souvenir girl. I had a swizzle stick that said "Havana Club," receipts from several museums and places of interest, stamps in my dive book, money for my coin collection, and worst of all, a package of cigars. I was going to bring a bottle of rum back, but we drank it on Roatan. I stashed my contraband in the odd pockets of my backpack, hiding them as best I could. The cigars gave me some trouble, but in the end I bought a package of tampons and stuck the cigars in the middle. I was sweating a bit and crossing my fingers, but I didn't get a second glance upon arrival in the States.

To be honest, I was glad for a small break at home, even though it was snowing and I didn't even have a pair of socks in my backpack. I spent Thanksgiving with my family, went to the mall, and watched football. We visited the Westside Market and Little Italy, family favorites, and that was almost like I was still travelling, but with a lot less effort. It was nice to be around people I knew and not have to go to a bar to find someone to talk to. I was still recovering from my illness, so I spent the week doing as little as possible. As long as I was nearly back home, I planned a quick stop on Kauai, then decided to go west to Australia rather than continue to South America. I'd get back there later, too.

My flights helped me realize another huge difference between American and Central American travel. All the employees on the Central American airlines were sweet and helpful, and there was always a free meal, good or bad, and free drinks – alcoholic ones. I didn't feel the love when I returned to the States. Everyone was in too big of a hurry to be friendly.

My seat was next to a larger woman in a track suit for the first half of the flights to Kauai. She had food, magazines, pens, and assorted miscellaneous stuff spread out all over my seat when I arrived, and took several minutes to move it all while I blocked the aisle. She looked at me as if I was intruding on her personal space. She repacked her purse and heaved herself out of the seat to let me in. Of all the buses, boats and planes I rode on my trip, I had yet to encounter anyone as ridiculous as this woman, even when it was so crowded that I was smashed between sweaty people. No one was this rude in Central America.

I watched her, fascinated, for the next few hours. She pulled several small bags of nuts out of her purse and ate them as fast as she could, while the contents of her purse were again laid out all over her lap and tray table. She paged through 10 different tabloids looking at pictures of celebrities caught by paparazzi. When the drink cart arrived, she got a small coffee and added six creams and six sugars, calling the attendant back twice to get more supplies. She made a mess, worse than the coffee bar in Starbucks after the morning rush.

It had been so long since I had encountered anyone so outrageous that I wasn't sure whether I should be offended by my fellow American, or laugh at such a perfect stereotype of us.

After watching her for four more hours and listening to the four nearby children scream, I got to Los Angeles and bought a first-class upgrade to Lihue. I ended up with two first-class seats and a nonstop flow of Pinot Grigio. Or, it was nonstop until I drank it all, then I had to switch. The attendant, friendlier now that I was in an upgraded seat, gave me a tiny wine glass at first, which she had to run back and forth to fill. Finally, she brought out a giant tumbler so she didn't have to make so many trips. I got a little tipsy.

Which brought up the question: which is the worse stereotype, the large woman in coach eating everything in sight, or the lazy drunk girl in first class? I realized I didn't have a lot of room to laugh at anyone else. But I was drunk, so I did.

KAUAI

I spent my time on Kauai catching up with friends, paddling, swimming and hiking the places I missed most. The main reason I wanted to stop home was to see my friend Kari, slightly older than me and pregnant with her first child. She Skyped me while

I was in Belize to let me know she was pregnant, and since I had never thought it would happen, I wanted to see her with her giant baby belly. That was worth the trip home.

I started to make my Australia itinerary and found a one-way ticket for $346 – almost too good to be true. The only catch was that I had to travel early on Christmas day, and flying over the International Date Line, I would arrive in Brisbane the day after Christmas, so I wouldn't actually have a Christmas day.

Brisbane is 20 hours ahead of Kauai, and wrapping my head around that was not easy. I had been through so many different time zones in the past five months that my phone, computer, and Kindle could never agree on what time it was, and I had alarms going off at all hours of the day and night. When my phone finally figured out what time zone it was in, it left all of my "to do" list on whatever time zone it was planned in, and there was no way to change everything with just one click. Australia was really going to mess things up.

On Christmas Eve I meant to do errands and catch up with people to say goodbye again. Instead, I ended up drinking tequila, eating leftovers, and watching old movies with my friend Mark. It was great, but I had to set my alarm to 3:30 a.m. so I could pack. Plenty of time to sleep on the plane.

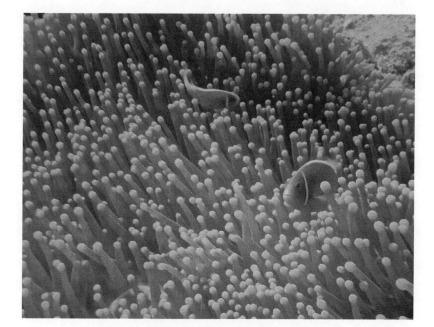

AUSTRALIA
DECEMBER 26TH, 2012

I'll never understand how drinking tequila instead of packing was a good idea. I snoozed my alarm three times before I realized I had a plane to catch. Luckily, packing was as easy as stuffing everything I currently owned into my backpack. Done.

As I sat in Honolulu, waiting for my flight to Brisbane, I realized all the things I had spent the past three weeks not doing. I never really made a plan for any of the places I wanted to go. I booked a few nights in Brisbane, and that was where I stopped for some reason. Planning just isn't my thing.

I only had one pair of pants for my travels, and I hadn't sewn the button back on.

I found the entire bunch of souvenirs I had smuggled home from Cuba still in the same hidden pocket. Now I would have to worry again when I came back. The cigars made it to their destination as a Christmas present, but if I had forgotten, I'm sure those would have been smoked well before I returned.

Minor things, but annoying.

BRISBANE

The flight was easy; it was only half-full, so everyone had a couple seats to sleep in. The food and drinks were nonstop since it was Christmas for such a short time. The movies sucked, which reminded me that I had forgotten to download new movies to my computer. I was constantly learning as I went.

Australia has the most involved quarantine of anywhere I had been to so far. After we landed, we had to sit in our seats while the crew sprayed the overhead luggage compartments and disinfected the plane itself. Following that was the longest line at immigration I had yet been in, and since it was a holiday, Boxing Day, only three people were working. The man was obviously annoyed at having to work; he stamped my passport right across France, Belize and Honduras as if I didn't have 10 blank pages.

The apartment I found through Airbnb was just outside of Brisbane, and it felt like I was in Portland. There were homey, tree-lined streets with sidewalks and cars parked on the sides of the road. Nothing like Kauai. Flowers were blooming everywhere, and the stores and restaurants were of the mom-and-pop variety. I nearly got mashed walking to the store for groceries; jet lag and cars coming at me on the wrong side of the road don't mix.

The one thing I was really curious about, being my first time in this hemisphere, was whether the toilets actually flushed in the opposite direction. The first thing I did was try. Maybe it was modern plumbing, but everything just went straight down; it was faintly disappointing. Maybe it's just an urban myth.

I was having trouble getting my head around what day it was. I left on Christmas morning, and later that same day it was the day after Christmas. I hoped it would make more sense after some sleep.

I started out my travels in Australia as a complete touron, someone on vacation who has left his or her brain at home. I just started hitting the main attractions. I walked to the nearest pier and jumped on the City Cat, the water transportation that connects Brisbane to the suburbs. The catamarans are giant blue boats that crisscross the Brisbane River, stopping at docks on both sides to pick up passengers. The more I saw of this city, the more I thought it was the Australian equivalent of Portland. It was a well-kept city with every mode of public transportation possible, most of it being environmentally friendly like the biking and walking paths that go everywhere, and super clean. Buses, rails, trains, boats, and everyone used them. There was hardly any traffic anywhere.

I rode the cat for 20 minutes to South Bank and walked to the City Botanic Gardens. They weren't a lot different from the gardens on Kauai. Across the river was downtown Brisbane, which contains 12 bridges, all of them pedestrian-friendly. I saw an advertisement for a bridge climb, but I thought I should save that for the giant bridge in Sydney Harbor when I planned to go there the following week.

The Queens Outdoor Mall was an incredible place for shopping, eating, or just people-watching. It took up several blocks in the middle of downtown, was several stories tall, and had nothing but shops and restaurants. Add in the street musicians and I could watch for hours. I generally dislike shopping, and had no need due to the limited space in my backpack, but I spent a good deal of time there. Apparently there was a fashion trend in Australia for women that comprised wearing shorts that button just under the boobs, but leave ass cheeks hanging out. It also looked like it was only for women whose ass cheeks you wouldn't be interested in looking at. I was definitely not shopping there, just in case.

For the most part, people seemed "metro;" every kind of city style was represented. It was easy to tell who was a tourist and who wasn't.

I found a bus called "City Sights" and hopped on. Its 19 stops covered all of Brisbane and the surrounding areas, and included a tour guide. I have never been a big fan of bus tours, but it was a great way to see everything in a couple hours and find places I might want to go back to. The coolest stop was the Mount Coot-tha Lookout. "Coot-tha" means "the place of wild honey" in the local Aboriginal dialect, and the site is 287 meters above sea level, the highest point in Queensland. It featured a restaurant, a café, and a lookout platform. I sat and ate ice cream.

Brisbane was possibly the cleanest place I have ever been. I don't think I saw a single piece of trash anywhere. The oldest buildings weren't very old – somewhere around the mid-1800s, so it might be the prettiest "modern" city I've been to as well. A lot of the older buildings have "convict built" signs, and all streets running parallel to Queen Street have girls' names; the perpendicular streets have boys' names.

After the city tour I walked back down to South Bank and rode the enormous Ferris wheel by the river. It wasn't entirely worth the money, but it was fun. Each of the cars was enclosed and air conditioned, and a tape-recorded guide pointed out the sites. The view was spectacular. I think I did all of the major touristy stuff in one day.

I spent the next day wandering through the suburbs and found a power yoga class that kicked my ass. I arrived early and watched all the women come in to warm up, and I was instantly appalled. They were all doing headstands and handstands and one-leg-over-their-head stands. I was hoping I could touch my toes. In Central America, I was a yoga rock star; I looked great working out with overweight vacationers trying it for the first time.

I started researching Sydney, and places to find sea dragons. I booked a condo near Sydney Harbor, ridiculously expensive since it was New Years and everything was already full. The hostels that had rooms required a 14-day stay over the holidays.

I found dive shops that advertised sea dragons, but again, nowhere to stay. What a bad idea, coming here with no plans.

There was no better way to grieve the death of my sea dragon dream than to hit the pubs. I tried the local beers and attempted conversation with the locals. It was a total failure. I couldn't get anyone to talk to me. I was the only woman in the bars I went to, and still, I couldn't get anyone to talk to me. A month ago I couldn't get guys to leave me alone. I found out a couple weeks later that pubs are mainly "a guy thing" in Oz. So culturally, I really was out of place.

Although I didn't like being ignored, one of the nice aspects of being in Australia was how I was treated. I didn't have men following me down the street telling me they loved me; it sounds ungrateful, but it really got annoying when they wouldn't leave me alone. I wasn't stared at everywhere I went. I could be anonymous for a little while, since I was only slightly taller than the average Australian, versus almost a foot taller than the average Central American. And no one called me "Blondie," even though my hair is clearly brown. I looked "normal" here. But I got bored with that soon enough; I've never been happy with melting into crowds.

I was glad to leave Brisbane for Sydney, where I could find all of the same activities, just bigger and better. I didn't much like my living arrangements; the ad on Airbnb wasn't truly honest. Sure, I had a nice, private room, but I wasn't told that I would have to share the house's one bathroom with eight other people. And my feet hung off the end of my bed; they must have bought it in Guatemala.

SYDNEY

The flight to Sydney was great; I loved flying on Virgin Australia. I shamelessly stole the window seat from a carbon copy of Ronald Weasley, and he was too polite to ask for it. Not only did I steal his seat, but when he told me he lived with his family in Sydney for a year I plied him with a thousand questions. My Lonely Planet Australia never showed up in the mail and I hated the Kindle version. I need to write in margins and dog-ear my pages.

The Weasley-looking boy was incredibly polite and happy to tell me about everywhere I should go, including how to get to my apartment by train. My host sent an email with directions: take the train, get off here, find the tram, get off here, take this number bus to here, then walk three blocks. No way could I figure that out any more than I can read Chinese. And the blue dot on my iPhone map wasn't working.

The train ride was quite nice, mostly underground until we approached the Opera House. From there I walked across a bridge, up a steep road, then got lost. I asked everyone I encountered where Cross Street was located and no one had heard of it. I wandered up and down the hill with my giant backpack, looking so out of place in what was obviously a yuppie sort of neighborhood. I finally broke down and turned on my phone to call the woman at the apartment, and she hadn't heard of any of the streets I was passing; all the money I saved by taking the train then walking a bit was given to AT&T. It probably would have been cheaper to take a taxi from the airport than talk on my phone.

Finally I stopped a Korean couple pushing a stroller, and the husband had a super high-tech map program on his phone; I was only a street away.

This wasn't a great start to my second experience renting a place from Airbnb, and it just got worse.

I found the apartment building and was let in by a woman who was also a guest. I was told by my "host" that I would share the apartment with her roommate, who would most likely be out of town for New Years. Not only was she home, but another family was staying with her, including a three-year-old boy who was running in and out of the rooms screaming and throwing things with his father chasing him, yelling his name over and over, and shouting, "Stop it!" and "Put that back!" incessantly. Since the family was staying there, they had the spare apartment key, and I got no key. The family finally went to the pool and I was by myself, trapped in a top-floor apartment with a fantastic view, like Rapunzel.

I tried to get the code for the Wi-Fi before they left, but no one could remember it. I was trapped with no means of communication. This was definitely strike two for Airbnb. At least I had my Snickers bar. I never travel without an emergency Snickers anymore.

I tried to nap and wait for the mess to get figured out, but that was ruined by the child camping outside my door and having a tantrum. They came back from the pool and I didn't even want to be social. I couldn't think of anything to say that wouldn't totally ruin their day. I still didn't have Wi-Fi to contact the owner; it was the middle of the night where she was, but I did get to meet the roommate. It turned out that the owner didn't tell her she was renting out her room for the holidays, so the roommate invited friends to stay. What a nightmare.

In the end, though, they fed me beer at the bar across the street and found the Wi-Fi password. I was happy again.

I met up with Pam's college friend Clare at the Opera House the next day. I had never met Clare before; I had to sit studying her Facebook picture and stare at the hundreds of people nearby. When I finally recognized her, we didn't go into the Opera House; instead we sat at the bar outside. It was the most crowded bar I've ever seen, and probably the biggest. There must have been 15 bartenders. The tables stretched for what seemed like a quarter-mile along the harbor, all of them full, and it was nearly impossible to get a drink. When I did, I spent $18 on one. I was definitely not in a third-world country anymore.

Clare showed me around the trendy suburbs of Sydney, and we went to several pubs. For dinner I ate kangaroo in a Jack Daniels sauce with mashed potatoes. I was told kangaroo is an eco-friendly, sustainable meat and thought I'd give it a try. It was really good, yet it made me feel sad, like I ate a koala bear. Several weeks later I told my Australian friend Kawika, and his response was, "I don't go to your country and eat bald eagles."

I found the IMAX Theater at the harbor, the biggest in the world, with a seven-story screen – playing the crappiest movies. I wanted to see something on a screen that massive, but for $31, I passed. Maybe if I came back this way before I left the country.

New Year's Eve was a giant riot of Australians setting up their barbies on every square inch of grass in the parks. It was an all-day drunken celebration. If there is one thing that stuck with me from my time in Australia, it's that Aussies know how to party.

My time in Sydney was short, thankfully, as I was ready to get to the Great Barrier Reef, so I did another city tour on a bus. I saw all the sights and picked out my spot to watch the fireworks. Seeing the fireworks from the Sydney Harbor Bridge was on my giant list of things to do before I die, and it was worth the hassle of being in a city on a major holiday. I walked to the park and joined thousands of other people at 9 p.m. for the children's show. It was good, but the real deal is always at midnight. I spent the next three hours wandering around, meeting new people and having a few drinks. Midnight came and the fireworks were spectacular, the best show I'd ever seen; it was so much better than watching it on TV.

When I returned to the apartment, empty now of all the people, I sat and thought about what an amazing year 2012 had been. I explored seven new countries, met a lot of new friends, learned a language, hiked, climbed and dove some crazy places, ate weird things, paddled the Molokai solo race, and made great memories. The year hadn't been without its loneliness, and I did turn 40, but overall it balanced out to the good.

I signed up for the Sydney Harbor Bridge climb on my last day in the city. I arrived and was assigned to a group of 14. They start each group five minutes apart so everyone needed to keep with the program. We filled out forms in case we died and blew into a breathalyzer. The next room was jumpsuit fitting, then a belt and safety leash, and onto the practice stairs to find out what it's like and to try using the safety equipment. Next was supplies, hats, croakies, handkerchiefs, jackets for the cold air at the top, then finally radios so we could hear our guide throughout the climb, and everything was neatly clipped to our belts. Every station had all the supplies in the exact order that we needed them; all the equipment was perfectly maintained. It was a great setup. They marched us through this with a very practiced, assembly-line efficiency. If a group of 14 leaves every five minutes, starting with the sunrise climbs and ending with sunset climbs and night climbs, there might be 2,000 people per day. If not for what I imagine are insanely high insurance rates, someone is making a fortune. I paid $250, more than the rest of my Sydney budget, but I had to do it. To be honest, the small amount of time that I had been in Australia had eaten away a giant portion of my travel money anyway. It's an expensive country.

No cameras were allowed for safety reasons, but I thought I would be able to sneak my camera on the climb. I don't go anywhere without a camera. Ever. I had it all figured out, exactly how I'd attach it inside my jump suit, then be the last in line and furthest away from the guide. And then we were marched through two metal detectors. Fail.

The climb itself wasn't very challenging; there were two sets of steps on the way up, then mostly just catwalks or gradual stairs. At one point we popped up between lanes of traffic on the bridge and that was fun, and on the way down I was walking between two trains.

The entire time I had a safety leash attached to a steel cord that ran the entire length of the bridge. I hooked on at the very beginning and there was no way to unattach, which I tried as well. The safety cord had anchors into the bridge steel every few feet and the leash end was a big ball with teeth; it went past each anchor without disengaging. I'd never seen anything like it and I was fascinated by how it worked.

The climb started slightly above ground level and the first planks to walk were right above the cars on the highway. A set of stairs took us to the upper-level planks where we were at the height of the Opera House and a few other taller buildings. The second set of stairs took us to the highest arch of the bridge, where we walked along the very top, level with almost all of the tallest buildings in the city. Except for the wind howling at what felt like 800 miles an hour at the top, it always felt safe.

Our guide stopped us every few feet to talk about bridge construction and people who died, and to point out landmarks. We saw the giant yellow rubber duck in the harbor; the guide didn't know why it was there, but it must have been two stories tall. What a great boat.

I found out later that the duck wasn't actually a boat, but a giant inflatable piece of art. It had been touring the world and gained an enormous following, while also being stabbed and deflated a few times. I was lucky to see it in Sydney, luckier still to see it from atop the bridge.

We took turns at the very apex for pictures. Our guide had a camera, and of course, we were welcome to buy the pictures for a stupid amount of money. Which I did. Then we crossed the top of the arch and walked down the other side. When we returned, we were marched through the stations in reverse order, returning all of our equipment and clothing.

Although the tour was pricey, it was worth it. And I had to do it. In total the trip was 3.5 hours, and well over half of that was on the bridge. I walked close to 1,400 steps round trip. A good day. I wished I had had the money to do it at night as well.

CAIRNS

I flew to Cairns, and it cost me almost double what I paid to get to Australia in the first place. That's what I get for not planning holiday travel, I guess. More and more of the Australia expense was going directly to my credit card by now. That was the beginning of the end of my trip, watching my money drain away. But I couldn't leave yet; I had to scuba dive.

Cairns wasn't a place I'd visit again unless I had a lot more money. I couldn't figure out how it was a backpacker's destination since all the hostels I looked at cost as much as my hotel room, minus the free Wi-Fi. I had noticed in my two weeks that Australia has very little free Wi-Fi anywhere. Some pubs have an hour pass if you buy something, and most hotels charge a fee. Just like cricket, I couldn't figure it out, and couldn't get anyone to explain it properly. At least Central America pretended to have free Wi-Fi everywhere.

The first thing I did in Cairns was find a dive shop and plan a day at the reef.

Diving on the Great Barrier Reef was in my top-five travel goals, and it was both fantastic and slightly disappointing. It was only a let-down because it cost way more money than Cozumel or

Ambergris or Roatan, but wasn't proportionally better. But that didn't stop me from enjoying it.

I walked to the dock early in the morning and was the first to arrive at the boat, as usual. It was a giant dive boat. I was told to show up a little early if I didn't want to stand in line for check-in, and I was so happy that I did; at least a hundred people had booked this dive, and I was sitting in the air conditioning drinking coffee for an hour by the time we were ready to leave the dock. The trip to the outer reef was an hour and a half, and we spent the time in safety briefings and were split into groups: certified divers, people taking the dive course, and snorkelers. Of the 100 people on the boat, only about 20 were certified, which surprised me.

We had a choice to go with a buddy or as a guided group for an extra $15 each per dive. I had already paid $180 for the three dives, but since I had no idea where we were I chose the guided group for the first one. There were only six of us, not too crowded for a group. When it was finally time to get geared up we went aft, where seasick people were sprawled all over the deck. The crew had to move them out of the way, and one poor guy had to be carried; he was so seasick that he didn't make it off the boat the entire day – he just puked until there wasn't anything left and passed out under a bench for hours. I'm so glad I don't get seasick.

The first dive was good. A giant Napoleon Wrasse, Wally, lives near the mooring and the photographer set up shop there for all of the people who wanted pictures with him. The fish was bigger than me and acted like a puppy. We weren't allowed to touch him, but the crew would grab him by the nose and guide him into the tourist pictures.

I saw the first shark in less than five minutes, a white-tip reef shark just cruising by. I saw tons of fish of every kind, corals, fans, everything I had dreamed of seeing. When I was back on Kauai for my sort-of-Christmas I had borrowed Mark's underwater camera. I got a few minutes of pictures before I saw a couple tiny beads of water creep into the housing. Crap. It started fogging, then a little more water, and I was so sure that it was sealed before I got in. I owed Mark a new camera, and I didn't even get a picture of Wally.

We had a couple out-of-control divers in our group to whom the guide had to continually pay attention, and when they were out of air he sent them to the surface while we continued. It was a much better policy than in other places.

We got back on board the boat just long enough to get our tanks refilled, drink some water, and decide if we wanted another group or a buddy. I chose buddy this time and was teamed with a guy and a girl. This was my first-ever unguided dive. I told them I wasn't a good navigator, that I couldn't make my way through a town even with a perfect grid pattern of streets. The guy didn't want to lead, and the girl weaseled out by not saying a word and refusing to look at us. By default, I became the group leader. Great plan. I decided I liked it, though, because it meant I could do whatever I wanted and they were just going to follow. And if we ended up a mile from the boat, I wouldn't mind the swim back. The crew had a great system of making sure that no one got left behind, a list with names and the number of dives or snorkels everyone was doing, and when I stepped on board I was instantly made to sign my name showing that I had returned. They did this after every dive, so regardless of how long it took us to get back, they wouldn't leave us out there. That gave me confidence.

On the first dive we headed out with the wall on our right; this time I went left. It was so strange to be out there by myself in the enormous space of the ocean. I felt like I was alone because we never saw anyone else and my buddies stayed behind me. It took me a while to believe they actually let people find their own way out here, especially me.

It was another good dive; we saw more great stuff, I checked on my buddies. When I tried to get some directional input the guy just shrugged and the girl wouldn't answer. I just kept going, hoping they at least had the sense to tell me when they were low on air. I turned us around a few minutes shy of our halfway time and realized that we had swum out with the current. Oops. A lesson to file away for future use. We swam back, slightly shallower, and I quit paying attention to my buddies except to note that they were still behind me. After a while, I started wondering where the boat might be. They didn't exactly park it squarely at the end of the reef. A few more minutes passed, no boat. I turned to ask the guy if he had any idea where the boat might be, he shrugged, no help at all. A couple minutes later it was time to do a safety stop and surface wherever we were and Wally swam up, welcoming us back to the boat. I was so happy to see that big fish.

It was lunchtime when I got back on the boat and I headed to the wheelhouse to eat. I sat with a Swedish woman who was also alone and we started chatting. She asked if I would be her buddy for the last dive, and I found out that she had just gotten certified 20 minutes ago. Hell no. I'm not the best diver in the world, but Queensland's rule is that no one can dive solo. When she ran out of air I'd have to surface as well, and this trip was too expensive to miss out on the last 15 minutes. I know it sounds ungracious, but she should have been diving in a guided group. What I dislike the most about diving is having to surface when I still have half a tank of air left, either because someone in the group is messing around and wasting air, or they're crappy diver, or new divers who are nervous.

Two crew members were sitting nearby and stopped talking just to listen to me squirm my way out of being her buddy, big grins on their faces. I carefully explained why she wouldn't want to dive with me. Overall, it was a super-awkward moment.

She gracefully accepted my decline, the boat moved to a new reef, and I was paired with the same guy as before. Thankfully, the girl was nowhere to be seen. The crew showed us a picture of the reef and told us which way we should head; it seemed pretty easy. I came up with a more comprehensive plan than on our first dive together. We agreed, and off we went. Find the wall, take a left, swim to 150 bar, turn around, swim back and explore the bay where the boat is moored until we're out of time. I thought it was a great plan.

It didn't turn out to be quite so easy, though. Finding the wall was the first problem. We swam over dozens of small reefs trying to find depth; we spent nearly 10 minutes at 5 meters, and I was already lost. The familiar panic set in early. I talked myself down, simply because when we surface so far out in the ocean, we couldn't get too confused. There was one giant boat and miles and miles of nothing else. So screw it, I would enjoy the dive and worry later if necessary. Eventually we found the wall, another shark, squid, huge pineapple sea cucumbers and giant clams that must have been three feet wide. I wish I hadn't destroyed Mark's camera.

I turned us around fairly soon so we could find the bay again. We didn't have compasses, which I did think of during our first solo dive, but I was too excited to remember to ask for one. We swam and swam and I knew we weren't going to surface anywhere near the boat. But again, who cares? I didn't bother to ask the guy's opinion, and I found out later he couldn't even work his dive computer, which only needed one button pressed to work. He did both dives completely blind, without depth or elapsed time; he just did what I did.

I tried to take mental notes of the time swimming in each direction, but when I saw something cool swim by I just forgot. We only had five minutes left until our safety stop and I turned to my buddy to let him know that I was completely lost. He shrugged. I kept going, determined to use every last moment to see everything I could, and just as I was signaling my buddy to start going up, I saw the boat. I had no idea how I found it again, and I was laughing underwater. Turns out that I'm a super navigator. Who would've guessed?

Cairns is a strange town – giant hotels, trendy shopping and travel agencies, and white-tablecloth restaurants. If you didn't know where you were you might not even guess it was Australia; there was nothing local about it.

I did try one upscale restaurant, but not really by choice. The Swedish woman I had met on the dive boat invited me out to dinner with a couple of her friends. They found an Australian fusion restaurant in their Lonely Planet. With my first glance at the menu, I wished I hadn't joined them; nothing was in my price range. But my companions were two Swedish engineers and a lawyer from DC, all with substantial incomes. The food was not amazing, as nothing really had been since Mexico, and it killed about a week's food budget. The word budget didn't even apply at this point.

Feeling sort of chubby again, I found a gym with an $8 daily fee as long as I went during the off hours, so I tried more power yoga. It was great in Brisbane and I was hoping it was the same here. The moment the instructor walked in with a headset in knew I would regret coming. Booty Camp, spinning, TRX, yes, scream at me over a loudspeaker, but not yoga. The class was full of people with New Year's resolutions. Instead of power yoga it turned out to be some sort of horrible combination of yoga and calisthenics. But for only $8, I wasn't too upset.

Cairns has a healthy population of bats and crazy birds. At dusk I walked through the center of town and watched thousands of bats waking up and terrorizing people with phobias. The entire sky was filled with them, and during the day I could see them hanging upside down from their tree limbs. I'm not sure if it was them, but I didn't get a single mosquito bite during my stay. The next night I watched the bats from the balcony of my hotel, flying off to the mountain range to feed. There was at least a mile of them, and more were still waking up and fluttering around the park. It was definitely on the list of coolest things I'd ever seen.

The biggest disappointment of Cairns was that I lived a few feet from the ocean but there was nowhere to swim. The water was only a foot or so deep for quite a ways out; birds were wading and picking at things in the mud. The esplanade along the coast was plastered with "Beware of Crocodile" signs. I kept looking but never saw one.

I spent some time working on my travel plans for the next few weeks. I found out Shanti and her family were vacationing in Cambodia and Thailand in a few weeks, and I couldn't pass up the chance to travel with a pro. I was hoping to learn something. I booked a live-aboard boat, another thing on my list, and some time in Port Douglas, and made travel arrangements to meet Kawika in Coolangatta. After that I had two weeks to amuse myself before Southeast Asia. Kawika has rooms full of surf boards, so it wouldn't be too hard to find something to do.

While waiting for my live-aboard trip, I jumped on another dive boat much like the first, spending an hour and a half with 100 other people to get to the outer reefs for three dives. The main difference was the wind; it was howling and the ocean swells were big, making the boat rock and roll and crash down over the waves. More than half the passengers were throwing up at some point, and many refused to leave the inside cabin when the crew tried to get them outside into the fresh air. One woman near me barfed and cried the entire way with her eyes closed, and no one could get her to move. If I could make it through those conditions while smelling and listening to people vomit and not get sick myself, I never will.

I went with the same company but still had to fill out all the same paperwork about experience and medical conditions and such. All the certified divers were grouped together, again only about 20 of us. One English woman with a high-pitched, whiny voice had dozens of questions for the crew. One of the questions in the paperwork was "Have you ever dived in the ocean?" and she immediately flagged down a crewman and asked, "Which ocean? This ocean? What if I've dived in a different ocean? Does that count? Are all the oceans the same? I did dive in one but maybe it doesn't count?" She had endless questions about the basic paperwork and the crewman sat down, realizing that he wasn't going to get away from her any time soon. I was sitting with a Canadian woman, Tamara, and we were practically rolling on the floor laughing.

When we arrived at the dive site, the certified divers were called back to gear up and my gear was set up next to the crazy woman's. She had trouble with her regulator, but not really, and called several crew members over to look at it. They all said it was fine, but she demanded that someone switch it out. Then we were seated, strapped onto our tanks and ready to go, when the boat ran over and severed the mooring line, which meant we had another 15 minutes to sit in full gear while they fixed it. Crazy woman started making small talk with me. "Have you dived here before?"

"Yes."

"Is this ocean salty?"

"Um, I think that's what defines an ocean, there's salt in the water."

"But is it really salty?"

"I don't know how to answer that."

"I'm asking because I'm really thirsty."

At that moment I knew that she would be assigned as my dive buddy. It was my fate.

Crazy did ask me to be her buddy while we were waiting for the mooring line to be fixed. I tried to weasel out like before, crossed my fingers, and told her that we get assigned and couldn't choose. I wished I had asked Tamara but completely forgot, and we were strapped into our tanks far away from each other. And, as luck would have it, I got Crazy for a buddy. I'm sure the crew was chuckling about being rid of her for a while. It was a group dive, but she was still my responsibility.

It was time and we finally jumped in. The first thing Crazy did was swim over and grab my arm; the dive hadn't even started and I was already annoyed. I did my best with hand signals to let her know that at no time was she welcome to touch me, and I headed to the bottom. In the minute it took to get there I received six OK signals from her.

I like to dive with a little space, so if people are crowded around the guide I'll hang back, or if people are doing their own thing I'll go up front, just as long as I can see what I want and not bump into people. Crazy never got more than two feet away from me at any point; no matter how hard I tried to make some room she would swim over and touch me. Every time I looked up to see what was touching me, I'd see her flash the OK sign. I wanted to give her the finger but thought that might be a bit much. She went so far as to swim up to my head and throw an OK sign in front of my mask. I wanted to turn off her tank.

I'm not a bad dive buddy, but partners need to check on each other only so much. I was always aware of where she was, even when she wasn't touching me; I looked back many times since she refused to swim in front of me, and she always seemed fine. That, in my opinion, is what was required of me.

There was a lot of great sea life on the dive, but my annoyance level was pretty high and I didn't enjoy everything as much as I could have. Forty minutes of OK signals.

We were back on the boat for our surface interval, getting our tanks refilled and our gear ready. I only wore a skin suit for the first dive and was kind of cold, so I was trying to find a half wetsuit to wear as well. Crazy sat down and started to lecture me on the proper way to be a good dive buddy. She didn't think I was doing my job.

"I'd appreciate it if you'd give me the OK sign more often when we're under water." I think I had given her one for the entire first dive. I let her know that I always knew where she was and she looked fine and I didn't feel the need for constant OK signs.

"How do you know I'm OK if I don't give you an OK sign?"

"Well, you're swimming along normally and looking at stuff and look pretty OK so I don't feel I need to ask."

"But how will I know if you're OK if you don't tell me you're OK?"

"Well, if I'm swimming normally and looking at stuff and I look OK then you should just assume that I'm OK too."

"You need to give me more OK signs on the next dive, I need to know that you're OK."

I had to turn and start talking to the woman on the other side of me because I was afraid I was going to hit Crazy.

We jumped in for the second dive and immediately I had my shadow throwing OK signs at me. I refused to give her even one for the entire dive; I get a little stubborn when I'm annoyed. I looked back at Crazy several times; I did my job. But this time I concentrated on the reef and all the wild things living down there and ignored her as much as possible. There were squid, white-tip reef sharks, turtles, rays, unicorn fish, another giant Napoleon wrasse, and huge groupers; completely excellent.

We had about seven minutes left to dive when I felt Crazy grab my leg and pull me backwards. That's fucking enough, time to turn off her tank for real. Her ear felt funny, she signaled, and I didn't give a shit. I got the guide's attention and signaled that my buddy was sick, then swam away in hopes that he'd send her to the surface. But she wasn't sick, there wasn't anything wrong with her ear, she just wanted attention, and after several more OK signals we resumed our dive.

During our lunch break I made it very clear that she was not to speak to me again.

The third dive was spectacular; I started it off by getting attacked by a good-sized triggerfish. It was mating season for them and they actually build nests and defend them ferociously. It would have been nice if the crew had warned us, since they dive at the same mooring every day. I was descending, minding my own business, when a big fish with pointy teeth charged at me. It was more funny than scary because trigger fish are so cute, but he wouldn't leave me alone. I tried to swim away but he kept nipping at me, and I could see Crazy having a minor underwater heart attack from the exertion of all the OK signals she was throwing at me, which I ignored.

Most surprisingly, though, on the third dive she mostly left me alone. I looked back for her here and there and she had given me several feet of personal space. Aaah. And when we surfaced, I never had to see her again.

I had one last day to kill before the live-aboard trip and I used it to take a rainforest and waterfall tour outside of Cairns, in the Atherton Tablelands. Specifically, we went to a highland tropical complex mesophyll rainforest. Even if I didn't need a map, I carried my waterproofed iPhone everywhere to take notes, or I would never have remembered that. And even knowing the proper name, I still couldn't clearly explain why the rainforest had that classification.

It wasn't a real intense tour – I got on a bus and drove a couple hours, walked on a path for 500 meters looking at plants, got back on the bus and drove a few minutes, walked 20 feet to a waterfall to swim, rode on the bus for five more minutes, looked for platypuses and drove home. It was a 12-hour trip, but nothing physically exerting happened at any point. Just a long day. Nice, but long.

My tour group was extremely diverse; there were people from Holland, Bangladesh, Italy, Brazil, Israel, Austria and Australia. It was fun to be the only American, although that didn't stop the American jokes – it just meant I got more attention, which I kind of liked.

The highlight of the first rainforest was the Cathedral Fig Tree. The original tree has long since been covered by other tree roots; all I could see was hundreds of smaller trees' roots, smaller meaning several stories high, then a trunk way up in the air, then leaves. It was a massive bunch of trees all grown together. I was amazed there were no mosquitos in the forest. I had blamed that earlier on the huge quantities of bats that live in Cairns, but I learned that they are strictly fruit eaters. And more correctly, they are Spectacled Flying Foxes. I never figured out exactly why there were no mosquitos anywhere.

Our guide was Bart and he loved to find us bizarre insects, not so much to show us cool things, but to scare the girls. We got to play with a Rhinoceros Beetle and leeches. Bart named every insect he found "Eric." After the second rainforest walk we were sitting in a park at Lake Barrine for lunch when Ashish, from Bangladesh, discovered that he had picked up a leech somewhere along the way. Not surprising, since we had all been playing with them earlier. It was between his toes and roughly 20 times the size of the ones we were messing with. After much fussing, Bart finally scraped it off his foot, blood gushed everywhere, and lunch was served.

Bart was also the first person in a long time with whom I could talk about American football. I hadn't been able to find football on TV since Honduras, so he gave me some play-by-plays of a few important games.

The first waterfall we visited was Milaa Milaa Falls, the most photographed waterfall in Australia, mainly because you could drive right up to it. The water was an icky brown color and icy cold, but we swam anyway. The cascade wasn't much more than a trickle, as it was near the end of the dry season. We swam behind the falls and took tons of pictures. I gave Marcio my camera and posed on some slimy, slippery rocks, which I then slipped off of, giving myself a giant bruise that covered my entire left thigh.

Milaa Milaa was the site of a famous shampoo commercial – to Australians, at least, because I haven't been able to locate it online – where a woman in the pool does a "hair flip." She has her hair in the water in front of her with her head bent forward, then flips her head backward making an arc of hair and water that makes for good pictures if you can do it right. We all tried it, and not just the girls. I just didn't have enough hair to make it work.

We went to another waterfall and climbed on rocks; I jumped from stupid places because I was with a bunch of 20-year-old guys and it looked like fun. The last stop of the day was at a river where platypuses were known to feed. We waited in total silence so we didn't scare them away, and finally saw a couple from a distance. They were much smaller than I had imagined, and way cuter.

On the way home a group of us made a plan to meet up and have drinks later that night. Marcio, from Brazil, knew Cairns nightlife best and took us to a bar he liked; it was loud and they encouraged everyone to dance on the tables. After that was the wet t-shirt contest. That's what you get when you follow a 20-year-old Brazilian guy to a bar.

It was finally time for the live-aboard trip. I originally intended to go out as soon as I got to Cairns, but because of the holidays, I had to wait a few days for an opening. The morning came and I was picked up and taken to the boat, another massive boat but with only 30 people aboard. After the worst-ever dive buddy experience, I was fairly nervous that I'd get stuck with someone I didn't like for all three days. I made small talk with random people for a bit, then a pretty cute boy sat next to me;

I took that as a good omen. We got our room assignments and I had to share a bunk with Iseta, a black Australian woman a few years older than me. She was perfect.

One constant in Australia was the vast number of Nordic people – Swedish, Norwegian, Danish – and close to half the population of the boat was from those countries. Cute boy Colin and I were the only Americans.

The initial trip to the reef was three hours, and we spent the time getting briefed on the plans, watching a safety video, and getting to know the people we were stuck with for three solid days. Very quickly, we separated into the small groups we would spend all of our time with, and I loved my group. I was with Colin, Darryl and Angela from Australia; Chiu-ki from Korea and her husband, Francesco, from France; Iseta; Linn and Annelin from Norway; South African Kerry and Swedish Lea. The crew members I spent the most time with were Veronica from Sweden, Warren, another South African; and Aric from Poland. The diversity was great, one of my favorite things about travel. We sometimes just referred to each other as the country we were from, and since I had spilled coffee everywhere in the first five minutes I was on the boat, Warren called me "Hawaiian Trouble." That became my name to the crew for the rest of the trip, even though I explained that I wasn't Hawaiian. But I tried my best to live up to it anyway.

We did four dives on the first day and they were amazing – white-tip reef sharks, rays, eels, anemone fish, giant clams, all the same stuff from previous dives, but in huge quantities. On the first dive I buddied with Iseta, but after that she started taking her advanced open water course and I couldn't dive with her again. For the second dive I buddied with Chiu-ki and Francesco, and at the last minute we grabbed Veronica, the crew member, since she had an hour free. Veronica and I ended up ditching the other two; Francesco was taking pictures and our forward movement was way too slow. The best part was that Veronica was the ship's cook, and after being her buddy she started making me my own private dishes that were onion-free, eventually making most of the menu that way. I hate onions.

I couldn't remember the last time I'd eaten that well. On the first day it seemed like all we did was dive and eat. Diving takes so much energy, and Veronica cooked up more food than could possibly have been eaten by twice as many people as we had aboard. If it wasn't meal time there was cake, fruit, cookies, and other snacks, but the meals were beyond expectation.

On the third dive I didn't want to go with the slow picture-takers again and asked Colin and Darryl if I could jump in with them. Darryl's main purpose of the trip was to swim with turtles. I had seen turtles on both previous dives, so he was happy to have me along as his turtle whisperer. He hadn't seen one yet.

For some reason, for every dive I'd done in Australia I ended up being the leader and navigator. I don't know why this happened since I have the worst navigation skills on the planet, but people were always happy to follow me. To my great surprise, I found that I was an underwater navigational goddess. I always found the boat again, even when I thought I was lost, which was most of the time. I'm still having a hard time reconciling this idea. Colin and Darryl were happy to let me lead.

Our first night dive was great – sharks everywhere, both white-tips and greys; we found a spotted leopard shark hiding in a cave. Starfish and shrimp were lurking in odd places. Navigating at night was easy, because all the boat lights were turned on and it glowed underwater.

The stars at night over the Great Barrier Reef were phenomenal; not a cloud in the sky and no lights in sight. I sat and wrote my blog, and was amazed that the boat had better Wi-Fi than all the hotels in the country.

Sleeping on the boat was a challenge for me. Sleep problems plagued my entire trip; every night I woke up several times wondering where I was, but the boat was hard. I didn't mind the rocking, but Iseta's and my cabin was near the loud generator, the air conditioning wasn't working so it was hot, and my bunk was about a foot shorter than I needed. I tried sleeping sideways, but the wooden bed frame dug into my legs. Iseta preferred our door open for some cooler air, but we couldn't figure out how to turn out the hall lights. Hot, bright, and a short bed; I slept about three hours on the first night.

We saw more great stuff on the first dive of the second day. I was with Colin and Darryl again, leading our group. Half an hour into the dive I was checking on everyone's air and Darryl told me that he was at about half, so I planned a meandering trail that would give us 15 minutes to get back to the boat. Super navigator. Obviously, though, I am not a super leader, because Darryl actually told me he was low on air and I didn't get it. I was leisurely wandering through some corals when he grabbed me and told me he only had 50 bar left, and we were 10 minutes from the boat. Oops. I still had over 100 bar so I wasn't worried about anyone dying; we could share if necessary. We made it back to the boat and they told Darryl's wife, Angela, to watch out, I was trying to kill him. I wondered if she had insurance, and whether she really loved him. Maybe we could work out a deal. We still hadn't found Darryl a turtle.

Colin and Darryl had been my buddies all day, but for some reason Darryl ditched us, possibly because he didn't want to die. He went with Annelin and Linn; they were more his speed in terms of air consumption, and Annelin wanted to see a turtle more than anything, too, and hadn't yet seen one either.

The second dive was fantastic. I'm afraid I don't have enough adjectives to describe diving The Great Barrier Reef. Great. Fantastic. Breathtaking. Spectacular. Still not enough.

Colin and I saw schools of sweetlips, bump-headed parrotfish, and rays. I was continually amazed that I could get dumped into an ocean with one other person, zigzag through coral formations, get sidetracked by animal-watching, and still find the boat when I needed to. I think I was beginning to develop an ego, and that's usually when everything goes wrong.

On the third dive, Colin and I set out to find a spot called "Clown Fish City." The plan seemed easy. Descend, find the mooring blocks, swim at 150 degrees through a couple giant rocks where turtles might be hanging out, then find a trio of huge coral formations called "Mickey Mouse," and right there we should find all of the anemone fish. Then we should continue to the wall, put it on our right shoulders and make a square back to the boat, returning at 300 degrees. No problem.

Even with an hour of discussion after the dive, we never quite figured out where we went wrong.

Part of the problem was that I brought my camera. Being the third dive of the day, we stayed fairly shallow, and my regular camera can go about 10 meters down and still function. I started off the dive by not paying close attention; there were pictures to be taken. Colin went swimming off after a turtle, and I didn't make a note of our new direction. We never found "Mickey Mouse" or "Clown Fish City," but we couldn't understand how exactly we had gotten so far off course. The only explanation that really makes sense is that we swam through a wardrobe to

Narnia. When we tried to intuitively make our way back we found ourselves in deep, deep water with no corals or other life in sight. At that point, we surfaced for visual confirmation and set our course back at 60 degrees, instead of 300, and the boat was about 400 yards away. That was the first time I was nervous while diving – no fish, no corals, just Colin and I in the deep, dark blue. It was a scene out of a horror movie. The spotters on the boat saw us surface, and when we finally made it back we were subjected to every diving joke imaginable. Everyone heard about our dive, and it was nonstop laughing at our expense for the rest of the trip.

Standing on the top deck afterward, we could see the entire reef in light greens and light blues, very close to the boat, and it didn't look like there was any way we could have taken a wrong turn. There must have been one single opening that we swam through to get to the other side of the reef, then we went the complete wrong direction.

After dinner we did another night dive, everyone on the boat reminding me that I should swim back to the boat lights, not the one light we could see miles and miles away. Ha-ha. But that didn't stop four other people from asking if they could join my group. Colin and I were the cool kids now.

We descended and instantly saw a dozen sharks circling under us; it was an intimidating sight at night. The highlight of that dive was the biggest turtle I've ever seen, who slept in a cave nearby. He was easily the size of a small car. Unfortunately, Darryl didn't rejoin our group and he never saw the turtle. And I didn't get lost.

Meanwhile, Iseta had gotten her advanced open water certification during the day and we celebrated with the bottle of vodka I had brought. We found some juice boxes onboard for the mixer and our group had a party. I thought that might help me sleep on the second night, but I was wrong. The crew had tried to fix the air conditioning in our room but couldn't get it to work; instead they cranked up the air and everyone else was freezing. It didn't help us. I ended up sleeping in the salon for about four hours before Veronica had to start preparing breakfast.

The final day of the trip consisted of three dives at Coral Gardens, and again I just don't have enough adjectives to describe how beautiful it was. Colin and I had great dives, and once again my navigation was perfect. Darryl had left Annelin and Linn's group because they hadn't found a turtle, and it was exactly as expected: the girls spent 20 minutes swimming with a turtle and Darryl's new group never found one. In the end, Darryl was the only person on the boat who hadn't seen a turtle, and I was happy that everyone could focus on him for the jokes instead of me.

Linn and I spent most of the trip home in the wheelhouse; she wanted to steer the boat. We had a last briefing before we got to port and the crew made plans to meet everyone at a bar for dinner and drinks. Aric drew up a navigational chart to the bar with directions in degrees just for Colin and me.

After our dinner and drinks I heard that there was a foosball table nearby, and we all headed that way. There was no foosball, but more wet t-shirt contests. Seemed like an appropriate way to end my time in Cairns.

PORT DOUGLAS

I caught a shuttle to Port Douglas, and the first thing I did was nap. Three days of diving with very little sleep made me miss almost my entire first day in the new town. I had gathered information about a six-man canoe team at the yacht club and I slept right through their practice. When I finally woke up I had barely enough time to walk through the town to get groceries.

Port Douglas is a beautiful town, and about as different from Cairns as could be imagined. It's quiet and residential, with miles and miles of perfect-looking beaches. There is no swimming allowed, but the beaches are there. The closest beach I found was 4-Mile Beach; it had a tiny area roped off with netting for swimming, and the rest of the miles had warning signs for crocodiles, sharks and jellyfish. I missed Hawaii.

One aspect of Australia I really respected was how environmentally conscious the country seemed to be – recycling bins, free outdoor exercise equipment at all the parks, local foods, signs everywhere educating me about the land and reefs and animals. I had a kitchen in my new room and I went to Cole's for supplies. The egg counter contained all sorts of expensive free-range eggs, and one tiny section of cheaper ones with the giant letters "CAGED" stamped on them. I was guilt-tripped into breaking my food budget yet again.

I had one day to plan before my diving friend Iseta returned to Port Douglas, where she lives, so I booked a final dive trip to the Great Barrier Reef with Poseidon Divers. I couldn't help but want to see it one last time.

The dives on the reef were further north than where I dove from Cairns. In retrospect I shouldn't have gone; the dives from the live-aboard were so amazing I should have stopped there. I spent an additional $250 on three dives and it wasn't worth it at all. The reef wasn't as alive, the visibility was much lower, and the crew was a bit weird.

Poseidon's crew operated with the idea that no one knows anything and should be treated as children doing their first dive. I'm sure a lot of people loved that; I asked around and the majority of people hadn't been on a dive in more than a year, or several years, so it was a good refresher for them. But after 80 dives in the past eight months, I had to sit through an hour-long briefing of "This is a BCD, this is a regulator, it goes in your mouth." It drove me crazy. I guess I'm a dive snob now. For nearly all of the 80 dives I had done, which is still a small number compared to people who have been diving for years, I had been completely in charge of all of my own equipment and I didn't want anyone messing with my gear, and I certainly didn't want to sit through the basics of an open-water course on an uncomfortable boat deck.

Every time I had my gear set up and ready, a crew member would come by and adjust something I had just set to how I liked it. I spent the day continually readjusting every piece of equipment. The worst was after the first dive. I was coming up to the boat; my normal procedure is to surface about 10 feet away, float and look around, relax and enjoy the scenery for a minute or two before I got out of the water. As I surfaced, I felt hands grab me, deflate my BCD and pull me under, so of course I started fighting. Apparently when I zoned out during our briefing, we were told to approach the ladder underwater, hang on, and the dive master would peel off our fins so we can climb up. I had never encountered anything like that before, and I thought these people needed to keep their hands off me; I am quite capable of taking off my own fins. Again, most people probably loved this, an extra step from an overly motherly crew, but I wanted nothing to do with it. I fought my dive master as he was trying to drag me back underwater to the ladder; I hadn't realized what was happening yet, and my brain went into fight or flight, I guess. My reaction was a bit more intense than he expected, but no permanent damage was done.

After I was back on board I had a talk with my dive master, a too-cheerful French guy. I asked him if I could be exempt from the normal boarding procedure; he agreed, and in turn had to tell every other crew member that on the next dive one person would be surfacing away from the boat, don't be alarmed. Everyone looked at me funny.

The next dive ended and there was a lineup underwater for the ladder. I surfaced about 10 feet away to float. Instantly the crew on board was frantic that something was wrong, even though I was giving them the giant full-arm OK signal. I was afraid someone was going to jump in to rescue me. When all of the divers were on board I swam to the ladder, but didn't realize my dive master was still waiting underwater for me. As I approached I felt him grab my legs and start pulling off my fins. I don't know why this bothered me so much.

After the third dive I surfaced in my spot, floated, reassured the onboard crew that I was neither drowning nor in need of any help, and watched my dive master underwater at the ladder. The rest of the divers were on the boat and he was waiting for me. Just once I was going to take off my own fins. There's that stubbornness again. I tried to wait him out, but he was watching me. He had a lot of paperwork to do on the boat so I thought he'd just go away. He didn't. So I peeled off my own fins 10 feet away and swam to the ladder. He was unreasonably upset. I don't normally try to be a troublemaker, but this was too weird.

The next day, Iseta picked me up at my hotel to go sailing at the Port Douglas Yacht Club. We arrived at 3 for a drink but the club didn't open until 4, forcing us to do a mini-pub crawl to kill time. We also needed to stock up on boat drinks, vodka and soda water. Mixed a bit too strong, perhaps.

Iseta is a favorite at the yacht club, and she had also been away for several months for a boat delivery, so everyone wanted her to sail on their boat. She picked a Sun Odyssey 40. Every Wednesday all the yacht clubs in Australia have an open sail for anyone who shows up. We sailed with the Australian boat owners and their friends, and a family from Scotland. There wasn't much wind and it was a bit cloudy, but otherwise a gorgeous evening. I was allowed to steer for most of the evening and I loved it. We sailed past a cruise ship and the six-man team; it felt a lot like home.

After the sail, we had dinner at the club and I got to know some of the members, which mostly consisted of me randomly sitting by people who looked like they had good stories to tell – the old, grizzled guys. My favorite was Steve, who had just that morning had an accident with a power washer, removing a good portion of the top of his foot. Steve crossed the Panama Canal in an odd way, and I love to hear canal stories. He was moored in the bay, waiting for his turn to cross, when a skiff of Russians pulled alongside; he thought he was being boarded by pirates. The Russians were taking a freighter through the canal and wanted to hoist Steve's boat onto the deck and carry him through. They charged him $1,000 less than his fee would normally be, and in turn they got to pocket that money. After they hoisted his boat, they cooked for him, kept him drunk, and did a mini-dry dock on his boat. They painted on some antifouling paint that's illegal in most countries, and Steve hasn't had to clean the bottom of his boat since.

Shockingly, I woke up the next morning without a hangover, and Iseta picked me up in her white 1972 Mercedes convertible. We drove up to the Daintree Forest Preserve for some beach time and trail hiking. The ride was an hour through tree-covered, windy roads along the ocean's edge. Being two women in a cute convertible, we had horns honking at us the entire way.

We stopped on the way at Iseta's house where I met her mother and sister. Her mother is 74 and had broken her leg badly five days before. She was up a ladder pruning her shrubs because she doesn't like how anyone else does them, and she fell off and knocked herself out. She was airlifted to the hospital and was recovering at Iseta's house. She was a serious world traveler and wasn't taking to bed rest very well. She had a history of packing up and camping in the bush for a week at a time, or hopping a flight to India or Asia with a tent and no plan. I want to be like her when I'm that age.

We were back on the road driving through the forest, and it smelled like freshness. Our first stop and the furthest point away was Cape Tribulation. We loved saying that word for some reason. Iseta asked me what it meant and I wasn't sure, but we decided that it sounded like a good boat name. When I got back to the hotel and internet access, I promptly decided that it wasn't.

Along the road there were "Cassowary Crossing" signs, but we never spotted one. A cassowary is a blue, 5-foot-tall bird. That would have been something to see running across the road.

Cape Tribulation is a point that juts out into the ocean; it's where jungle meets water. There is no swimming due to jellyfish, crocodiles, and other nasty things in the water, but it was quite pretty. As we walked up the beach we could see miles in either direction, and there was only one other person around. It happened to be Bob, one of our buddies from the live-aboard. His main purpose in life after he retired was to take pictures of stars and celestial events through his telescope. He came to Australia on a cruise that catered to astronomy buffs; they had sailed to the best location to see the last solar eclipse. We sat on the beach and looked through Bob's eclipse pictures.

Iseta and I walked a bit more, then headed back south to find more of her favorite spots. Iseta was a great tour guide. We didn't see any cassowaries or crocodiles, but the scenery was unbelievable. It really impressed upon me how giant the country is – endless miles of beaches, tree-covered mountains, swamps and forests; it seemed never-ending.

Our bathroom stop in the jungle was surprising in a couple different ways. First, Australia was constantly reminding me of how clean it is. We were in the middle of nowhere, and the bathroom was sparkling. Definitely unexpected. As I was reaching for toilet paper, a giant spider jumped down and landed on the very last square sticking out of the roll. He startled me, so of course I jumped, which made me pee down my leg and all over the floor without being able to get any toilet paper. I had just been complaining to Iseta that I hadn't seen any wildlife and there it was, in the most inconvenient place imaginable. I flicked the paper; the spider ran up an inch. I pulled it down, flicked again, and the spider ran up another inch. I repeated this over and over until eventually I had enough to clean up my situation. I smelled faintly of urine the rest of the day.

We went to lunch and a couple more lookouts, ate the best ice cream ever made, then went for a quick swim in a river in Shannonvale. I was hoping that the river smell would overpower the pee smell. The river was flowing over the top of a bridge and kids were running back and forth on the road diving from both sides, screaming, pausing just long enough to let a car go by. This was where I learned what the word "Billabong" meant. I had previously thought it was just a brand of surf clothing started by a stoner.

I said goodbye to Iseta, sadly, and caught a shuttle back to Cairns for the airport and some surf time with Kawika.

COOLANGATTA

Kawika lives in Coolangatta, which is on the border between Queensland and New South Wales, making it the most confusing place I've been. There is an hour time difference between the two states and the border isn't straight, so as we drove it was 6 o'clock, then 5 o'clock, back to 6 o'clock. On one side of the street all the stores and restaurants were closed, then we crossed and everything was open. It wasn't bad for wandering around, but I found that making an appointment, booking a flight or going to see a movie involved some research. Kawika set my phone to Queensland time, but it didn't help when I couldn't remember which was which.

I met Kawika online, through Facebook actually; I thought he was someone else and friended him. Shortly after that he visited a friend in Hawaii where I met him in person, and we kept in touch ever since. Kawika works two weeks on, one week off in another country on a protection detail, and was due to fly home the day after I arrived. His roommate, Scotty, picked me up at the bus station and showed me around town.

I was awakened around 5 the next morning; Kawika was thoughtful enough to bring me coffee and croissants in bed. He had another friend in town, Claudia, who also happened to live on Kauai; I'd just never met her. We surfed Snapper Rocks and Byron Bay, and the waves were small and easy, perfect for an out-of-shape surfer like me.

I got a lot of my Oz to-do list done during the week. I tried vegemite, which was like licking a beef bouillon cube, finally figured out cricket, and saw all the animals that had been eluding me.

Kawika dropped me off at Currumbin Nature Preserve. I'm not a big fan of zoos, but I had to find a cassowary, along with all the other animals that make me think of Australia. The nature preserve was very park-like. It contained a lot of poisonous and bitey things, snakes and crocodiles, a field of endangered cassowaries, koalas, kangaroos and Tasmanian devils, each in its own habitat. I saw a dingo; I hadn't known that they were just wild dogs. I went to a bird show, an aboriginal dance, and a crocodile feeding.

An hour into my visit my flip-flops finally broke, and it was actually a sad moment. Cynthia had given me those shoes; she had found them the night before I left Kauai and they fit perfectly, and I'd worn them every day since. They'd been up volcanoes, down rivers, and walked towns around the world. Now I was barefoot in a nature preserve at the hottest part of the day in the hottest month of the year in the hottest year on record. It wasn't pretty. I went to sit in the shade and have lunch, and my french fries were violently attacked by an ibis, worse than the wild chickens at home because they have 5-inch beaks. I moved to get away from the crazy birds and spotted a gift store with a rack of slippers for sale. For the rest of my trip I wandered around in bright blue palm tree slippers that said "Australia."

The final day was a big day at the house. Kawika was getting ready to go back to work, and Scotty had taken a job in South Australia as an emergency medical response guy at a mine. They had a lot of shopping to do and I followed along. I was wandering through the mall, window-shopping since I couldn't fit anything else in my backpack, and saw a home store with dishware on display. I found myself staring at it, jealously wishing that I had matching dishes and a kitchen to store them. That was a sign that it was time to consider going home.

HOBART

I had one more week until I was supposed to meet Shanti and her family in Cambodia, so I decided to check out Tasmania.

When I was planning, I asked Kawika and Scotty about it, and neither of them had ever been there, nor knew anyone who had been there (which immediately prompted me to resupply my tampon stash while still in the city, I was traveling into unknown territory again). I hadn't even known it was an Australian state until I started researching. I emailed a scuba company that promised sea dragons and set up a dive, so that was where I reserved a hotel room. All of the hostels were sold out, again, and the hotel in Hobart was officially the most expensive place I have ever stayed. Stupid holidays.

As I flew into Hobart, I realized that I hadn't done any proper research. I was looking for sea dragons and nature; in my mind I saw mountains and lakes and rivers, adventures and surf and scuba. It never occurred to me that I was going to the capital city of one of the Australian states. A big, horrible city.

I was the last drop-off for the hotel shuttle, so I got a small tour of the city. I felt like I was in downtown Seattle, not the small beach towns and backwoods laziness that I envisioned. And I had to walk several blocks from my hotel to find a Wi-Fi connection at a pub. I really need to learn how to properly research destinations.

According to my emails with Sue at Underwater Adventures, sea dragons lived in the harbors around Hobart. On my first morning in town I was supposed to meet her at the docks at 7:45, along with one other woman who was equally excited to find them. I arrived at the dock at 7:40, early as usual, and Georgina got there at 7:43. We waited, made small talk, waited more, and no boat. Finally, Sue motored up at 8:20; apparently a cruise ship motored past while she was loading tanks and the wake knocked two of them overboard and she had to dive for them. A shaky start to the day.

The boat wasn't very well-kept; it was kind of messy with stuff everywhere, with six tanks sort of bungeed to the sides, but Sue was nice. She didn't have any crew so she wasn't going to dive with us, which immediately annoyed both Georgina and me. It's way easier to find things underwater with someone who's been there before. Getting directions in Cairns for a colony of clownfish was bad enough; now we had to locate an animal that looks like kelp in darker water.

We travelled 50 minutes to our first site at Betsey Island. The sky was grey and rainy and the wind was picking up. There were dozens of crayfish pots in the area where Sue wanted to drop anchor, so it took us a while to settle in. She gave me a selection of 7 millimeter wetsuits, all of them covered in dog hair. They probably would be comfy to sleep on. After trying a few, I finally found one that fit, which meant I could fasten it properly and still manage to breathe a little. I was worried that in darker water a tight wetsuit might make me feel claustrophobic and I'd freak out, but I continued getting ready – boots, hood, gloves, and 32 pounds of weights. I could barely move. Georgina was using a dry suit; Sue didn't have one in my size. It took us an hour to gear up for the first dive.

Then came the moment I was dreading – touching the water. It was 16 degrees Celsius. In a 7-millimeter wetsuit, it still felt like 16 degrees. It was fucking cold. Like getting wrapped in ice, then buried in snow. Then stabbed in the head with icicles. I couldn't remember ever being that cold in my life. Every time I turned my head to look around, some water would channel straight down my back. I just kept telling myself that I was doing this for a good purpose: sea dragons.

The visibility was around five meters in the greenish water. The underwater landscape consisted of kelp forests and a lot of strange plants, but I didn't find many fish. I saw a wrasse, a box cowfish, anemones, starfish, a rockfish, and a couple crabs, but mostly just plants floating back and forth with the current. I was praying for a sea dragon.

"Please, God, let me see one so I don't ever have to get back in this water. Pretty please? I'll be good, I promise."

The first dive lasted 48 minutes and by the end I was shaking uncontrollably, my teeth were chattering, and no sea dragon. Sue kept asking if we saw the felled tree where some live, or the backside of the reef where others are. That was why we had wanted a guide.

We left for the second dive site, the blowhole in Blackman's Bay. There was no way I could take off my wetsuit between dives, so I put a jacket over it and jumped up and down to try to get warm, but it didn't work. I ate half a box of Tim-Tams, possibly the greatest chocolate cookie in mass production, thinking that might help. Maybe it was just a good excuse to eat so many.

On the second dive I was cold going in, and thought I would die the moment I hit the water. I vaguely remember wondering if my nipples could cut through a 7 millimeter suit. This dive was a little shallower and I was too floaty; I had to swim back to the boat after 20 minutes for more weights. I was now carrying 38 pounds; the most I'd ever used before was 14. It was good incentive to start working out again; my legs had a hard time standing under the extra weight.

We saw more kelp and more cute cowfish, but it was 48 more minutes of no sea dragons. As we swam back to the boat, Sue yelled that we should try one more time a little further down, maybe swim until we have about 40 bar of air left. Obviously, sea dragons were way more important than following strict PADI dive rules. We dove back down on the other side of the reef for a total dive time of 63 minutes with no sea dragons. I was pretty sure my fingertips were going to break off.

I was told that we were only doing two dives, and although I was upset that we didn't find a sea dragon, I was OK with getting dried off. The weather had gotten worse and the sun hadn't come out all day; it was just windy and rainy. All I could think about was a hot shower and obscene amounts of food.

But Sue felt bad and suggested a third dive. Georgina gave the decision to me since I was the coldest, but not by much since her drysuit had a small leak. I came all this way to Tasmania, was half-frozen, and I'd probably never make it back. Another 20 minutes wouldn't kill me. Sue's rationale was that the first site gets battered by storms, the second site had a bunch of spear divers a few days ago, but the third site never gets much traffic. And that was when Georgina got pissed. Imagine an older, shorter, English housewife getting really angry. But I agreed with her. Why did we go to the crappy sites first, especially when the pristine site was only 15 minutes from the dock?

The third site was Boronia Beach. Sue was begging us to dive just a little while, even though one tank only had 100 bar and Georgina had to use her tank from the last dive. We decided to go for 20 minutes or until one of us had no air left. By then we had left PADI standards far behind. I think Sue felt bad because she usually gets in the water with the divers and can find the sea dragon hangouts; maybe her crew called in sick, but this wasn't a great day for diving. I had been carrying my camera and decided to leave it on the boat for the last dive since it wasn't doing anything but wearing down the battery.

Sue dropped us at the edge of a reef with instructions, "Go in here where you can see the reef, swim with it on your left; if you go around that corner into the other bay that's OK, I'll follow your bubbles from the boat." Georgina and I swam, freezing. I started thinking that I really was going to die, then OH MY GOD A SEA DRAGON!

It was the weirdest animal I've ever seen in my life. It had a snout like a seahorse, a fat little body with teensy, fluttery, useless-looking fins, and a long tail that started off fat and tapered to very skinny. It was a male, carrying eggs. In total, it was about 14 inches long, and every color in the crayon box. The sun had just come out, and every time he moved, different body parts turned different colors in the light. He had two lumps on his head that looked like horns, and two long side fins that just dangled and looked like kelp. There was another set of tiny, fluttery fins where I thought his ears should go. The overall impression was like a flying elephant with a couple tinker-bell wings. Totally ridiculous.

And of course, I didn't have my camera. I signaled to Georgina that I was going to the boat and I'd be right back. I sprinted in my 7 millimeter wetsuit. By the time I got back I was so out of breath that I had to float on the surface trying to breathe; my suit was too tight for a proper breath. But there was a sea dragon, so I went down anyway.

Georgina and I spent 25 minutes watching him. He just swam back and forth between a couple big rocks and showed off for us, like he was on a sea dragon catwalk. I completely forgot that I was cold.

I managed to get a room at a hostel and finally figured out why I had so much trouble finding places to live. There was a Christian youth group of nearly 500 kids in town, the wooden boat show was coming up, and there were sailing races. If I ever make it back to Australia, I'll be sure to book everything months in advance.

My new hostel was overpriced and crappy, but still cheaper than the hotel room. And it was the first place that had decent Wi-Fi in the entire country. I was looking at a room above an Irish pub; it sounded romantic and fun, but I was too lazy to move again when it became available.

Australia Day came and went; I think it is comparable to our Independence Day in terms of celebration. Everyone got as drunk as possible by a barbecue. This year, though, there were bush fires, a cyclone, tornadoes and record flooding in many places, so it wasn't a great weekend for a lot of people. There was a giant street market and I did my best to refrain from buying more stuff to haul around. I did buy the cutest skirt with owls on it; the tag said "Handmade in Tasmania." When I got back home to Kauai and unpacked, I found the real tag that said "Made in Cambodia." I bet I paid 20 times more than if I had found it in Cambodia. I went to an "Invasion Day" protest, the aboriginal version of Australia Day, much like Native Americans would do on Columbus Day. I saw very few people who looked like they could be native to Tasmania, and the only thing I could understand they wanted was to change the date of Australia Day. I didn't get it.

The Moscow Circus was also in town. I couldn't remember going to a circus in the past 30 years, so when I saw the brightly colored, striped tent when I first came to town, it just demanded my attendance. None of the performers looked particularly Russian except for their clothing, which all had "CCCP" and sickles on them. It was a strange experience.

There was one ring, and between acts two "clowns" would do skits while the sets were changed, and they were great. There was knife throwing, a trapeze act without swings – the guy hooked his feet under a bar and became the swing for the girl – trained ponies, a troupe of acrobats on trampolines, a woman doing an aerial act that was something between gymnastics and stripping, and for the big finale, a motorcycle cage. Five guys on motorcycles fit into a small steel sphere that was moved and anchored onto the stage only moments before. The performers must have had an immense amount of trust in their coworkers.

With only two days left before my flights to Cambodia, I had to hurry to see more of Tasmania than just the city. I took a day trip to Freycinet National Park to see Wineglass Bay, supposedly one of the most beautiful beaches in the world. For the first time, I was the youngest person in the tour group by far. It was slightly dismaying, but a group of Italians always turns out to be fun.

The only other younger guy on the bus was Bob, from China. Of course Bob was only his English name. Someone asked him to say his Chinese name and it reminded me of when Darryl Hannah tells Tom Hanks her name in "Splash." My mouth can't make those sounds.

The road to the park was covered in dead wallabies. I hadn't been this sad about road kill before. I saw dead chickens all the time on Kauai, but I hate to say it, who cares? These were like miniature kangaroos, or dogs with really long tails. The speed limit at night is half that of during the daytime because of all the animals on the move, and even that doesn't help, especially with all the road trains – semi trucks pulling three trailers – they have here. The only rule about road kill is that if you hit a wallaby, you have to stop and check its pouch to see if there's a joey inside, and if so, bring it to a vet.

I didn't see any dead Tasmanian devils; they are getting scarce because of a fast-spreading cancer with no cure or preventative. The government was collecting healthy devils and making parks for them to breed, hoping that the cancer would wipe out the rest, allowing the healthy ones to repopulate the island. Officials predict the wild devils will be extinct in two to three years.

Speaking of extinction, I asked our guide about Invasion Day, and the mostly white scene at the protest. There are no native Tasmanians alive anywhere, and anyone I thought who might be aboriginal was not from there. When the English were settling, they had trouble with the natives and formed a giant line of men, the "black line," that spent weeks walking the island and killing them all. Some got away to a smaller nearby island, but eventually they all died.

We arrived at the trailhead to Wineglass Bay lookout and beach and faced a choice: the hike to the lookout was 40 minutes uphill and the hike to the beach was an hour and a half. The old Italians opted to tour in the van while some of us hiked; the guide drove them around to accessible lookouts to other bays. The two Australian women only wanted to go to the lookout, and Bob wanted to go all the way to the beach. I couldn't decide. The four of us started off together up the trail, carved from rock that ran between two peaks in the mountains. One of the women had chronic fatigue so Bob and I took off, planning to meet them at the lookout.

We hiked up for half an hour until the trail started to slope down. I made up my mind to only go to the lookout, not all the way to the beach; I had gone running the day before and my legs were sore. But Bob and I walked and walked and there was no lookout; pretty soon I stopped and could hear the ocean. I saw an old lady making her way slowly down the rocky trail with a cane and figured she couldn't be going all the way to the beach, so we kept going.

The area we were wandering through had been hit by a wild-fire the previous week and the smell of burnt eucalyptus was very dreamy. It soon became apparent that we had missed the lookout. The sound of the waves was loud and we were far too low for any sort of vantage point. Not the first time getting lost reshaped my plans. We were going to the beach.

Wineglass Beach was miles of white sand and clear blue water. The wind was strong and there was a gnarly beach break, probably close to 10 feet. We were told to bring our "swimmers," what Australians call bathing suits, but of the eight people on the beach, no one dared to go into the ice-cold waves. I had seen a lot of beaches on this trip, many of them called "the most beautiful," but so far nothing had been prettier than Hanalei. Wineglass wasn't even close, although it was definitely nice. It wasn't even shaped like a wineglass; our guide thought it might have been named that because it had been used for whaling and the water was always reddish in those days.

Bob and I hiked the beach, climbed rocks and took pictures. We did find the lookout on the way back; it was painfully obvious. I couldn't understand how we missed it, especially since dozens of people were there and we could hear them talking from half a mile away.

I had one more day until the long flights to Cambodia to meet Shanti and Pablo, so I chose one last tour, this time to the Tasman

Peninsula and Port Arthur. I wanted to see penguins and the historic penal colony, neither of which I ended up seeing.

Port Arthur is the home of Australia's worst mass murder; a man gunned down 58 people in 1996, killing 35 of them. This led to Australia banning semi-automatic shotguns and rifles.

The trip began on another van with some random sightseeing. Tasmania grows opium poppies, and produces 25% of the world's legal supply for medicine. I had no idea.

Most of the trip down the coast was through the recent wildfire areas, which started with a farmer burning a stump on his property; he wrongly thought it was extinguished, and there were strong winds the next day. Weeks later, 110,000 hectares, around 275,000 acres, and a couple hundred homes, schools and businesses were destroyed. I bet he feels like crap.

The landscape was literally black. Crews were out removing the larger trees before they fell over, people had tents set up next to the remains of their houses, and the state was setting up emergency trailers to be used for the elementary school until it could be rebuilt. As we drove, we saw perfectly preserved houses and yards with summer flowers blooming, surrounded by destruction. It was interesting how small areas escaped such a massive fire. Our tour guide was on the wrong side of the fire when they closed the roads, and he and his group of tourists had to spend a week away from home and hotel.

Our first historical spot was Eagle Hawk Neck, home of the infamous "dog line." The Tasman Peninsula held the worst criminals from Australia, and Eagle Hawk Neck is a thin strip of land connecting it to the mainland. Authorities chained lines of half-starved dogs across the Neck to prevent escape attempts.

We boarded a large raft to visit the sea cliffs and Tasman Island. This was the point where I realized I wasn't thinking too clearly before I left and was wishing I had packed more clothes, and wasn't wearing flip-flops. They gave us knee-length waterproof jackets, but I was freezing again. Other tourists were pulling hats and gloves and scarves out of their bags, and what would you think was in mine? A bikini. Because I was going on a boat ride. We were pretty far off the mainland and only 2,000 kilometers of open ocean and cold wind separated us from Antarctica. And I brought a bikini.

The boat tour was three hours and went down the Tasman Peninsula to view the highest sea cliffs in the southern hemisphere, about 300 meters high, and finally to see Tasman Island before heading back. The cliffs were beautiful, but nothing compared to amazing Na Pali at 1,200 meters. I really need to stop comparing everything to Kauai.

I didn't get to see penguins, but there were cormorants, and if I squinted they kind of looked like penguins. There were also albatross with 9-foot wing spans, and fur seals. I was so cold I wouldn't have thought twice about clubbing one of those seals for its fur if I had a baseball bat, or at least trying to get it to snuggle up with me. It started raining and it was like having thumbtacks thrown at my face. Again, my research sucked.

I asked the boat crew for more clothes and eventually ended up wearing three coats, with another wrapped around my feet.

After sightseeing it was time to zip back, and the crew took this time to talk about wildlife. The seabirds migrate, and every year there are fewer and fewer of them. Researchers find all types of plastic junk in the dead ones, and estimate that even if there isn't another single piece of plastic added to the ocean, all the birds will be extinct in 20 years. There was also a medical waste dump nearby that officials haven't been able to contain that's leaching into the water, killing the fish. And the phytoplankton, important for creating a huge amount of oxygen, is on a severe decline. I know it's crucial to educate people about environmental issues, but between half-freezing and learning all of the depressing information, it didn't end up being a cheerful trip.

The harbor we left from is the only harbor in Australia that doesn't have limits for amounts of fish caught, so fishermen come here to catch as much as they can. The crew said the Japanese come here to catch every last southern bluefin tuna so they can get hundreds of thousands of dollars per fish when this type is extinct. I don't know how true that is, and if these guys were so conservation-minded, that seems like something easier to fix than plastic or toxic waste.

After lunch we went to a chocolate factory, a cherry farm and a "remarkable" cave. About halfway through, I realized I had made a mistake and didn't book the Port Arthur historic sites. I took the wrong van. The rest of the day was somewhat boring and annoying; a small group of women from Sydney took at least 300 pictures everywhere we went. First the group of all four girls, then in couples, then singles, then all over again with each person's camera, squealing the entire time. We waited an extra 20 minutes everywhere we went for them to finish posing.

I was happy to be done with this trip; I had the evening to finish up my Tasmanian wine and chocolates while I packed for my early morning flight. I had become friends with the owner of the hostel, an older man from Portugal who has lived in Tasmania most of his life. He asked me most nights why I hadn't brought home any Tasmanian guys, to sample more of the local flavor. It seemed to be one of those "the odds are good but the goods are odd" kinds of places. He even offered his services in case I was feeling like it was something I had to do. Instead, I just let him drive me to the store when I was too lazy to walk.

SUVARNABHUMI AIRPORT, BANGKOK
FEBRUARY 4ᵀᴴ, 2013

I haven't written yet about an airport like it was a destination, but Suvarnabhumi airport in Bangkok deserves its own chapter. It felt like a city. Leaving from Sydney, I had a 10-hour layover before my flight to Siem Reap. I was deciding what to do with my time, maybe take a taxi to the city and explore, but

I landed shortly after midnight and was outrageously tired. In my first few minutes at the airport, I realized that I could happily kill several hours in that crazy place. I was going back to Bangkok in a few days with Shanti and her family, and could check out the city then, rather than get lost at night by myself and miss my flight.

The airport was amazing. I felt like I was on a four-story Rodeo Drive with bits of Thailand stuck here and there. I wandered through duty-free shops, cute little restaurants, Thai specialty stores and massage parlors. I spent my first two hours walking just to take it all in. It was 2 a.m., everything was open, and people were everywhere. Intricately carved and painted statues and pagodas and dried fruit stands were scattered amidst Dior, Rolex and Coach stores. I could have lived in that airport for weeks. It had shower rooms and bed rentals and travel stores for anything travelers may have forgotten.

I had walked roughly a quarter of the airport in my first two hours and thought a nap would be good. I had passed hundreds of people sleeping wherever there were chairs. There were areas with small couches and comfy-looking recliners, mostly full, but I found a couple of nice padded chairs, pulled them together, and made a pretty nice bed.

I had gone through another time zone change and had no concept of what time it might be at the airport or in Australia, at home, or at my parents' house. I was falling into blissful sleep with my daypack as my pillow and my arms wrapped around my giant backpack, so I could worry about what time it was later. I wouldn't have been upset if I had slept through my flight, but I only slept for three hours.

When I woke up, the first thing I saw was a giant, glowing Chanel sign and it made me feel like a bum in a cardboard box waking up in Beverly Hills. Coffee was the first thing on my mind and surprisingly, some cafés were closed at 5 a.m. Most places never closed; I just had to wake up the person napping at the counter. Starbucks was open, of course, and it was the first one I'd ever seen without Wi-Fi.

After another hour of wandering, it was time for my first Thai foot massage. I did have to wake up the masseuses, but they were amazingly cheerful for that. My foot and leg massage was 40 minutes and cost $12. Since I still had three hours until my flight, I was considering a full-on Thai body massage; it was the same price. Travelling makes me so sore. But I felt good enough after my foot massage to continue my exploration through booze and cigarettes and chocolates and perfumes and shoes. The only things I bought were dried mangoes and ginger, a healthy breakfast, and more coffee. Then I found a comfy seat to watch the sunrise.

It was the greatest airport ever.

CAMBODIA
FEBRUARY 5ᵀᴴ, 2013

SIEM REAP

It took a total of 29 hours to get to Siem Reap from Tasmania. Sambo, an employee at the Golden Mango Inn, was waiting at the airport for me with his tuk-tuk, and I immediately found Shanti, Sol, and Pablo when I arrived. It was so wonderful to have travel buddies again. We took it easy on our first day in Cambodia, and as the Golden Mango was a little far from town, Sambo dropped us off for lunch. We wandered around a bit, Pablo got a haircut, and Shanti and I stopped at one of the dozens of foot massage parlors for half an hour of wonderfulness. One dollar for 15 minutes. The main streets have rows of chairs set up along the sidewalks and tiny women yelling "foot massage, lady?" We also saw giant tanks of pedicure fish – you sit on a wooden plank, dangle your feet in the tank, and fish nibble the dead skin off of your feet while you drink a beer. No thanks. In heat worse than Panama, that just screamed "foot fungus."

I had scheduled a full-body Khmer massage, pretty much the same as Thai massage, for the evening. It was my third foot and leg massage of the day, probably unnecessary, but it was only $6. In total I spent $20 for two hours of massage, and since it was way too hot to run outside, I thought this might be the way to stay in shape, like what hospitals do for people in comas, or the bedridden.

When we went to dinner we had to learn how to cross the street. It wasn't as easy as it sounds; it was more like a real-life Frogger. There was no point in looking both ways – it only scared us. There was a line down the middle of the road, but it was only a suggestion; buses, trucks, cars, motorcycles, tuk-tuks and bicycles were on both sides driving in both directions, and at first it just looked like a thousand accidents about to happen. After a few minutes of observation and watching locals, we tried it ourselves. The basic idea is take a deep breath, step into the road when there's a small space, and keep moving at an even pace. If you stop you're screwed. Just keep moving and don't panic, and everything will be alright, no matter how much traffic there is. All the drivers were hyper-aware of what was going on, and as long as we didn't make any sudden course changes or stop dead, they could anticipate where we would be and go around. It made a terrifying kind of sense.

Our first road trip together in a tuk-tuk proved our traffic theory. We were headed 15 minutes out of town to Angkor Wat and hired Sambo to drive us around. The tuk-tuks in Cambodia are four-person carts with a roof attached to the back of a motorcycle. We watched cars and trucks driving straight at us on the wrong side of the road, but everyone gave way to allow others to get where they were going, all extremely polite. Horns were only used to let other drivers know that you were there, not used in anger like in the States. Polite toots helped choreograph the crazy free-for-all, and it was no problem at all for someone who had driven there all their life. I didn't think I was ready to rent a car in the city, however. I probably never would be.

Sol loved the tuk-tuks. He was only one and a half years old, and it was the first time in his life that he didn't have to get buckled into a car seat. I doubt we could have found a car seat anywhere in the country. While we swerved through traffic, one of us held Sol, one made sure our bags didn't fly out, and one took pictures. Fun.

The first temple we visited was Angkor Wat, the largest religious building in the world. It was massive, an entire complex of buildings surrounded by a moat. The walls were completely covered with carvings depicting battles, history, and so much more.

Pablo and I got in line to climb up to the main temple while Shanti stayed with Sol. I was turned away at the steps for not meeting the dress code. I had worn what I thought of as a modest outfit, considering what I'd been wearing to the beach for the past few months, but too much leg was showing below my shorts, and too much arm below my sleeves. It would have been nice to know that I had to have my shoulders completely covered, and my legs covered down to my knees. So I got to sit with Sol while Shanti and Pablo climbed to the temple. No big deal though, there were ruins everywhere. That one just happened to be further above ground.

In two hours we saw only a small portion of Angkor Wat before it was time to find Sambo and move to the next ruin. We hired Sambo for three days, and since the temples are a good distance apart, he waited with all of the other tuk-tuk drivers. There were dozens of them parked in the shade, waiting for their tourists. We learned the importance of memorizing something unique about Sambo's tuk-tuk. Some drivers were listening to music, some were playing an impossible version of hackeysack, but most had hammocks attached to the roofs of their vehicles and napped until it was time to move on.

Our next stop was Bayon, known for the 216 faces carved into the stone looking down at tourists. If there was a picture of surreal in the dictionary, it would be Bayon. We did a downwind run at this temple; we hiked in through one side and Sambo was waiting at the opposite end.

Our last stop of the morning was Ta Prohm, known to most people as the "Tomb Raider Temple." The Cambodian scenes were filmed there and it was every bit as impressive as it looked on the big screen. Giant trees were growing over the ruins of the temples, with long, smooth roots running over the rocks down to the ground; it was quite dramatic. It was hard to get any good pictures because of the huge amount of tourists; someone was always in the way, or a dozen someones. But it didn't really matter – seeing it was enough.

The windows of the temples, if window is the correct word – maybe "openings" is a better term – were spooky. They were made so precisely, and the long corridors were such exact duplicates to each other, that I thought at first the openings were mirrors until someone on the other side moved and I realized that I wasn't looking at us. Everything was so precisely built in mirror images that it was sort of creepy, and easy to get lost.

It was slightly after noon and steamy hot; we were dripping sweat and it was time to go back to the hotel pool and recover before our sunset hike. Sol was a trooper; he was sweating as much as the rest of us, but still managed to find the energy to climb on the rocks and play in the dirt. He added a new phrase to his vocabulary: Angkor Wat was a "broke house."

We only bought three day passes to the ruins and saw parts of three of them on the first morning. I don't think we realized how enormous Angkor Wat is, but we did realize that if we spent every waking moment there we'd still never see it all. We did get to see the sun set over the temples, along with hundreds of other tourists. It's a very popular tour to sell, apparently.

Our second day walking through temples was incredible as well, but we only lasted for the morning. Sol got so hot that he projectile-vomited out of his nose.

We had to switch hotels in the early afternoon to one closer to the town's center; we arrived shortly after noon only to find out that the power would be down on the block until 5:30. No air conditioning, no fans, no lights, nothing. My new room was near the road, so the windows were blacked out and I was lying in bed naked, sweating in total darkness. I had to use the light from my iPhone to figure out how to take a cold shower. Shanti and I left sleeping Sol with Pablo and we went to get our feet rubbed again. It was too hot to do anything else. A bit later we went for a short walk, but it was still too hot to be outside.

We were back before 5 p.m., still no power. We went to the pool to cool off and Sol vomited again and had diarrhea in the pool. Oops. But that's how hot it was. At 6 p.m., we heard "Yes, the power will be on in half an hour." It didn't happen; we took showers by candlelight this time. When the hotel staff realized we wouldn't have light any time soon, they gave everyone a candle. We went up to the roof and spotted a mall, but it only had mild air conditioning and nothing good to eat. Still no lights at our hotel. We walked, practiced crossing the streets, sweated, and swore because every other block in town had lights. We wandered into an internet restaurant with great air conditioning, had dinner and lounged until it was clear that Sol needed to go back home, and as we left the entire city lost power. Siem Reap was lit entirely by headlights. The full Cambodian experience.

The biggest surprise of the night, besides the projectile vomiting, was turning the corner toward our hotel; our block was now the only block that had power. The staff was blowing out the candles as we walked in. I ran to charge my phone, camera and laptop before the power went out again.

By our fourth day in Cambodia and third day at Angkor Wat, Sambo had taken us to so many different temples that I could no longer remember which was which. My favorite three were on the first day, and everything else was just extra fun. Cambodia in general was overwhelming for such a small place. The garbage, pollution and heat were what I noticed the most, except for how wonderful the people were.

Shanti and I climbed up to one temple that was so steep that I couldn't believe it was allowed. The stone stairs were about 6 inches wide and slanted slightly downward. Climbing up was so sketchy I almost had to crawl, using my hands to pull myself as I went higher. I wished I had recognized what it would mean to get back down. I walked around and saw the views, then started down. And stopped. For the first time ever, I thought I might throw up from the height. The teensy, curvy, broken stairs didn't inspire a feeling of safety at all. Shanti scrambled down like a little mountain goat, but she's a foot shorter than me with feet about half the size of mine, or that's how I'm justifying my inability to climb down. I walked to the other side of the temple where the steps seemed better somehow, and I crawled back down slowly on my butt, like a giant baby.

Just like in Mexico, I was amazed at what is legal in some countries, how I haven't heard news reports of tourists tumbling off ruins to a bloody, broken death. I can't imagine that it hasn't happened.

Sol was with Pablo, so Shanti and I wandered through the ground-floor corridors of another temple, Preah Kahn, and found a small toothless man beckoning us to walk through a tiny opening in the walls. Most of the openings were blocked by rocks that had tumbled down, but the one he wanted us to go through was open, so we went. He didn't speak any English, so we couldn't tell what he wanted us to see. After a couple small passages, we came to an altar with a beautiful carved stone statue adorned with bright yellow silk cloth. I put a dollar in a bucket and we were given incense and allowed to make a prayer; we convinced the man by mime that he should take our picture. A woman standing guard over the offerings put a thin yellow and orange string bracelet on my wrist, and over a year later it still hasn't broken off; maybe it's waiting for my prayer to come true. I wish I could remember what it was I asked for. With acres and acres of ruins, I can't even imagine how long it would take to find all the secret alcoves and passageways.

Sambo took us to a couple more temples, but by this time it was outrageously hot and Sol was starting to have a hard time. Instead of exploring, we stopped for pictures and kept moving. On the way home, we came across a big family of monkeys, which was probably the highlight of Sol's morning. They were playing on the side of the road and so happy to see us. They loved Shanti's skirt and kept trying to climb her; Pablo had to run back and forth chasing them away. They seemed fun, but it was possible that they actually wanted to eat us. After we left, Sambo said they only bit "sometimes."

We went back home for the usual late-morning swim and to hide from the sun. We went to a great vegetarian restaurant with some of the best pumpkin curry I've ever tasted. Shanti and I got another foot massage, the best $6 I ever spent, and did some shopping at the markets.

And then everything went to hell. Almost instantaneously, Shanti and Pablo started throwing up, and diarrhea followed soon after. I guess the restaurant wasn't that great. They were sick for the rest of the night. I took Sol to play for a couple hours and left them to vomit in peace.

I felt great. I went back to the mall and bought a bottle of Khmer Palm wine after they went to bed, and sat on the balcony drinking and watching the city. I felt bad because I felt so good and they were miserable, and hoped that they'd puke it all out before we started our drive to Bangkok in the morning. That could be an awful seven hours.

THAILAND
FEBRUARY 8ᵀᴴ, 2013

Buses cross the Cambodia-Thailand border daily, but we thought with Sol and family being sick we should take a private taxi to make life easier, and it wasn't that much more expensive.

Our first taxi picked us up at Passagiero in Siem Reap at 7:45 a.m. Our driver didn't say a word during the trip; he just gunned it, layed on the horn and blew through all the towns. Shanti mentioned that she'd probably never used a car horn as many times in her entire life as our driver did during that three hour ride. Every car, truck, motorcycle and bike we passed got honked at to make sure they knew we were flying by. It was awesome.

Shanti and Pablo had pretty much gotten over whatever sickness they had; thank God, because I was envisioning several stops at the side of the road for bodily functions that needed attention. We only stopped once so the driver could have a cigarette. They both felt horrible, but nobody was leaking.

The rest of Cambodia was flat, dry, and dirty; our eyes stung from burning garbage and leaves. Between the small towns filled with markets and shops lacking a single sign written in English, the fields were populated with hundreds of anorexic-looking cows.

Our driver dropped us off near the border and we were instantly mobbed by Thais wanting to sell us a bus ride or food, or offering to take our luggage; it was a mob scene. Between the three of us we had three giant backpacks, three smaller daypacks, three small bags of food, and random shopping items, and one hot, unhappy child. We hauled everything to the departure lines and stood in sweltering heat with dozens of other people to get processed out of Cambodia. That first line was an hour long. Sol dealt with the heat and chaos very well, but Shanti and Pablo felt like they wanted to die. I was just overly warm.

After departure came a quarter-mile walk through no-man's land to the Thai immigration offices. The difference between the countries was incredible; one bore the weight of crushing poverty, while the other was merely poor. They are both kingdoms, which I hadn't known before my trip. Cambodia had pictures of the king here and there, but Thailand featured them every 5 feet on buildings, bridges, everywhere we looked.

We found the line for immigration and it was even longer than the Cambodian departure line; we must have arrived at the same time as the buses. Again, we stood in line in the heat with all of our bags; Sol got his diaper changed while Pablo was about to fall over from not eating for two days. Just when we were getting near the front of the line, a second line opened; the first one had gotten so long it went into the road. Now we weren't in the front anymore; the people from the rear filled in and pushed us to the middle. We were slowly becoming unhappy.

After an hour in line, we got into the building, which was packed with more people standing in more lines; at least this time it was air-conditioned. Shanti, Pablo, and Sol fell into chairs while I held our places in line, this one about half an hour. As we approached the front we saw signs in Thai with dollar amounts and we started to worry that we didn't have enough money to get into the country and would have to start all over again. I had some Thai baht from my luxurious night at the airport, but not enough for all four of us. I wished I would have read up on the border crossing. I just couldn't learn the lessons from my lack of research in the previous nine months.

We didn't end up needing money and got through customs. We were mobbed again on the other side with people trying to sell us everything ever made. We settled on a tourist agency to get a taxi to Bangkok and finally started to relax. It took three hours in the horrible smoggy heat carrying all of our bags, with a tired little boy and two sick adults. The day was truly a test of patience, and we made it.

We had 10 minutes until our taxi left, so I took the opportunity to find a bathroom. Way back near customs was a building with "toilet" written on the side. In retrospect, it would have been more pleasant to pee down my leg than to enter that building. The toilets were bowls on the ground next to tubs of water with scoops. The floor was flooded over my flip-flops, and the smell almost knocked me out. The woman next to me was scooping water and the splash was hitting the floor, bouncing up and dripping down my legs and arms. I couldn't figure out what she was doing. I got outside and rubbed antibacterial lotion all over my body. I had to pay three baht for that experience, to add insult to injury.

Our second taxi driver wasn't as nice as the first. He had packed his entire trunk full of other people's things to deliver and told us we had to keep all our bags in the car by our feet. Hell no. I got a little bossy with him and told him to get his crap out; we were not sitting smashed in a car for another three hours. We paid for the entire car. It was only a regular five-seat taxi. The driver tried and tried to make everything fit and sneak things in our seats, but we won in the end and the driver took a load of packages back to the taxi office.

After another three hours of wild trucks and cars and highways and bridges with giant portraits of the king, we made it to Bangkok only to sit in traffic, stopped dead. No one moved for several minutes at a time; we were so close, but we just couldn't get to our hotel. The driver wanted to drop us off in the middle of the street; he said our hotel was right around the next corner, but after almost 12 hours we were going to get to the front door or sit in his car until it ran out of gas.

Finally, we got to our hotel, which was much more than "just around the corner." Street vendors and massage parlors and bars were everywhere, and surprisingly, the air quality was much better than Cambodia, even with the nonstop traffic jams and highrise hotels. It was time to check out this crazy place.

BANGKOK

We wandered around looking at the city, but our main goal was to buy a train ticket to one of the islands. We found the train station and bought tickets on an overnight train, to a bus, to a ferry, to Ko Phi Phi. Back at the hotel we got online and checked every hotel and travel site and realized that every hotel on the island was booked. We spent hours searching, even the over-priced luxury places.

Research, again. When will I learn? There was no worse time and place to be traveling, and it began in Australia. It was so hard to find hotels or hostels due to Christmas, then New Years, then the Australian holiday month, and boat races. The prices were so inflated that I spent more money in the five weeks in Australia than I did in five months in the rest of the world. I was so relieved coming to Southeast Asia; I thought I'd get back to $20 rooms, cheap food and plenty of space, but that turned out to be incred-ibly wrong. Happy Chinese New Year. The entire week was spent searching for places to stay, modes of transportation that weren't sold out, paying much more money than normal, and worrying a bit about homelessness.

So we had tickets to an island with nowhere to stay. Pablo and I went back to the train station to change our tickets to Ko Tao on the eastern side, a shorter trip, but we didn't get any money back. There were a few hotels available and we scrambled to book the first decent one we found.

We only had one full day in Bangkok and we spent it explor-ing. We took the train further into town and wandered until we found the ferry station. I had taken ferry rides, like water taxis, through Brisbane and Sydney, but Bangkok's water transportation was a whole new world. Instead of the giant, new, high-powered catamarans of Australia, these boats were long, wooden, and rickety, and jam-smashed with people. Everywhere in the dirty brown water there were wild looking old boats of every description flying in every direction. Some were long and pointy, and some had roofs that made them look like old houses. There was definitely no speed limit, and the wakes from all of the boats made the docks rise and fall and tilt. When our boat arrived, it barely slowed down. As it approached the dock, a man whistled, jumped off the back, and hooked a line over a metal pole; then the captain threw it in reverse and slammed into the tires on the dock. We had about 10 seconds to jump onto the boat before the crew whistled again and we were off. A woman pushed her way through the crowd jingling a box of money and somehow found every new person to collect the fare. This was the chicken bus of the sea.

We got off at Wat Pho, Thailand's oldest and largest temple, and also the national headquarters for traditional Thai medicine and massage. It holds the largest collection of Buddha images in the country. The area was walled in and contained several temples and ornately decorated buildings, all of which had pictures and statues – more Buddhas than can possibly be described. Some of the temples had altars with people praying; some were just rooms with statues lining the walls. We had to remove our shoes to enter each of them, and in one I was given a shawl to wear because once again, I was not wearing a sufficient amount of clothing.

The main attraction for tourists at Wat Pho was the giant reclining Buddha, measuring 138 feet long by 45 feet high. It was enormous, and enclosed in a room that barely contained it, so people were jammed inside taking pictures. Its eyes and feet were covered in mother-of-pearl, and the bottoms of the feet held more than 100 images of Buddha in various life stages. I was very happy that Shanti wanted to see the statue, because with the sky train, transfer, and walk to the ferry, I never would have made it by myself. Chinese New Year festivities were taking place at the temple, which made it a pretty intense morning of crowd-dodging, so after a couple hours we decided to go back to the hotel and recover. I napped. It was a great day.

Pablo was the first of us to get a massage in Bangkok. I offered to buy him a "happy ending," but sadly, he wanted nothing to do with that. He limped back to the hotel an hour later in more pain than when he left; the little Thai ladies went nuts on him. My theory is that they are such tiny women and when they see big people like Pablo or me they feel they have to work extra hard to make it an effective massage. But when they use elbows and knees and jam them into your soft places they really don't need to add any effort. Pablo actually had bruises on his back. Shanti and I heeded his warning and only got our heads, necks, and feet massaged.

Our train left the next night, but we had to check out of our hotel hours before departure. We stored our luggage and headed to the outdoor markets. Bangkok has the largest outdoor market in Southeast Asia, which sort of follows one of the themes of my travels. I kept running into the largest this or the deepest that or the biggest whatever, which is kind of cool. This market was huge; we could see tents and stalls well before the tram stopped at the station. It was very much like the market at Chichi in Guatemala, just rows and rows or everything you could imagine. I passed street food, clothing, shoes, tools, jewelry, sunglasses, and pirated cds, and every once in a while, dirty-looking men with tables of condoms and vibrators. I bought a couple t-shirts for $3 each, but we still had yet to see the market in Chiang Mai so I didn't want to add anything else to the pack for now. One thing here and one thing there and I'd been carrying way too much for way too long.

I wanted to get some food, but the smells from the street, sewers, dirty water, and unwashed people made me think it might not be the best idea for the night I had to sleep on a train.

We picked up our luggage in the afternoon and went to the train station. It was a big deal because it was Sol's first real train experience. We'd been on the subway and the sky rail, but not a train like he plays with at home. Shanti and Pablo had been getting him excited about it all week, and every once in a while for the past few days he'd just say "all aboard, choo choo!" like Thomas the Train in the videos he watches.

We got to the station early and had dinner, possibly the hottest curry I'd yet eaten. They don't make anything "gringo hot;" it's full-on Thai hot.

I enjoyed the small bit of Bangkok that I saw, but I wish I had been able to see more. I get so lost in big cities that I didn't want to travel this one alone and was thankful I had Shanti and Pablo with me. I simply can't figure out how to get where I want to by rail; the pictures of the routes just don't make sense to me, and a taxi was useless here in the bumper-to-bumper traffic. Instead of going out alone, I behaved myself and stayed close to home. Bangkok will remain on my list of places to visit with a single friend. There were too many things missed with a child, including the famous nightlife. The bits I did see were reminiscent of Panama: older, fat white guys with gaudily dressed 20-something girls on their arms, girls who didn't really smile, but sort of grimaced. This was definitely not a place where I had to worry about guys hitting on me too much. The single men here were looking for the child-sized Thai boy or girl of their dreams. I was pretty grossed out. I don't think I would have cared if I'd seen a white guy with a girl who was within 25 years of his age, but all the old men wanted teenagers. Gross.

It was time for my first overnight train ride. Actually, I think it was my first train ride ever. We had booked our tickets so late that Pablo and Shanti got the last spot in first class, a sleeper cabin, and I got one of the last in second class. I got a seat that folds out into a bed in a whole car full of people, and honestly, I hadn't been looking forward to it. It sounded like an entire night with no sleep. We each had our own space, but it was very hostel-like. My nearest neighbors were French guys; they were nice, but not interesting enough to spend the evening talking to, so I caught up on my blog.

I had wanted a drink to help me sleep; it felt pretty weird to be sleeping on a train on a cot with only a thin curtain separating me from dozens of people. The waiter told me the only juice on board was orange juice, so I ordered a screwdriver. When he returned I couldn't help but laugh, and everyone nearby immediately thought better of me. On a large tray I received a bucket of ice, two large plastic bottles of orange juice, and an entire bottle of vodka. Apparently they don't mix the drinks for us. It was only a few dollars, but I wouldn't have returned it anyway. The French guys had a bucket of beers, and as I sipped my drink they increasingly became cuter and more interesting. I had been a little annoyed that I couldn't get a first-class bunk, but screw it – slumming it with the rowdy crowd was the way to go on a train. I wasn't going to get any sleep anyway.

The train ride was almost nine hours, and I finally tried to get some sleep after I spilled vodka on my computer.

KO TAO

The trip from Bangkok to Ko Tao was an adventure in third-world transportation. The train got old fairly quickly; I was tipsy, there was no air-conditioning, and the fans couldn't get rid of the fumy smell. Pablo came to wake me up at 3:45 a.m. after I had just fallen asleep. I thought I could sleep more on the bus to the ferry dock; I envisioned a cushy tourist bus like in Mexico, but it was an open air truck with long benches in the bed, like a troop transport.

I enjoyed the truck. Several of us piled in, then our bags were stacked at the back all the way to the top, effectively blocking our only escape route if, say, the truck caught on fire. We rode for 20 minutes to the dock; it was around 4:30 a.m. and completely black outside. When we arrived dozens of people were already lying all over the ground waiting for the boat. I started to get a feeling that our tickets weren't completely legit; this seemed like way too many people for one boat, so I wandered down to the dock to check, and actually ended up being first in line to get our boarding stickers – we got first pick of the seats. We naturally chose the cabin that said "air condition" and got comfortable while the giant crowd trickled on. It was hard to tell what the boat looked like, but our section of 30 seats wasn't bad, just a bit run-down.

Sol was having the best day of his life. He slept on a choo-choo, then got to ride in a big truck, much scarier for mom and dad than him, and now he was on a boat. He kept saying "bye bye, caboose." He might be the cutest boy I've ever met.

The giant mob was finally on the boat, but we didn't get to leave; we just hung out on the dock. I asked around and found out that we were waiting for the next truckload of people from the train station. That's what happens when all the boats are sold out for the holidays: we got tickets with the only company that Lonely Planet doesn't like, and they smashed as many people aboard as there was deck space. We were thankful to get seats in the only air-conditioned area.

Shortly after we pulled away from the dock, a Thai man came into the room with a sign that said "air condition 30 baht per person," and had a bowl to collect money. What a great scam. People were grumbling because the sun had come up and it was already hot in the cabin. The man behind me argued, but paid in the end, demanding that they now turn on the air since he gave money. When the man had collected from everyone, we learned that the air conditioning had been on the whole time, it was just broken. We paid extra to sit in a hot room. It was a better scam than I thought, since now there wasn't a single other spot on the boat to sit, and no sign of the man with our money.

A few minutes later when it became obvious that the cabin was going to be a furnace, we made the crew open the two small windows. Although there was a bit of a breeze, the room quickly filled with diesel fumes. I think that was what lulled me into a 20-minute nap. When I woke up, Shanti had taken Sol onto the deck in the front of the boat because the smell was making him sick. I stayed inside to watch our bags and Pablo followed them out; he wasn't feeling very well either.

Fifteen minutes later, Pablo stuck his head through the window and asked for his bag. And what he described was the funniest thing I'd heard in days, something I truly wish I had seen.

According to eyewitness reports, Shanti had gone to the front of the boat to get Sol some fresh air, but none of the people would let them have a seat. She wanted to lean back against the pilot house and nurse him. She ended up standing at the very front of the boat nursing, with a strong wind rushing past. There were about 10 people behind her. The moment Sol was done nursing, he vomited, which Shanti described as taking a glass of milk and throwing it into the wind. It instantly coated the people sitting behind her. As they sat there in shock, milk running down their faces, Sol barfed again, the wind caught it, and the crowd got another dose. And then he did it once more, just to make sure everyone was covered. I would have given anything to see that.

Shanti's milk was dripping down people's foreheads; they couldn't see out of their sunglasses and it was all over their clothes. I hope they'll all think twice before refusing a nursing mother a seat again.

The fumes had gotten to be too much for me and I started to make my way outside. I hadn't been outside the cabin since the sun came up and the boat looked exactly as I would picture a refugee boat to look: in complete disrepair, every inch of space crammed with people. It was truly the picture of those tragic ferry accidents that appear in the news every once in a while: "Overloaded boat capsizes in channel, killing all 800 aboard."

I opened the cabin door and banged it into a woman; three people had to move so I could get out, then I had to tiptoe my way between arms and legs, apologizing the whole way because I couldn't help stepping on them. Two guys had to hang over the side of the boat to let me past so I could reach the bow where I found Shanti, Pablo, and Sol, along with some unhappy people that smelled like spoiled milk. So much fun before 8 a.m.

We made it to Ko Tao without any further incident and found a pickup truck to take us to our hotel. We were exhausted after 17 hours of travel and weren't inclined to start our sightseeing. We did see a bar with an all-you-can-eat pizza sign and made plans to nap and go there for dinner.

Pablo and I were unnaturally excited for pizza. At 199 baht, close to $6, we figured we could do some real damage, and were betting on who could eat more. We showed up to a crowded restaurant, all 30 tables full. It looked like everyone had the same idea, but it didn't matter; the place had a great-looking pizza oven and we were starving. Given our experiences so far in Southeast Asia, I'm not sure why we expected it to be like home. Perhaps starving ourselves for pizza had dulled our sense of reality.

We didn't properly assess the situation until after we had ordered. Thirty tables sat three to four people each, one guy was making one pizza at a time, and one waitress with one six-slice pizza served single small slices to six different people, then ran back to get the next pizza from the oven, cutting it and serving six more people. She seemed to remember whom she had served last, so it worked out that Pablo and I each got a tiny piece every 8-10 minutes. The restaurant was full of people staring at empty plates, their gazes following the waitress with longing, in hopes it was their turn.

At the rate that we got our slices, we were digesting faster than we were eating, so "all-you-can-eat" became impossible. We could have sat there until closing and waited everyone out, but after an hour we just gave up. The waitress came by once when Pablo had taken Sol for a walk; I stole his piece from his plate and ate it, so technically I won the bet.

Life on Ko Tao was pretty laid-back. We hired a water taxi to take us all the way around the island, stopping at some snorkel spots. Sol had become proficient with his water wings and he was blowing bubbles floating on his back. We bought goggles so he could watch fish swim by.

The last stop on our boat tour was a beach resort on a nearby island. It was a pleasant place for lunch and swimming, and it featured a lookout with a great view. Unlike most beach spots, no music was blaring and people were really mellow; it was a super calm, quiet place. We were lazing in the water waiting for our taxi pickup when out of nowhere two fighter jets screamed over the islands. It was so loud it was shocking. There isn't air transportation of any kind on Ko Tao, so it really took us by surprise. There was no Wi-Fi, so we couldn't even check to see if the next world war had started. That night I received an email from Lynn, a friend at home, telling me that the state department reported possible terrorist activity at the U.S. Embassy in Chiang Mai, our next destination.

I set out on my own that night to watch the Muay Thai fights at the stadium. The word "stadium" is used very loosely here; it was a ring surrounded by plastic chairs and metal benches in a field. The seven fights weren't as bloody as I'd imagined. I used to practice Kung Fu and Muay Thai and was super excited to be there. I especially loved the side of the ring smashed with screaming Thai men. That was exactly as I'd imagined.

The women's fight was disappointing; a Norwegian girl, undefeated after several months of fighting throughout Thailand, was up against a local girl. She kicked the local girl's ass up and down the ring but lost on decision. Completely fixed. The biggest surprise of the night was an English guy named Charlie; his name alone seemed funny in that place. I saw him posing for pictures before his match and I thought maybe there was a tourist division; he looked like a computer programmer: pasty white and a little goofy. But he was in the main bout and put up a good fight against a giant, oiled, ripped Thai guy who eventually crushed him.

I spent a good portion of the next day sleeping while Shanti and Pablo rented an ATV and explored more beaches. I did manage to go out long enough to get a massage and a haircut. I've gotten my hair cut by drag queens when I lived in Seattle, but this was the first time I'd gotten one from a man actually in drag at the time. It was an awesome new experience. Cheap, fun and maybe the worst haircut I've had since my father cut my hair before my sister's wedding many years ago.

The next morning, Pablo and I went scuba diving. After Belize, Roatan, and the Great Barrier Reef, this was pretty unremarkable, but I had to do it to check it off the list. The visibility was poor, it wasn't the right season, and there wasn't a lot of underwater life. I still enjoyed it; I love diving.

My group included a dive master and two scuba instructors from other countries. It was a small group to keep together, but so many other divers were at the sites that it was overcrowded. Towards the end of the first dive, I saw my dive master duck into a swim-through; I was a good distance behind him, and the other two men were far behind me. I hung back to show the guys where we were going and another group, Pablo's, actually, entered the swim-through in front of me. When I got to the other side I looked around and we couldn't find our dive master; he hadn't looked to see if we were behind him and probably went into another swim-through. I wasn't going to dive into a hole that possibly didn't go anywhere, and we didn't see any sign of him, so we hung out to wait for him. He appeared about six minutes later to collect us. When we got back on the boat he was pissed at us. "If you don't want a dive master just let me know," he shouted, like it was our fault he didn't wait for us.

It was still a good day, though. Shanti and Sol met us for lunch on the beach, followed by more swimming, then naps, sunset and dinner on the beach. The restaurants at the water's edge have cushions directly on the sand, so we actually ate on the beach. It was Valentine's Day and men were selling giant lanterns shaped like hearts for people to write messages on and send them burning off into space. They didn't look very environmentally friendly. I got my Valentine's kiss from Sol and we called it a night.

The next day, our last on Ko Tao, had a very promising start. Pablo rented another ATV for his family, I got a scooter, and we all went exploring. The roads on Ko Tao were a mix of pavement, dirt and rock. There were a lot of hills; nothing too extreme, but I hadn't driven a scooter in years, so it took a little while before I was totally comfortable. Shanti and Pablo had their system down from the other day – Sol up front standing and holding onto the padded bar, Pablo driving, and Shanti behind, making sure Sol didn't tumble off the side. Sol had a cute little helmet with a visor and looked like a true biker baby, except none of the local babies wear helmets; they're only for tourists.

We went up and down some pretty steep hills to get to our first beach on the other side of the island. We went to this particular beach because our boat taxi driver took us there the first day and showed Pablo a huge rock he could jump from. After swimming out and climbing the base, Pablo had to climb a rope anchored to the top, a few stories tall. Another tourist attraction where I expected people to die. But he made a successful jump, Sol practiced his new swimming moves, and we sat at a restaurant to escape the unexpected rain.

As soon as the rain stopped, we loaded onto our vehicles to find another beach. We motored up and down more hills, some of them pretty sketchy on my scooter, and ended up driving fairly vertically towards a resort with a view. It was called Eagles Nest, and that's pretty much what it was. I wasn't looking forward to going down the giant hill we climbed to get there in the rain, but my scooter was new with good tires, so I wasn't worried that I'd have any problems. It did occur to me that if I did any damage to the scooter I wouldn't be able to hide it since it was so shiny; when we were at the rental agency we had to sign forms with the price lists for replacing damaged parts. We also had to leave our passports as a guarantee so there wouldn't be any ducking out of payment.

We pulled up to the resort just as the rain started coming down hard, as good a time as any for lunch. The Eagles Nest was an open-air restaurant with a metal roof and cushions on the floor by the tables. As we were looking out over the incredible view, the storm really blew in and it was a total whiteout, pouring rain blowing onto us wherever we sat. Sitting in the only building above the treetops, high on a hill during a thunderstorm under a metal roof made for an exciting lunch. The food was good too.

The storm lasted about an hour and blew off to the other side of the island. We were ready to get back home for Sol's nap before we headed out again for the evening. To add to the excitement, the giant hill we climbed was soaking wet from the storm as we slowly started making our way down.

Shortly after we started our descent, I heard squealing tires behind me, guys yelling, and before I could look, an ATV plowed into me from behind. The guy had the whole open road to fly out of control, but he had to steer right into the tiny bit I was already using. He was fine, but I was laid out under my scooter, so mad that "fuck" was the only word coming out of my mouth, over and over. Another guy ran up to help get my scooter off of me and the idiot on the ATV was just sitting there staring. I yelled at him. A lot.

The guy didn't even ask how I was. After assessing my arms and legs for damage, I started looking at the damage to the scooter and thinking about how much it was going to cost, and that I shouldn't have to pay for it. I told the guy that he needed to pay for all of the dents and scratches, and my adrenaline was spiked pretty high so I wasn't being very nice. He didn't once ask if I was ok, which pissed me off even more; if he had just said sorry or expressed any concern whatsoever, I wouldn't have been so mad.

His friends were much nicer and we decided they would follow us back to the rental agency to pay for the damage to my scooter. We had seen warnings about these agencies charging outrageous amounts of money for minor damage, so I was not anticipating an easy time. If the guy ditched us on the way, I'd be stuck paying or lose my passport. To add to my worries, I didn't want the guy to drive behind me down the giant, wet hill; we were still at the top, but his friends assured me that they would stay between us. The guy and his friends were covered in fresh, bloody scrapes from earlier in the day, which did not inspire confidence.

We made it to the bottom of the hill and across town without incident, although I was shaking with post-accident energy the whole way. The rental agency had an entrance with a steep incline, and as I gunned my scooter to make it up I smashed right into an ATV parked at the top that I didn't see. That caused me to dump my scooter again, this time right in front of the doorway of the shop, about two feet from the owner, who was sitting on the stoop. Fuck.

Instead of having the guys deal with the damage by themselves I had just put a fresh set of scratches on the front fender.

The owner brought out a price list, which I had ignored when renting the scooter, and the amounts were ridiculous. The list also contained a clause stating that no matter what damage was done, the price charged will be to replace the entire part. My front fender, which only had a few scratches that could be sanded out and good as new, was going to cost me 4500 baht, or $150. The mirror and exhaust cover damage from the accident also had scratches that weren't too horrible but the owner demanded 3500 baht, $115. So began an hour of arguing and bargaining, and I was pretty sure I was going to have to break into the shop at night to rescue my passport.

The argument went round and round and the owner was not willing to come down in price below 4000 baht for all of the damage. In my opinion it was stupid that a few scratches would make him insist that each part needed total replacement. Some sandpaper and paint and the scooter would look brand new, but he wouldn't budge.

Pablo had come with me to help and I was grateful for that; I was almost useless because I was angry and bruised and didn't feel like being nice. Pablo took charge and was amazing with the stubborn man. The guys from the accident finally realized that they were going to have to pay something and gave me 2000 baht for their part, and we let them go. The next problem was that I didn't have any money. I was supposed to come up with 2000 baht for my part and only had 1350 in my wallet. Pablo had dropped off his bags with his family at the hotel and was without money as well. We were stuck at the agency because I couldn't come up with any more money, which pissed me off even more. If the guy hadn't hit me in the first place I never would have rammed the ATV. But what was done was done.

Pablo was being reasonable and respectful, and I began apologizing and telling the owner and an old woman, probably his mother, that I didn't have any more money, and please accept what I did have. They kept refusing. We just stood there getting nowhere.

After another 20 minutes, the old woman said something in Thai to the man, she took my money, and we called it done. I was supposed to have the scooter for the rest of the day, until 9 a.m. the next morning, but I was worried they would forget I had paid for the damages and have to start this all over again, so I exchanged my key for my passport.

I think what I was angriest about was that both my knees and my ankles were bruised and sore, which put an end to cheap leg massages, my new favorite pastime.

CHIANG MAI

We had a hard time getting tickets out of Ko Tao; all modes of transportation, as crappy as some were, were booked solid. We did find a travel agent to get us connected to Chiang Mai; it turned out to be a bus, then a boat to Ko Samui, another bus to the airport, a plane to Bangkok, then a plane to Chiang Mai. We decided that one overnight train ride for Sol was enough, and even though the train was cheaper, it would end up taking two nights to get there.

Our first flight left an hour late and we only had a two-hour layover in Bangkok – the smaller airport, not the cool one. We would have to collect our bags there and check in again. Shanti spoke to an airline clerk and she arranged to have someone meet us to help expedite our connection. We arrived in Bangkok and a tiny woman in a golf cart loaded us up for the trip to our gate, and it was a good thing she did; it was a seriously confusing airport. She wasn't a very aggressive driver and we ended up driving exactly as fast as people were walking. But she already had our boarding passes and assured us that our bags would find us. I wasn't convinced, but I had yet to lose my backpack in nine months. We made our flight with a bit of shopping time to spare; there was a bizarre clothing store where everything was $2 or $3, and that was it.

Our bags arrived in Chiang Mai at the same time we did, as promised.

After settling into our not-so-wonderful hotel, we hit the Sunday Walking Market, the biggest in Chiang Mai. The city closes some streets and there are blocks and blocks to walk through. It was big but not like Bangkok's, and open until midnight. I had gotten up at 4 a.m., so I wasn't too keen on staying late; we got just enough of a taste to last us until the next market, which was the following night. There was a market somewhere every day, so we didn't worry that we'd miss anything.

Monday was the long-anticipated zoo day. We had been getting Sol psyched up about it and it turned out to be the coolest zoo ever, for all of us. We could interact with all of the animals except the lions, tigers, and bears, and other assorted dangerous stuff. We fed giraffes, hippos, and elephants and got to touch them. The only zoo "security" were the guys selling food, 10 baht or 30 cents for a bowl of cucumbers and radishes to dump into the hippos' gaping mouths, another 10 baht for cucumbers and sugar cane for the elephant and its baby while trying not to get trampled, and 10 more for long beans for the giraffes with unexpectedly long tongues.

For 20 baht, Pablo bought a bunch of bananas to feed the monkeys. There was a moat between us; we couldn't touch them, so Pablo would get a monkey's attention, throw a banana, and the monkey would catch, peel and eat it from its tree branch.

One of our daily activities was reviewing the day's activities with Sol in hopes that he'd be able to remember some of it as he gets older. We were explaining what the monkeys were doing and this caused Sol to form his first grown-up sentence. He said "Dadda throw monkey banana." Subject, verb, object, indirect object. Perfect, for an almost 2-year-old. Better than my Spanish at that point.

After the zoo, we went to Khun Churn, a great all-Thai vegetarian restaurant. It was an enormous all-you-can-eat buffet – a real one, not like the pizza – and most things were labeled for tourists. The deep-fried pumpkin almost killed me with delicious-ness. When we ate all we thought we could, we hit the dessert table. I spotted the most wonderful-looking chocolate pudding and helped myself to a giant bowl full. I'm used to finding choco-late pudding at salad bars and was extra-excited, not only because I have a chocolate addiction, but because it had been quite a long time since I'd had chocolate pudding. I put the first heaping spoonful in my mouth and it was the most extreme opposite of what chocolate pudding should taste like. After several tries at communication, I was able to understand that it was a type of dark, fluffy vinegar. That was the closest I'd come to vomiting on my trip. Shanti had a similar experience with her "raspberry jello," which was a spongy, smoked meat in disguise.

We ended our day at a night market stuffing ourselves with crepes and gelato and buying knockoff sunglasses and flip-flops. Ray-Bans and Hawaiianas for $5 each; it didn't matter if they only lasted a month.

Shanti and I spent a day learning to cook at the Siam Rice Thai Cookery School. Shanti signed us up for a full-day class to learn a seven-course meal, eating as we went. There were mul-tiple options for each course and I picked chicken coconut soup, pad thai, mango salad, sweet and sour vegetables, red curry, pine-apple red curry, and pumpkin in coconut milk. I learned how to enjoy pumpkin in at least 15 new ways in Southeast Asia. Shanti picked other options so we could try everything, and all the dishes we made were better than any Thai food we ever ate at restaurants in the States.

Our group was eight people, and we started at the prep table cutting and dicing our ingredients. We prepared two dishes at a time, then went to the gas stoves to cook. Even though we all chose different dishes, each course started with the same basic ingredients. After cooking our two dishes, we went inside to eat while an army of kitchen helpers magically cleaned our stations and readied them for the next round. We were lucky to have the owner of the school as our teacher; her English was great and she had a thorough understanding of how sexual innuendo can be applied to food.

The curries were fun to make; no matter what color curry we made they all started with the exact same ingredients. Only the final ones differentiated red from green from yellow. We diced our veggies and spices, dumped them into mortar-and-pestles, and got to work grinding. The motion we were taught for the grinding looked very naughty; if we did it with a smile, we could be considered for "best wife" status. I was the only unmarried girl at the table, so I'm not sure how I could qualify for "best wife," but my curry was ground the best, so maybe I got "best kinky girlfriend."

Shanti and I ate all day, way more than we thought possible. We had to take some of our creations home in to-go containers. I couldn't even taste a couple dishes I made until the next day, I was so full. I have to say my pad thai was exceptionally good, my soup was fully awesome, the pineapple curry incredible, and the coconut pumpkin dessert was something I could eat every night for the rest of my life.

On the second-to-last day of my nine-month trip, we went to the Chiang Mai Tiger Kingdom, and the 420 baht was well-spent. Pablo and I signed up to snuggle the big cats, and Shanti went with Sol for the cubs. Oddly enough, it cost more to cuddle a baby tiger than a full-grown one. Children under a certain height aren't allowed in with the big cats, I'm guessing because the children look too much like food.

I was nervous going into the tiger cage. Five big tigers, about 300 kilos each, were walking around and waiting for people to lay on them. Pablo and I went in together with a guide who carried a stick; if a tiger did anything that looked even remotely aggressive or impolite, the guide gently tapped him on the head and the tiger behaved. All but one tiger in our pen was male; the female was pacing back and forth making little growling noises the whole time. I seriously had considered asking at the reservation desk if it was OK to go into a cage with wild animals while I had my period; I couldn't help but wonder if they'd think I was either ready for mating, or an injured animal they could snack on.

There was a sign on the cage door that we were required to read before entering, conveying helpful information like "No poking or prodding," "No antagonizing," and "Approach animals from behind so they don't think you're coming to play." We were careful to stay away from all those teeth, signs or not.

The tigers were very relaxed, and made for comfy cushions. They mostly just laid there while we petted and scratched and draped ourselves on top of them for pictures. One of the tigers was named Roy, and I couldn't help thinking of the circus guy who got his throat ripped open by his own pet.

Altogether we spent 20 minutes in the cage, and it was quality time.

We wandered down to the baby tiger pens for Shanti and Sol's turn. The cubs were the size of small dogs, about three months old, and very playful. Shanti and Sol sat by a sleepy one and petted it as Sol made his "rowr" tiger sounds. They got 20 minutes as well, with Pablo and me watching from outside the fence. At one point Sol was more interested in the guy running a hose because all of the tigers decided to pee on the floor at the same time. There was a lot going on for him to process.

After possibly the only scary tuk-tuk ride we had, Shanti and I went out for some serious shopping. We first headed to the grocery store and I loaded up on shampoo, toothpaste, and typical beauty aisle products, because they sell the same things in Thailand at a fraction of the price on Kauai. We bought plenty of spices and Thai products that we couldn't get at home. I checked out the tampon selection; I didn't need any, but was curious about how Thai tampons compared to those from other countries. All I could find were Japanese brands with pink and blue wrappers, decorated with childishly drawn flowers. And not a word on the box in Thai; I've never read the packaging of U.S. tampons, but at least I'm given the opportunity to learn more. I had to buy a box.

The market was next – more spices and gifts and bargaining fun. I spent close to $100, which buys a lot of stuff in Thailand, and then had to buy a giant bag to carry it all home. I made up for nine months of almost no shopping.

I got my last foot massage and first pedicure to end my day. I truly miss that aspect of Southeast Asia; I was in the spa for two hours and it only cost $13. The spa I went to, Chiang Mai Women's Prison Massage Centre, only employed women from the prison to give them stable jobs and help them stay out of trouble. As I watched the women, I tried to imagine what each of them might have been in prison for, but I was having a hard time imagining anything that was illegal in Thailand.

And so ended the last full day of my trip. I was sad to be going home the next day, but relieved to unpack my backpack and live in one place for a while.

For the final adventure of my trip, we went to the Baanchang Elephant Park. I was feeling so burnt out from travel that if Shanti hadn't been organizing activities I might have skipped everything the last week and taken up residence in a massage chair, so I was truly thankful she organized my last days.

Our van pulled into the park and the first thing we saw was a field of elephants of all sizes and ages, each chained by the leg so they didn't touch one another. It sounds sad, but they looked happy and healthy. Sol was in heaven. We were given matching uniforms to wear, and after a short briefing our first task was to feed them bananas and sugar cane. We were shown which animals we couldn't touch: the blind one, the angry one, the people-hater. Each of the elephants had come from a working environment where they were mistreated; they were at the park to recover and give rides to tourists.

We grabbed bunches of bananas and as much sugar cane as we could carry and walked to the different animals to feed them. Their trunks were so cute. As we approached they sniffed us out; if they found food, the trunk would make snuffling noises and grab. It was like an alien being; very weird.

After our group went through several bushels of food, it was time to learn how to sit on an elephant. We were going to ride them bareback, so learning to climb on and off was important. Many of the elephants at the park were recovering from being tourist transports with giant wooden platform seats on their backs, which are not healthy for them. We learned the command to sit, but no matter how loud we yelled it the elephants only listened to their trainers. The elephant kneeled down, I stepped on the front leg, threw myself on top and the elephant got up. I can't equate that feeling with anything else I've ever done – maybe like climbing a small mountain during an earthquake? I sat high up on the neck with my knees tucked behind his ears. The tigers were much comfier.

After practicing sitting, we learned how to steer the elephants and did a practice loop, turning in both directions. The command to go is "pai pai," while kicking both of the elephant's ears. Not hard kicking, more like flapping them. To turn we yelled "kwek," and kicked the ear on the opposite side of the way we wanted to go, like a giant turn signal. Stop was "how," and we squeezed the neck with our knees. The elephants humored us by making us think they were listening, but really they've done this loop a million times in their lives and didn't even notice we were there. Sol's first elephant ride was a success. Pablo climbed up, I passed Sol to him, and they did a loop while Shanti took 8,000 pictures. Sol loved it.

After lunch was the real fun, the jungle walk. We boarded our elephants; Shanti, Pablo and Sol shared one and I had my own, and we were each led by the animal's personal handler. Some people's elephants were a little rowdy and had to be led by a rope, while some handlers used their spiky axe-looking thing for reminders of manners, but my elephant, Tong Toom, was excellent. All she did was follow her guy, and never did anything naughty.

Riding an elephant bareback is something that everyone should try once. It was an incredible experience. I locked myself on with my knees, sort of; my hands were on her giant head for balance, and we lumbered around for an hour and a half. The skin and prickly hairs were so fun to touch. Her eyes were beautiful and old and sad, with 2-inch eyelashes. She did have some scars from her past life, but she was super healthy-looking otherwise. Occasionally she would wander to the side of the trail and scrounge for a snack, chomping as we walked.

The commands we learned were just to make us feel important; the elephants didn't listen to a word we said. Tong Toom's trainer walked directly in front of us, and every time he stopped she stopped, whichever path he took, she followed. I still pretended to steer.

I tried to look back for Shanti, but turning around on an elephant was not easy. I relaxed as much as possible, but balancing on an elephant was far different from anything I've tried before; I kept sliding off the side of her neck. Maybe I would have had it with another hour of practice.

Elephants have a clever, yet gross, air conditioning system. As Tong Toom walked, she stuck her trunk into her mouth and sucked water, spit, slime, and food bits out of her throat and sprayed herself down. And me, too. It sounded like a 2,000 pound man hocking a giant spit wad through a 4-foot-long nose. I don't think I could describe it any better than that. Trunk in throat, sucking accomplished, Tong Toom alternated spraying her sides and bottom, whichever part was hot. After our ride I was soaked with elephant phlegm, but it did keep me cool – stinky, but cool.

After the jungle tour, it was time to wash our elephants and let them rest. We ended the walk at a pond of brown water and floating elephant poop and waded in. We received buckets and scrub brushes, although I didn't see how any cleaning could be accomplished in poopy water. The elephants laid down and we scrubbed them. I enjoyed this part almost as much as the walk, because my trainer let me lay on my elephant and strike calendar poses while he took pictures. He let me stand on her, too. But I scrubbed, and washed, and loved. Shanti, Pablo and Sol were having a blast washing their elephant, Moon; she snorkeled water and sprayed them the entire time.

When the trainers started organizing the elephants to lead them in for the night, my trainer let me ride Tong Toom one last time. That was an unforgettable experience.

And that was the last adventure of my trip; I said my goodbyes and packed for Kauai. It was time to think about a place to live, a job, a boyfriend, what I was going to do with my life now that my first real travel experience was complete.

HOME
FEBRUARY 23ᴿᴰ, 2013

Life after the trip was not as I'd imagined it from the road. I was desperately craving a house of my own where I could unpack my storage unit, spread out my possessions, and nest. I came home to over-inflated rental prices for studio apartments that were not only out of my price range, but mostly didn't include a real kitchen.

I had envisioned myself working at an outdoor adventure-type job and was turned down for what I counted on as a sure thing, a job I really wanted. I was lucky to find an accounting job that allowed me to pay my rent, but I had sworn to myself that I'd never sit behind a desk again. It's now more than a year since I've been riding a desk.

I had to get a loan to buy a used truck, and combined with my rent and credit card debt, I was broke. I couldn't afford to eat out or go for drinks nearly as often as I was accustomed to before I left.

I thought that my complicated relationship issues were worked out and I would start a life with the man I loved; we have now broken up and gotten back together at least five times since I've been home.

Getting back into sports was not easy; nine months of minimal exercise, a lot of drinking, and too many cigarettes left me with little motivation to jump into the daily grind of working out and competition.

While I was gone I lost touch with many friends, and the ones I did stay close to all had babies or small children now. My drinking buddies were gone, and it was hard to find anyone to stay out with past 8 p.m.

Nothing was how I imagined it would be when I returned home. Everything had changed, most of all myself, and I was disappointed. I thought that the high of a world travel adventure would make everything in my life better, fix all of the problems that I had before I left. Instead, that high made my return to day-to-day banality a harsh come-down, and I was depressed. My job, my house, my personal life, everything left me feeling as if I shouldn't have come home, or shouldn't have gone in the first place. I spent nearly five months on my couch crying and watching reruns of Buffy the Vampire Slayer, hoping I'd find something that would cheer me up. I thought writing a book about my adventure could be the start to a new career, a new life. I became even more depressed thinking that I had a way to a better life, but was too depressed to get it done.

With the help of a good friend, I learned to appreciate the things I have, even if they aren't perfect. I have a roof over my head; I love my boss and I can pay my bills; I can enjoy watching my friends' children grow up. Eventually I was able to start writing, which I doubted would ever happen.

My new perspective also gave me a new appreciation for an adventure few are fortunate enough to embark upon. I really began to understand how amazing my trip had been, learning about new cultures, meeting so many great people with whom I still keep in touch, and gaining a new confidence that I really can do anything. I experienced great moments with fellow travelers. I didn't get mugged or lose any important possessions. There were moments of extreme loneliness, like in Guatemala when I couldn't find anyone I wanted to talk to and had no internet access to call home. Over time, one song on my iPod became my theme song, the 80's rock anthem "Here I Go Again." I played it as I changed locations; sometimes I'd cry, sometimes I'd "woo hoo!" with excitement to leave the last familiar place. Traveling ran me through every possible emotion, in every degree imaginable. Looking back and reliving the highs and the lows taught me one absolute fact: I couldn't outrun my original problems. They were with me the entire time, just waiting for me to notice. They shaped every aspect of my travel.

I didn't learn how to navigate bus systems or find my way around cities, and I didn't learn how to plan any better. But I did learn something so much more important: how to be happy.

This book would not have been possible without the help of so many: The Burovac Family, always there when I need you; Soren Velice, editor; Don Schlotman, cover art; Pamela Brown, consultant; Kristin Markling, consultant; Stacey Wisiorowski & Shanti Manzano, support crew; and all of my RocketHub supporters: Robert Burovac, Donna Burovac, Clare Burovac, Chris Mattaliano, Andrew Evans, Frank Burovac, Kristie Burns, Ben Silver, Karen Palting, Mike Watts, Elle & Bryan Miyake, Lynn Bingman, Nicole Schwartzkopf, Mark Boetticher, Michael Espenan, Eva Smietana, Don Schlotman, Michelle & Brian Paul, Linda Sherman Gordon, and Tracy & Kipp Wingo. Thank you to all.

Finally, to all the great people I met on the road – I hope to see you again.

For trip pictures, go to www.wanderwithmelissa.com